AN UNBELIEVER'S GUIDE TO THE BIBLE

Also by Leslie Scrase:

An
Unbeliever's
Guide to
the Bible
including the Apocrypha

Leslie Scrase

UNITED WRITERS
Cornwall

UNITED WRITERS PUBLICATIONS LTD
Ailsa, Castle Gate, Penzance, Cornwall.

British Library Cataloguing in Publication Data:
A catalogue record for this book is
available from the British Library.

ISBN 9781852001469

Printed in Great Britain by
United Writers Publications Ltd
Cornwall.

This book is dedicated to Don Liversedge, who lit the fuse; to Edward Gwinnell, who made me feel that the effort was worthwhile; and to my brother Aubs, who manages both to criticise and to encourage – such a rare combination.

Read the Bible as you would any other book – with strictest criticism, frankly determining what you think beautiful, and what you think false or foolish.

John Ruskin (*c.*1877)

Acknowledgements

I owe a considerable debt of gratitude to Malcolm Sheppard of United Writers Publications Ltd. This is now the fifth time we have worked together. He began by publishing my three autobiographical novels *An Evacuee*, *A Prized Pupil!*, and *A Reluctant Seaman*. Then he published my best known book *Coping with Death*. And now he has taken on this, the most difficult task of them all. I'm deeply grateful to him.

Contents

Part Two: The Apocrypha

Part Three: The New Testament

Preface to the Whole

The Christian Bible is divided into three parts.

The Old Testament comprises the holy books of the pre-Christian Jewish tribes. These books were written in Hebrew and in Aramaic. The modern English texts are based on the studies of Jewish scholars, but the discovery of the ancient Dead Sea scrolls and other ancient writings has enabled scholars to do some fine tuning and to clarify the meaning of some parts of the old Testament and also the old Apocrypha.

The Apocrypha comprises books mostly written in the second and first centuries BCE in Hebrew and in Greek. They were more popular with Jews scattered throughout the Mediterranean (known as the Diaspora) than in Palestine where the religious authorities tended to be more conservative.

The Old Testament and the Apocrypha together (in a Greek version) comprised the Septuagint. To the early Christians this was the whole Bible. But in due course they added to it the books of the New Testament, written in Greek (though it was often Greek with an Aramaic or Palestinian accent).

For Jews, the first five books of the Old Testament were of supreme importance. These contained the Torah, God's law finalised in 458 BCE. The Jews refined their understanding of the Torah and gave added definition to it in the Mishnah (*c*. 200 CE) and the Talmud (*c*. 550 CE). As God's law it commanded complete obedience.

Christian use of the Bible changed with the Protestant

Reformation. Protestants down-graded the Apocrypha and most of them tended not to use it at all. I was an adult before I even knew of its existence. But they gave the rest of the Bible a new status. It became their supreme authority, a fact which has given them considerable problems in recent times.

For Catholics and in a different way for Eastern Orthodox Christians, the supreme authority has always been the Church. That remains their position. But, apart from extreme fundamentalists, Protestants find that they can no longer regard the Bible as their supreme authority. They tend to look to 'the Bible as interpreted by the Church as inspired by the Holy Spirit' (the third person of the Christian Trinity).

That sounds fine but in practice it can mean all things to all people. It leaves many thoughtful Protestants with no firm or clear foundation on which to build their faith.

To an atheist none of these things matter. Neither Church nor Bible has any authority for us. And since we do not believe in gods, the Holy Spirit has no authority either.

If we read the Bible at all, we read it as the 'holy' books of Jews, Christians and to a lesser degree moslems too. All sorts of questions may fill our minds but there is only one that really matters. Is there anything in these books that can help me to live my life in the best possible way? At once there are other questions. Is the Bible worth reading for its stories, poetry and so on? But although I have no doubt that I shall often be side-tracked and sometimes I may indulge in a little gentle mockery, that is the only question I want to try to answer in the pages that follow.

So, why bother?

There seem to me to be a number of reasons.

Thanks to the historical coincidence of the invention of printing and the Protestant Reformation both coming at about the same time, the Bible has been incredibly influential in European history. Wherever Protestant Christianity has known a period of dominance, the Bible has had a powerful impact. As a result, a reading of the Bible should help towards a greater understanding of the society to which we belong.

A study of Greek and Roman literature adds to our understanding of our society in much the same way. All have been major contributors to our culture and tradition.

Secondly, a study of the Bible should help towards an

12

understanding of the Judaic religions and their followers. Parts of it are of importance to Jews and Moslems and all of it is important to Christians.

We shall soon discover that religious people themselves look at their scriptures in different ways. At one extreme are the people who take the view that the books have been virtually dictated by their god and that the authors are little more than clerks reproducing his materials. Others see the books as human and fallible attempts to express the mind and will of their god through poetry, history, law and prophecy. This kind of person takes into account the historical and environmental circumstances which helped to mould the books and acknowledges that they were written over the course of about 1000 years by many different authors. Believing that the books contain messages of eternal value, s/he will attempt to apply the voice of the past to the present.

So I'm going to bother with the Bible because I hope to add to my own understanding of my European and specifically British background, and because I hope to add to my understanding of my religious friends.

There are other reasons. The Bible contains passages of great literature. When Sir Arthur Quiller-Couch was guest lecturer at Oxford for a year he used the Authorised Version of the book of Job as a textbook for English literature.

And of course, many authors still use the Bible as sources of ideas for their own work. Perhaps the best known present day examples are Tim Rice and Andrew Lloyd-Webber with their musicals of *Joseph and the Amazing Technicolour Dreamcoat* and *Jesus Christ Superstar*.

I hope that I shall find other reasons as I go along. Above all, I hope that I shall find it all worth the effort. We shall see.

Many years ago, when I was a Christian, I read a book called *A Christian Agnostic* by Leslie Weatherhead, one of the best known English Protestants of his day. In his book he claimed that it was a waste of time reading large parts of the Bible. At the time I was shocked, but he was absolutely right.

My book may help curious atheists and perhaps some Christians too, to skip the barren acres of print (or should that be hectares) and concentrate their attention on those passages that are helpful in our quest to live life well.

Perhaps my pages may also help those religious people who are prepared to listen, to discover that atheists are no different from anybody else. They also want to live their lives to the best of their ability. And if religions have anything to teach them they are willing to be taught.

Few of us are scholars. We do not come to books as scholars. We come simply to read. The printed page either makes an impact on us, or fails to do so.

That is the way in which I shall approach my task. I am not interested in dates or authorship or accuracy of text or any of the other things over which scholars agonise. I shall simply read the text of the Bible; allow it to say what it has to say to me; and comment on what I read. Like it or lump it, that is the way it will be.

Leslie Scrase

Part One

THE OLD
TESTAMENT

Section One

The Pentateuch

The first five books of the Bible are sometimes known as the Torah (the Law) and sometimes as the Pentateuch. They are of especial importance to orthodox Jews who believe that they contain the law of their god and the history which gives them a special relationship with that god. But Jews do not restrict Torah to the things found in these books.

The books are also important to Christians and Moslems.

Genesis

Accounts of the creation

The Bible begins with accounts of the creation of the world. At once we are faced with the question of creation or evolution, or both!

Darwin's *On the Origin of Species* posed immense problems for religious people. They could defend the indefensible and live in a world of make believe, or they could accept the truth of evolution and move on.

We now call the former 'creationists'. They are an aberration, unworthy of our attention and I shall not bother with them.

Sensible religious people fully accept the truths of Darwinism. For them there are only two questions left. Did their God envisage and initiate the evolutionary process? They would say

17

that he did. Has their God still got his hand on the tiller? They would say that he has.

Frankly, these things are unknowable (given the present state of human knowledge). The religious person has as much right to his belief as the atheist has to his unbelief.

With that by way of preface, let us get down to the Bible itself, noting in passing that the chapter and verse headings are no part of the original manuscript. They were added for our convenience and they were not always added very sensibly or well.

Genesis begins with an account of the creation of the world by God in six days. No wonder he took the seventh day off as a day of rest. Sabbath and Sunday customs and laws all derive from this. Many of them were foolish and pernickety and we have spent a great deal of time and effort getting rid of them. But we forget the underlying principle at our peril:

Humans need regular rest and refreshment.

No one in his right mind takes this account (Genesis 1:1–2, 3) literally any more. But it is worth reading for its sheer literary beauty and order. It has the same kind of structural beauty as a Renaissance work of art, the same clarity and beauty and purity of line.

It contains one verse which troubles many people today. 1:28 has God giving humans dominion over all other living things. If these words are treated just as the words of a beautiful poem, they don't matter. But if the verse is treated as the word of God, it has serious implications.

This verse in Genesis suggests that we humans are the lords of all we survey. There is a growing awareness among those of us who care about the environment that that kind of attitude has done, and is doing, enormous damage in the world.

We need to learn that the world does not exist for us. We are interdependent beings. In fact we are even less significant than that. We are utterly dependent beings, relying on a host of other living things, from the humble bee through a wide variety of plants and insects and animals, for our very existence.

The human race can only survive if it learns that lesson and unlearns the Biblical one. We shall only survive if we learn to share, cherish and nurture the world we live in.

Genesis 2:4–4:26 — *Creation Stories*

Genesis now offers us something quite different – an account of creation and human beginnings told in story form. These are the famous Adam and Eve stories and they are great fun.

Adam and Eve, the first humans, are placed in a beautiful garden. They are perfectly free except for one prohibition. They must not eat of the fruit of the tree of knowledge. Since they are human, it is inevitable that before long the forbidden fruit will prove too tempting. They eat. But of course, God knows what they have done.

When he questions them he receives the classic schoolchild response: 'Please sir, it wasn't me sir, it was her sir' and then from Eve in desperation, looking around to see who she could blame, 'Please sir, it wasn't me sir, it was . . . the snake sir.'

Unfortunately for them God proves to be the classic school-master: 'You are all guilty and you will all be punished (including the snake!).'

These stories are only stories but they do raise one or two questions. God's masculinity troubles some people nowadays. People go to such silly lengths to try to rectify the situation. Why can't they simply accept that God is portrayed as masculine because of the society which is portraying him. As the ancient Greeks pointed out, if we were horses we would portray God as a horse, though they didn't go on to tell us whether horses would portray God as a stallion or mare! Such questions are not worth bothering with.

But we SHOULD bother about the rule laid down in the garden of Eden. Adam and Eve were not to eat of 'the tree of the knowledge of good and evil'.

Wherever there is power, there is always an unwillingness to share knowledge. Religions have always loved what they call 'mystery' – the mystery of the apostolic succession, the mystery of the sacraments and so on. Royalty loved to claim a similar mystery from the anointing of the coronation. And all Governments are obsessed with secrecy.

The less we (ordinary people) know and the less we think, the better for all of them. It is far easier to govern and rule an ignorant people than a knowing people. When ordinary people discover that their priests and prime ministers are no more than Hans Christian Anderson's Emperor dressed in his new clothes; when we learn that they are no wiser than we are and that they are just as foolish as we are, then we begin to stand on our own feet and to dispense with their services.

Genesis 4:1–16

In Genesis 4:1–16 there is a story about Cain and Abel, two sons of Adam and Eve. It is a story to point up the age-long hostility between nomadic shepherds and settled farmers. Since the early Jewish tribes were nomadic shepherds, Abel the shepherd is the goody and Cain the farmer is the baddy.

At one level this story can be summed up with the song from the musical *Oklahoma*: 'Oh the farmer and the cowboy should be friends.'

But there are important things to consider in this story. In the story Cain murders his brother. Although he is punished, there is no death penalty and God also specifically opposes the kind of vengeance killing which can lead to feuds continuing from one generation to another. It is remarkable to find such an enlightened approach in such ancient literature. (Sadly the Bible is not consistent and is often thoroughly unenlightened. Only a few chapters further on in Genesis – in chapter 9 – we shall find God regarding capital punishment as a fitting punishment for murder.)

At the heart of this story, when God questions Cain about his brother, Cain tries to get away with things by pleading ignorance. I find his words among the most haunting words in the whole Bible: 'Am I my brother's keeper?'

The simple answer is that we are not. Each individual is responsible for his or her own life. But the simple answer is not enough. This is surely a question that should always be at the forefront of our minds. What are our responsibilities towards other people?

It is when we use the Bible in this way instead of asking the old chestnut about where Cain's wife came from, that it begins to be a valuable resource. Just as many children's stories used to end with a moral, so there are moral questions contained within many Biblical stories and passages which are worth examination and continuing thought.

But we can now skip to chapter 6. . .
Biblical writers were fascinated by (invented) genealogies and
that is more or less all we have here. So although this chapter
provided me with the starting point of one of the poems published
in my book *The Game Goes On* it need not trouble us – except
perhaps for one sentence.

I sometimes like to mention that in Britain there were people
who, as far as we can make out, lived without religion for
between 50 and 60 thousand years. A tiny verse in Genesis 4:26
suggests that there was also a time in the middle east when people
did without religion: 'At that time men *began* to call upon the
name of the Lord'! Perhaps the earliest human beings were wiser
than we have been ever since.

Genesis 6–10 — *The Great Flood*
In Genesis chapters 6 to 10 we have the story of Noah and the
flood. If we read it simply as a story we shan't be side-tracked by
its impossibilities. I once read figures which someone had worked
out showing how long it would take a sloth to get from South
America to Noah's ark!

Anyone who has known what it is to be flooded will know
what a devastating experience it can be. The loss of possessions,
the ruining of homes, the deaths of cattle, sheep, not to mention
wildlife, and sometimes the human fatalities make floods
experiences people never forget. It is no wonder that many
ancient societies have stories of terrible floods (including, for
example, the American Indians and the ancient Greeks).

The point of the Bible story is God's promise never to inflict
such a flood again, a promise guaranteed by the rainbow. Those
who have lived through present day natural disasters may wonder
how much God's promise is worth.

During the course of the story, God binds himself to the *whole
of humanity* in a covenant relationship. Such inclusiveness is rare
in the Bible. Sadly it does not even outlast the Noah story.

In chapter 9 there is the sad picture of Noah getting drunk and
being seen drunk and naked by his son Ham. Such an old man
naked cannot have been a pretty sight. Ham reacts as many
children would have done. Full of mirth he comes out of his
father's tent and says to his brothers, 'Come and look at this.'

The fact that they didn't, either tells us something of their quality, or it tells us what prudes they were. I'm never sure which!

Noah was furious with his son. Like many elderly people he expected to be treated with respect by his sons. Why is it that the elderly expect respect just because they are old? Why do we expect respect just because we are parents? Why do we expect respect for our achievements, such as they are? Unlike most of us, Noah also expected respect because he was 'a righteous man, blameless in his generation.' (6:9) After all, hadn't God given him respect?

What he fails to recognise is that, at every moment of life, respect has to be earned. His drunkenness had forfeited his right to his son's respect.

But he cursed his son. 'A slave of slaves shall he be to his brothers.' (9:25) And now see the incredible perversity of human logic. This curse of Noah was used by white Christians as an excuse for enslaving black Africans – or rather as a justification. The argument went something like this:

Ham was cursed by Noah and by extension by God with perpetual slavery.

Black Africans are slaves. Therefore Ham's descendants were black Africans. Therefore it is God's will that black Africans should always be slaves. Therefore the slave trade is the fulfilment of God's will.

This is a vivid example of the tortuous reasoning by which religious people often seek to justify the evil that they do. There are times when the Bible, or rather the misuse of the Bible, has a great deal to answer for.

Genesis 11:1–9 — *The Tower of Babel*

In Genesis 11:1–9 there is the story of the tower of Babel. In the story, people have one language and work harmoniously and co-operatively with one another until God steps in. God sees that 'nothing that they propose to do will now be impossible for them' (11:6) so he scatters them throughout the world and destroys the unity of language that has enabled them to co-operate.

Religious people interpret this passage as a story of God's hostility to human pride. But if you come to the story without religious beliefs, the picture is rather different.

22

Human life and work are good without God! He becomes the baddy of the story, jealous of human accomplishments and of the fact that they have no need of him. Their co-operation renders him unnecessary and he can't stand being redundant. So he sets about destroying human unity by destroying their unity of language. This does not sound like a God worthy of our worship.

Fortunately modern technology is enabling us to overcome language barriers and to work together once more – something we have achieved without God's help. So perhaps the moral of this story is; if we do without divisive religious beliefs and the gods behind them, we shall manage to achieve real co-operation and harmony.

Genesis chapters 12–50 — *The Patriarchs and Joseph*

The whole of the rest of Genesis features four people, four generations of the same tribe of nomadic shepherds. Abram (who becomes Abraham), Isaac and Jacob are all tribal chieftains. The fourth, Joseph, breaks the mould. The stories told about them may possibly have some basis in history, perhaps on a par with the stories of King Arthur and Hereward the Wake. They are a record of ancient folklore with all the romance, confusion and embroidery that belongs to the genre. Nevertheless, there is a consistency about the characters of Abram, Jacob and Joseph that rings true.

Read simply as a story this whole chunk of Genesis makes for some good reading. But the Bible is supposed either to be or to include the Word of God. As a result, when we read we are expected to be on the lookout for things that should get us thinking, things that should enable us to live our lives in the best possible way.

I do not propose to provide a chapter by chapter, verse by verse commentary but rather to focus on those stories which caused me to stop and think. Other people would pinpoint different stories and examine them in different ways.

Genesis 12:1–25, 18 — *Abram = Abraham*

Abram is the most important of the four men. He is revered by both Jews and Arabs as the father of their race. He is honoured by

Jews, Christians and Moslems as the first in a long line of those who are a part of what is seen as God's plan to save the world from sin.

In most of the stories he comes across as a genuinely decent, honourable, god-fearing man, capable of real depth of love, genuine personal sacrifice and great nobility. In his relationship with his nephew Lot, he is revealed as a man of great generosity, a decisive man of action, but supremely as a generous and peace loving man totally without greed. And in the rather nasty stories about Sodom and Gomorrah he is revealed as a man who is both fairer and more compassionate than the god he serves.

His story begins in Babylonia near the city of Ur. It begins with God's instruction to him to move and with God's promise to bless him. So Abram sets off with his family and takes his nephew Lot with him. They settle in Canaan and God tells them that is to be their permanent home. But famine drives them into Egypt and presents us with a first story which doesn't paint Abram in a very good light – it is a story that is repeated twice more, once with Abram's son Isaac and his wife as the chief characters. The story looks no better the second and third times round! In this version Abram looks to protect himself by surrendering his wife Sarai to be taken into Pharaoh's harem as Abram's 'sister'. God steps in and plagues Pharaoh until he realises that Sarai is the problem and returns her unharmed to Abram.

The stories that follow in chapters 13–15 show Abram in a better light – generous, unselfish and peace-loving but ready to take decisive military action in order to save his nephew's family.

Chapters 16–18:15 are all about Abram's need for an heir and it is here that his name is changed to Abraham, 'the father of a multitude?' His wife's name is also changed from Sarai to Sarah. Told that they will have a child in their old age they both laugh, so the child is named Isaac meaning 'he laughs'.

Prior to the conception of Isaac, Sarai takes matters into her own hands and persuades Abram to have a child by a serving maid – Ishmael the father of the Arabs. From such small beginnings what troubles have arisen!

During the course of the stories about Abram we find that God's covenant relationship with all mankind has been narrowed significantly. It does not even include all Abram's descendants. Only the children of Isaac (the Jews) share the covenant relationship with God – a relationship marked by male physical circumcision.

Apparently male circumcision is not as daft as it seems. In the *London Review of Books* (20.9.07) Hilary Mantel wrote: 'Circumcision seems to cut a man's risk of contracting the (aids) virus by at least 50 per cent. It is also protective of his sexual partners.'

But why does God only protect the Israelites? Here are beginnings of racism, of divisiveness and exclusiveness. Do we blame God, the same God who divided people at the tower of Babel? Do we blame religion? Do we blame humanity?

Looking at the world as it is today, it is clear that we have learned nothing in 4,000 years. Religions and the gods have certainly played no part in binding peoples together. They are divided against themselves. At the very least they must share the blame, and often bear a major portion of that blame.

But in the end it comes down to people. We are responsible as human beings for our relationships with other human beings. It is as human beings that we have to find common ground with one another. We are the ones who must find ways to end all those things which divide us: race, colour, creed, class. We have to begin with ourselves.

Chapters 18:15 to the end of 19 — *Sodom and Gomorrah*

In chapter 18:15 the horrible stories of Sodom and Gomorrah begin. Having destroyed the earth with the Flood, God has now become more selective. He announces to Abraham that the two cities are to be destroyed because of the wickedness of their inhabitants.

But Abraham proves to be both fairer and more compassionate than the god he serves. He persuades his god that if there are any good people found in the cities, they should be saved.

And now, through to the end of chapter 19 we have the horror story of the destruction of Sodom and Gomorrah. Those who wrote the story will have seen it in a very different light to the way we see it today.

It expresses an ancient rural hostility to cities. In black and white terms, nomadic rural life is good and urban life is bad!

The story is about ancient traditions of hospitality. Abram's

b

nephew Lot is the goody, first because he extends hospitality to the visitors and then because he strives to protect them from the mob. The fact that he offers his own daughters to satisfy the lusts of the mob is not something to get worked up about. Daughters were regarded as expendable!

We see this story in a very different way. We recognise the lusts of the mob because we have become accustomed to the sight of mobs maddened by their sense of injustice and the futility of relying on governments and legal process; or just plain bored and looking for a bit of fun.

And whether people come to this country as refugees or simply as immigrants looking for better lives, there is a growing hostility to the ancient traditions of hospitality towards the stranger in our midst.

But the story raises other questions too – questions about the place of women in society and questions about sex. Women have fought long and hard to be given their rightful place in society but there are still many societies where their fight has barely begun, and some religions are particularly unhelpful to their cause.

The same is true of homosexuals. The Sodom and Gomorrah stories condemn *lust*. It is the lust that is condemned, not the homosexuality. Religion has failed to make that distinction, or has been happy to take other passages from the Bible where homosexuality *is* condemned. The prejudice and hostility of religion towards homosexuals is itself both ignorant and evil and it continues.

Homosexuality is as natural to homosexuals as heterosexual behaviour is to heterosexuals. ALL sexual behaviour should be judged by the same standards. It should be a private matter between consenting adults. The only elements that are essential are privacy and willing or eager consent. Beyond that, permanence is perhaps the ideal and there is no doubt that many homosexual relationships are as permanent and companionable as the very best heterosexual relationships.

However important sex may be, stories such as the Sodom and Gomorrah stories are replicated daily in the worst of the newspapers, and all give lurid support to all those hysterical people who love to judge, condemn and hate. SOME sexual activity *is* hateful. Things like rape and child abuse ARE vile. But a great deal of sexual activity is pretty trivial and neither psycho-

26

logically nor physically harmful. Often the physical act has no real emotional content at all and can happen almost incidentally or accidentally. I am reminded of the 19th century cockney family who all slept in one bed. I turned a conversation between father and daughter into verse:

> 'I'm sorry Glad
> I forcher was yer muvver.'

> ' 'as all right Dad,
> I forcher was me bruvver.' !!!

Curiously, the Sodom and Gomorrah story ends with another sexual episode which is often by-passed as if it were insignificant. The destruction has robbed Lot's daughters both of their mother and of their prospective husbands. So on successive nights they get their father drunk and lie with him to make sure that they have sons to continue their line. Do we condemn this reverse incest? Do we condemn the girls for taking out insurance for the future, for that is what they are doing. Or do we simply chuckle at the devious cleverness of these young women? The story itself contains no condemnation of their behaviour.

There is one more element in these stories which I want to refer to. Before the cities are destroyed Lot and his family were told to flee for their lives and not look back. Lot's wife looked back and was turned into a pillar of salt.

Similarly Orpheus bringing Persephone out of the place of the dead, looked back and lost her. There is a New Testament saying of Jesus: 'No man who sets his hand to the plough and looks back is worthy of me.'

Addicts of all kinds would acknowledge the importance of the 'don't look back' principle. One drink, one shot, one cigarette is enough to send people back to the addiction they thought they had conquered. All their struggle has been in vain. As in 'Snakes and Ladders' they are back where they started from. If we want to kick any kind of addiction there is no room for backward glances.

Genesis 22:1–19 — *Sacrifice*

The next significant story in Genesis is the story of God's testing of Abraham. In the story God requires Abraham to sacrifice his son Isaac ('your son, your only son Isaac, whom you love'). Such is Abraham's devotion to his God that he sets out to do just that. The story is told with great skill but Abraham's willingness to sacrifice his son comes in for a great deal of criticism nowadays, as does the idea of a God who could ask such a thing.

In fact the story marks a real advance! Many ancient peoples believed that the gods required sacrifices, mostly of birds and animals but sometimes humans too. This story is an attempt to teach people that the God of Abraham does not require *human* sacrifice. As such it is a small step in the right direction.

But as an atheist I look back with sadness at the terrible things religion has expected people to do. And I look back with considerable cynicism at a 'godly' priesthood laying down careful rules about animal and bird sacrifice to ensure that the priests never went short of the best cuts of meat!

Christians relate the non-sacrifice of the only son Isaac to the story of the sacrifice of Jesus the only son of God. What God did not require of Abraham he was prepared to go through himself on behalf of all of us.

There ARE vicarious sacrifices which are noble. The death of someone who gives his life saving someone else from drowning is an example. But this Christian picture of vicarious sacrifice is one that I find revolting, nor am I alone. Many Christians find it revolting too. The whole business of the sacrifice of the body and blood of Jesus, a sacrifice commemorated in the central Christian rite, is one which many Christians as well as many of the rest of us who are not Christian, find unacceptable. No doubt when we look at the New Testament we shall look at this all over again.

But how did humans ever come up with the horrible idea that the sacrifice of humans, birds, animals, could cleanse us from sin. To religion our most trivial misdemeanours are treated as if they were important to the gods, so important that we are expected to be riddled with guilt over them; so important that things must die to cleanse us. It all beggars belief but of course, it gave the priests great power for thousands of years – and it is power and wealth that religion is really all about.

Genesis 24 — *A wife for Isaac*

As we have seen, Genesis is full of good stories, many of them full of psychological insight.

One of my favourites is in Genesis 24 where a family retainer is sent to find a wife for Isaac. The man himself is utterly loyal and faithful, scrupulously honest and full of that rare wisdom which we call common sense. The wife he finds is hard working and decisive and, inevitably, beautiful. It is a lovely story.

Sadly, she has been found for a husband who is such a nonentity that we can turn immediately to consider one of their sons.

Genesis 27–38 — *Jacob*

Isaac and Rebekah had two children, twins. The hero of the next few chapters in Genesis is the younger of the twins, his mother's favourite, Jacob. Painted in strong colours he stands in the pages of Jewish literature honoured as a patriarch – a Jew honoured among Jews. Yet he is everything you will find in an old style, preholocaust European caricature of the Jews. Given the widespread influence of the Bible, he is perhaps more responsible for anti-Semitism than any other single person you can name.

Jacob has all those traits or characteristics with which non-Jews have typecast Jews. However unfair it may be; however wrong it may be – and it is both wrong and unfair – Jacob is the image set up by anti-Semitists as typical.

He was devious, crafty, cunning, deceitful and treacherous. Too clever by half, he was capable both of great courage and of great cowardice. His approach to the saying 'women and children first' was to put them first in the line of danger, giving himself the best chance of escape. He almost always looked after number one. He trusted no one and was utterly untrustworthy himself. He is a model only of how to achieve success by unscrupulous means. As you may gather, I have no time for him at all. If I were a Jew I would want to remove him from the pantheon of patriarchs and consign him to the outer darkness.

Jews dislike Shakespeare's Shylock and often feel that he has been the cause of much misunderstanding and anti-Semitism. Shylock was of course only a reflection of the way people thought about Jews then but Jews have every right to whinge at that particular image. However, their own image of a patriarchal Jew is infinitely worse than Shylock. If we take Jacob as a model of the Jews, Jews have only themselves to blame.

Since the holocaust it has become impossible for anyone to risk criticising Jews. It is not politically correct. But it is the Jews themselves who are making some of us feel that the time has come for simple honesty to raise its head. The state of Israel calls for condemnation on a host of different counts. Jews cannot hide behind the holocaust when they themselves are responsible for so much oppression, poverty, deprivation and death.

Genesis 29

Genesis chapter 29 has the story of how Jacob came to marry two sisters. The following pages show some of the problems people face within that kind of marital situation.

We have grown accustomed to thinking of the ideal marriage as the lifelong union of a man and a woman. But we have learned to tolerate the idea of single sex marriage, and we are perhaps beginning to learn to respect such marriages when they are stable. With a fifty per cent divorce rate and a good deal of unfaithfulness in the other fifty per cent, isn't it time that we did a complete rethink of our attitudes to marriage?

For me personally, the lifelong union ideal is the best though I haven't managed to live up to it and am now on my second marriage. But I don't see why that ideal should be regarded as the only possible ideal. Marriage is a unique human relationship. It presents problems and opportunities in human relationships that no other friendship knows.

I see no reason why we should not allow within the legal framework of our society all sorts of different kinds of marriage. Why should a man not have more than one wife at the same time? Why should a woman not have more than one husband? Why should we regard monogamy as the only right form of marriage?

My own preference is for monogamy and for heterosexual relationships. But that is a matter of preference and probably a measure of prejudice too. I can't see any real reason why any form of marriage should be taboo. As long as there is genuine care and consideration all round; as long as stability is aimed at; as long as children are provided with a stable, secure and caring environment; any form of marriage or relationship should be acceptable.

All kinds of marriage are subject to immense strains for marriage is a unique relationship. Perhaps monogamy has advantages over other kinds of marriage precisely because it has the simplicity of one to one. And perhaps a one to one relationship can reach depths of love that can be found in no other way. But even if those perhaps are true, none of us has any right to dictate to others. Given the conditions I have outlined above, ANY form of relationship should be acceptable.

Genesis 38 — *Tamar's Vindication*

I want to jump now to chapter 38. It tells the story of a very courageous woman. It is a story I never remember being told in Sunday School! Many teenagers would love it but they would probably miss the things that really matter about the story.

We have been looking at the stories of Jacob. Jacob had a son called Judah who married a Canaanite woman called Shua. Their marriage produced three sons, Er, Onan and Shelah.

Judah married the eldest of the three to a girl called Tamar, the heroine of the story.

Tamar's husband Er was a bad lot. His badness is not defined but it was so serious that God killed him leaving Tamar a childless widow.

Ancient tradition required that when a widow was left childless, the next brother in the family should give her a child who would be treated as his dead brother's child. Judah gave his second son Onan to Tamar but Onan was not prepared to play ball. He lay with Tamar but he practised coitus interruptus, withdrawing just before ejaculation and spilling his semen all over the bedroom floor.

God was not pleased. Instead of telling Judah what was going on and letting Judah sort his son out, God killed Onan. (Nice God these people worshipped.)

Judah took precisely the wrong message from this. He blamed Tamar and assumed that she was bad news. So when his third son Shelah was old enough to be given to Tamar, Judah held back. So Tamar was left a widow with no heir. What on earth should she do?

The story shows her ingenuity and courage. It also shows how Judah got his comeuppance. It is a thoroughly good story and it is a story which demonstrates very forcibly that morality is not always simple or straightforward. So what did Tamar do?

She obviously knew what a randy beggar her father-in-law was. So she placed herself on his route dressed and heavily veiled as a prostitute. He couldn't resist but he had no money! Could she trust him. Of course she could trust him provided he left his signet, his waist cord and his rod with her. (Note that there is no hint of criticism for Judah's behaviour. As a man he can do as he likes.)

When he sent a servant to pay her she had disappeared but in due course he learned that his wicked daughter-in-law had become pregnant. How evil can you get! She must be stoned to death for her sin.

'As she was being brought out [for stoning] she sent word to her father-in-law, "By the man to whom these belong, I am with child," and she returned his signet, his cord and his staff.'

What incredible courage! But she really did know her father-in-law. Ultimately he proves to be an honourable man, acknowledging his possessions and more than that, acknowledging that his daughter-in-law 'is more righteous than I.'

As I mentioned, I never heard the story in Sunday School but I never heard it from the pulpit either! But then, the God of the story is pretty awful and the morality far too complicated to be risked in public.

Genesis 37 and 39–50 — *Joseph*

I can skate over the remaining chapters of Genesis very lightly. They are the stories of Joseph, favourite son of Jacob by his favourite wife. If jealousy between wives is one of the problems of polygamous marriages, jealousy between children can be another – although jealousy between children can be a problem in any form of marriage.

As a boy, Joseph was a cocky little beggar who got away with it because he was his father's favourite. He riled his half brothers so much that they sold him into slavery and pretended that he was dead.

In slavery his underlying quality and virtue surfaced and

enabled him to triumph over adversity and achieve great things both for his Egyptian overlords and in the end, for his own people too.

These stories show the wisdom of good housekeeping in national affairs and the importance of using the good times to ensure that we can cope with the bad times. They offer basic wisdom for every level of human life.

And they are terrific stories of enmity, of wrongs done, of genuine affection and ultimate reconciliation (and they have earned Andrew Lloyd Webber and Tim Rice a pile of money).

For the writers of the Bible their chief purpose was to show why the great-grandchildren of Abraham left the promised land and ended up in Egypt. Faced with famine, they came to Egypt in search of food and pasture. They found both but over the course of time they became little better than slaves. The next book of the Bible (Exodus) will show how they recovered their freedom.

How much genuine history lies behind these stories no one knows – probably not very much.

Exodus

Genesis ended with the Israelite tribes in Egypt enjoying the privileges Joseph's protection brought them. Exodus begins with them still in Egypt but by this time they felt that they were a persecuted slave race. They may have been. But we should remember that all Egyptians were subject to three months conscript service a year, working on the great building works of the Pharaohs. This would not have gone down well with nomadic shepherds.

Egyptian civilisation and religion were far in advance of anything else in the western world. It is interesting to speculate on how much influence it had on the Jews and also on the early Christians. What follows is *only speculation* but it seems to me to be significant.

I'm told that the events of Exodus are probably to be dated round about 1300 BCE. From 1352 to 1336 Amenhotep IV carried out a short-lived revolution in Egyptian religion. He reduced the gods to just one: Aten the faceless one. Under Moses, the ancient

Jews were taught that their god was the only real god. Moses carried the Egyptian revolution just one stage further. No image at all was to be made of this god.

As we shall see later in our study of the Bible, until the Hasidims, the predecessors of the Pharisees, the Jews had no real belief in life after death. How much were their later beliefs influenced by the Egyptian obsession with life beyond this one? And how much does the Christian resurrection story owe to the myths of Isis and Osiris? Iris went to the place of the dead before being resurrected by Osiris.

And how much does the Catholic veneration of Mary 'the Mother of God' owe to the Egyptian worship of Isis the Universal Mother? There is considerable similarity between images of Isis suckling Horus and the Madonna with child.

But all of this is a considerable digression. Exodus tells the story of Moses who became the leader of the Israelites (the early Jews) and led them out of Egypt to freedom and to the borders of the country they hoped to make their own. It provides the Jews with the myths of their birth as a religious nation, myths which underlie some of the most important rituals of their calendar.

The well known story of Moses in the bulrushes has parallels in other cultures. It is an enjoyable read as is the story of the call of Moses to leadership many years later. God calls Moses to become the leader of his people and chapter 4 has a delightful account of his attempts to dodge the column, ending with Moses' final plea: 'Oh my Lord, send I pray some other person.' (4:13)

The following chapters are not particularly edifying. They are full of magic and signs and wonders. There is a good deal of unpleasantness and cruelty. Although God describes himself as 'merciful and gracious, slow to anger and abounding in steadfast love and faithfulness, keeping steadfast love for thousands, forgiving iniquity and transgression and sin', there is precious little sign of it.

Unless we regard these pages as holy scripture, we should expect them to be pretty primitive in their ideas. The god portrayed is dishonest, capricious, cruel, jealous and violent. He is a god who frightens people into obedience. He is unforgiving and unjust. He 'will by no means clear the guilty, visiting the iniquity of the fathers upon the children and the children's children, to the third and fourth generation.'

If the book of Exodus has any interest at all, it lies in the fact that it is from the events described in Genesis and Exodus that the Jews derive their sense of nationhood and their idea that they are the chosen people of God, 'a kingdom of priests and a holy nation'. (19:6)

But that is an idea which raises many, many questions. As applied to the Jews, it was rejected by Christians who saw themselves as inheritors of the title. And then it was rejected by Moslems who, in their turn, saw themselves as inheritors of the title.

But if this god is god over all, why would he choose *any* single nation or religious group? When he was so busy choosing the Jews what was he doing throughout the rest of the African continent, or in Asia or Europe, Australasia or the Americas? Out of all the people in the world was he only interested in a few thousand roaming the desert areas of Sinai?

Exodus describes the origin of the Jewish Passover festival and the giving of the ten commandments. In general terms most of us would go along with the last six of these:

'Honour your father and your mother . . . You shall not kill. . . you shall not commit adultery. . . steal. . . bear false witness. . . covet.' (20:12–18)

Notice that most of the ten commandments are negative. Many years ago I listened to a child psychologist who spoke of the changes that take place in our language towards children as they grow. We begin by spending a great deal of our time with Joyce Grenfell's Primary School Teacher saying 'Don't do that.'

As children grow older we begin to find ourselves switching from the negative to the positive – often a pretty forceful positive – 'Do as I tell you!'

But it isn't long before the voice of authority doesn't work any more and then comes the more thoughtful, 'This is the kind of person it is worth striving to be.'

So we move from 'don't' to 'do' to 'be'. The ten commandments are direct commands for people who are incapable of thinking things out for themselves. They are for young children even if they retain their basic relevance throughout our lives. That is why they are so popular with both priests and politicians. Both these groups of people like to treat us as if we were children instead of engaging us in thoughtful debate.

Some of the ten commandments are about our relationship with God. For an atheist these are completely meaningless. But an atheist will also have a different attitude to the commandments to which I have given a measure of approval. If they are divine laws then they are absolute. But if they are not divine we shall not think of them as in any sense absolute. For example, Victor Hugo's novel *Les Miserables* demonstrates very forcibly the fact that there are times when the command 'thou shalt not steal' should be set on one side. But having said that, six of the commands are a pretty good rule of thumb basis for a good deal of life. The world would undoubtedly be a better place if we all took them seriously.

Perhaps today's world also needs to take more seriously the requirement for one day off work each week. We have forgotten lessons learned in the mid 20th century. Overloading people leads to a deterioration in their standards of work. The same is true of long hours. We all need regular rest and refreshment. Whether that rest time is spent in religious worship is up to each of us to decide. Those of us who have no religious beliefs are that much freer to pursue our favourite leisure pursuits.

After the great escape from Egypt across 'the Red Sea' (probably not the Red Sea at all), the Jewish tribes spent forty years getting to Palestine and they grew rather fractious in the process (who wouldn't). So when the commandments were given, they were given in a (volcanic?) context that left people with a terrifying image of their god's power. Fear of their god was intended to persuade them to keep the law. But fear does not last. *Laws have to commend themselves to us if we are to be persuaded to keep them.*

There are a large number of laws in Exodus. Many of them (see chapter 21) were fairly humane for their time and with one exception chapter 23 verses 1–12 was so far ahead of its time that even now we do not attain its standards in some of our everyday living. The exception is in verse 5 where consideration is given to an enemy in trouble but no concern at all is shown towards his poor, overloaded donkey.

I have done my best to give praise where it is due. But there is one law which has been used as an excuse to put to death thousands of innocent women – and I mean thousands. That is not an exaggeration. It is the law in 22:18; 'You shall not permit a sorceress to live.'

In its application of this law and its treatment of so-called 'witches' religion has been diabolical, encouraging ordinary human fear and superstition and also human nastiness.

Most of the rest of Exodus is concerned with the manufacture of the tent of worship, the box which was to carry the ten commandments, and priestly and ceremonial regulations – the trappings of worship. It has no relevance for today at all.

Did the events described in Exodus actually happen? There is virtually no evidence. What little evidence there is suggests that they could not have happened in the way described. Throughout this period Egypt ruled over Canaan and had a strong military presence there including Egyptian garrisons throughout the Sinai desert. There was nothing to stop nomadic tribes wandering in the desert and having their own beliefs and customs but we should not think of this book as real history.

Leviticus

With the possible exception of chapter 19, there is no point in reading this book at all.

Leviticus is a book of laws – divine laws. One of the problems with divine law is that it is unreasoned and unreasoning. We are told what we should do and (far more often) what we should not do but we are almost never given the reason why.

Some Moslem friends of mine claimed that we have no business to ask. God has spoken and that is enough. I'm afraid that it is not enough for me.

The law in Leviticus is often a law of retribution. Worse than that, the death sentence is pronounced on a whole range of offences including blasphemy. If these laws from Leviticus were enforced in full, multitudes of us would have been put to death long ago. It is, I suppose, one way of dealing with the world's population crisis for religions opposed to sensible methods of birth control.

There are also quite a lot of laws concerning slavery. Slavery was regarded as perfectly normal and acceptable for non-Jews but not for the Jews themselves. They were God's chosen people.

If we regard this book as containing the law of God, then we are in trouble. But if we regard it simply as a set of laws fashioned by a primitive people we shall not even bother to read most of them.

We shall ignore chapters 1–17 which are mostly full of ceremonial and ritual law, and also include Jewish dietary laws.

It is also likely that we shall skip chapter 18 which gives rules about forbidden sexual relationships. Prohibited relationships include those between close relatives, between humans and animals and also homosexual relationships. The Bible is consistently hostile to homosexual relationships. In consequence the Judaic religions are also pretty hostile.

This is sad in itself and sometimes worse than sad – evil. But it is particularly sad for those homosexuals who crave the ritual that is at the heart of much religious practice.

They will find no comfort in Leviticus which makes it very clear (in chapter 20) that most sexual 'crimes' are punishable by death!

In the whole of Leviticus perhaps the only chapter worth reading is chapter 19. Here humanitarian concerns break through.

So having dismissed practically the whole of Leviticus, let me end by paying attention to some verses in chapter 19:

19:3 and 32 encourage reverence for parents and the elderly.

19:13 reminds me of a row I once had with a boss of mine when he was tardy in paying an impecunious member of staff: 'The wages of a hired servant shall not remain with you all night until the morning.'

Most of 19:14–15 seems obvious enough: 'You shall not curse the deaf or put a stumbling block before the blind. You shall do no injustice in judgement.'

Do you find that puzzling? Why would anyone curse the deaf or put a stumbling block in the way of the blind?

We have to put ourselves into the mind-set of religious people of the time. Deafness and blindness were not looked upon simply as tragic, disabling limitations. They were judgements of God upon sinful people – the fact that the sins were not known was completely irrelevant.

So these words mark an advance on the general thinking of the time. And the next words are worth thinking about too: 'You shall not be partial to the poor or defer to the great.'

Today's society, no less than any other, needs to be reminded not to defer to the so-called great and good. But should we not be 'partial to the poor'? Those are words worth more than a moment or two of our thought. I often watch well-meaning attempts by charities to do things for 'the poor' and find myself asking, why have the poor not done these things for themselves? It isn't just a lack of resources. We need to beware of undermining people's responsibility to stand on their own feet, and their capacity to do so.

Kindness and generosity to the 'deserving' poor needs to be thought about very carefully and needs to be both enabling and uplifting as well as supportive.

In this tedious book, at last we have found things worth our attention. Verses 16 and 18 give us two more:

16: 'You shall not go up and down as a slanderer among your people, and you shall not stand forth against the life of your neighbour.'

19:18 is one of the two laws which Jesus regarded as all important and as a summary of all the rest:

'You shall love your neighbour as yourself.'

I have seen sensible, critical comment on that law which suggests that there are better ways of loving our neighbour than loving them as we love ourselves. It may seem like a rather petty quibble but it is worth thinking about. It should not distract us from the essential importance of the acknowledgement that decent people will strive for a good relationship with their neighbours, will care about them and sometimes even care for them.

And Leviticus also has something valuable to say when it includes 'the stranger who sojourns with you' (19:34) as one to whom this law of neighbourly love applies.

Verse 31 tells us not to place reliance upon mediums or wizards and verse 35 tells merchants to give honest measures. A swift jump to chapter 25 brings us to some laws about property and slavery, the proper use of land, and also laws about caring for others within the family (verses 35–37).

But although these passages are useful reminders to thoughtful people of our responsibilities towards our families, our guests, the stranger or migrant in our midst, and the world's disadvantaged, most of Leviticus is not worth the effort required to read it.

Numbers

I suggested that the book of Leviticus was not worth reading. I can't recommend the book of Numbers either. Apart from one story and three verses in chapter 6 it is thoroughly unedifying. It contains all sorts of stories about the time Jewish tribes wandered in limbo before invading Palestine.

The god of this book is very quick to anger and very ready to destroy. Several times Moses has to point out to him the folly of the destruction he has in mind. I remember reading once that the gods of Homer were just like humans only more so. That is also true of the god of the ancient Jews. Abram was more compassionate than this god. Moses is sometimes wiser, out only sometimes. Like his god he can be utterly ruthless in violence and slaughter.

This is true whether we are dealing in individuals or nations. In 15:32–36 we read of a man gathering sticks on the sabbath day. For this 'crime' he is stoned to death. In chapter 25 Zimri is killed for marrying a Midianite woman. She is also killed of course.

And of nations: 'They utterly destroyed the Canaanites and their cities. 'Israel slew Ammon [ie the whole tribe] and took possession of his land.' 'They slew Og, king of Bashan, and his sons; and all his people until there was not one survivor left.'

When they fought the Midianites (c. 31) they killed every male and took the women and children captive. But that was not enough for Moses. All the male children were slaughtered and their mothers with them. Curiously enough, in a nation so obsessed with racial purity, the virgins and female children are allowed to live: 'All the young girls who have not known man by lying with him, keep alive for yourselves.' (v. 18)

The story of Balaam's ass:
And so we come to the story of Balaam's ass in chapters 22–24. I doubt if many people read it today. The scene is already set. Land-hungry Israelite tribes are on the march. A settled Moabite

tribe feels threatened and the king and his elders are scared stiff. So they turn to Balaam who is some kind of witch-doctor or holy man. The king sends messengers asking:

'Come now, curse this people [the Israelites] for me,
since they are too mighty for me;
perhaps I shall be able to defeat them
and drive them from the land;
for I know that he whom you bless is blessed,
and he whom you curse is cursed.'

In the following verses (22:9–14) Balaam asks God whether he should go and God says 'no'.

King Barak tries again, sending his messengers to Balaam, hoping for a better answer. But Balaam is an honest holy man so he passes on God's message which this time is, yes, you can go to Barak 'But only what I bid you, that shall you do.'

So Balaam saddled his ass and went, and having told him to go, God is angry with him for going!

God sent his angel with a sword to block Balaam's path but only Balaam's ass can see the angel. So the ass turns off the path to avoid the angel and Balaam beats her for doing so and forces her back onto the path.

Meanwhile the angel has moved to a narrower bit of path. It is more difficult to get past but the ass tries and Balaam's foot gets hurt against the rock as the ass squeezes past, so Balaam strikes his ass again.

The angel moves to a still narrower spot and the ass can't get past so she lays down to protect her master and gets a third beating. So far God has not bothered about these beatings but now he gives the ass the power of human speech. With wonderful economy of narrative the ass taxes Balaam with his injustice and Balaam acknowledges his fault. (22:28–35)

Since God has now made it clear to the man as well as to the ass that he has changed his mind and doesn't want Balaam to go to the king, Balaam offers to return home, at which point God changes his mind again 'so Balaam went on with the princes of Balak'. After all that the ass has suffered, we are back to square one.

Advised by Balaam, Balak offers the required sacrifices to

41

God and then asks for God's message, expecting it to be favourable, but it isn't. Instead of the Israelites being cursed, they are blessed. Balak decides to try again on another hill-top. Perhaps he can twist God's arm if he offers more sacrifices, but the attempt is fruitless. The message from God is the same only more so. God is for the Israelites.

In desperation Balak tries once more. Surely his persistence and his sacrifices will pay off. But the message from God, via Balaam, is even more unequivocal. Incredibly, the king, in spite of all his disappointment and desperation, proves to be an honourable man and allows Balaam to go home.

And the denouement? In chapter 31 we are told of the slaughter of the Midianites including every male child and all women except virgins and female children. 'And they also slew Balaam the son of Be'or with the sword.'

If people read this story at all, they will remember it for the ass more than for anything else. It is significant that I remember it as the story of 'Balaam's ass'. The ass certainly deserves to be remembered. There are many stories in life and in literature of animals, notably dogs and horses, saving their owners' lives because of their greater awareness of the environment. This must be one of the very first such stories. Balaam's ass should go down as one of the first known life-savers.

She is nobler than her master and far nobler than the God of the story. God is fickle. First he tells Balaam not to respond to the king's summons. Then he tells him to go. Then he condemns him for going. Then he tells him to go. You don't know where you are with this God. And finally, when Balaam has done all that God requires, God allows him to be killed by his bloodthirsty chosen people when they destroy the Midianites. Not a nice God at all.

Balaam himself is a man of complete courage and integrity, absolute consistency and firmness of purpose. He is incorruptible and fearless. Nothing will deflect him from doing his job and speaking what he believes to be the word of his god, no matter how unpalatable that word may be. He shows us that the best of men and women have far more to offer us than gods created in our image.

That leaves us with just three verses in the whole book which I treasure. They form a beautiful blessing in chapter 6 verses 24–26:

'The Lord bless you and keep you. The Lord make his face to shine upon you and be gracious to you. The Lord lift up the light of his countenance upon you, and give you peace.'

I can understand words like that meaning a tremendous amount to people who believe in God. Blessings used to have considerable power in superstitious ways. The Genesis story of Jacob stealing Esau's blessing points this up very clearly. Words were thought to have a power greater than themselves – a power to bestow what they wish for.

In attempting to modernise, the churches have often failed to sustain the power of language. Many modern translations of the Bible and many modern service books use language as flat and banal as could be.

There is a seduction in language that can be dangerous, and superstition is something to be resisted and opposed. But having said that, we all want to express our good wishes – again and again. The greetings card industry depends on that desire.

Some of us who are not religious conduct ceremonies for other like-minded people. We could not use the passage in Numbers, beautiful though it is. But its beauty and charm may well inspire us to find ways in which we can express our own good wishes carefully. It is good to send people away from a ceremony with positive, cheering, comforting words for their future happiness and well-being.

Deuteronomy

The word 'Deuteronomy' is probably best known today as the name of one of the cats in an Andrew Lloyd Webber musical. That demonstrates how far knowledge of the Bible has been sidelined in modern society.

The book purports to be Moses' farewell speech to his people. For simplicity's sake I have called them 'Jews' and will continue to do so. They were actually a group of Semitic tribes known by a common overall title which has changed several times throughout history.

Chapter 4:1–30 has an impressive depiction of the power of God and his relationship with his people. It includes a condemnation of graven images 'in the form of any figure, the likeness of male or female. . .'

One wonders what Moses would have made of Christian crucifixes with their images of the man they call God the Son, pictures of the bleeding heart of Jesus, statues of the virgin Mary, not to mention the farce of weeping statues, holy shrouds, relics of wood or bone – the tourist (pilgrimage) trappings of the centuries.

There are works of art among them which we can appreciate for their quality. But most of them are common, vulgar and tasteless, pandering to human superstition and ignorance.

Deuteronomy 5 repeats the ten commandments and then in chapter six we come to the most important verses in the whole of Jewish law (6:4–9). They are known as the Shema and are the very heart of the Jewish religion and also of their sense of nationhood. They contain the words: 'you shall love the Lord your God with all your heart, and with all your soul and with all your mind.'

For Jews, as for Christians and Moslems, their god is unique. Their lives, not just their thinking, are intended to be centred upon this god with a devotion that is the supreme devotion of their lives – greater even than the devotion to their closest human companions. I don't suppose anyone can really understand this without becoming involved – without actually becoming a devotee.

But without that kind of involvement, it may be that this passage has valuable things to say to all of us. All the three religions I have mentioned regard their god as the supreme good. If we replace the concept of god with our understanding of the good these words suddenly seem to become more relevant; you shall love the *good* with all your heart and with all your might, and teach your children to do the same.

44

Curiously enough there is no reason why we should not pop in an extra vowel. The Jews regarded the name of their god as of such holiness that it should never be pronounced. Since they wrote without vowels no one knows for sure what the vowels in the name of their god JHVH or YHWH should be. Some call him Yahweh and some Jehovah.

If we really did focus on the good, how much better the world would be, how much better local society would be; how much better our own lives would be. Jews who take their religion seriously repeat the Shema constantly as a reminder of the central focus of their lives. Might it not be a useful idea to encourage a similar focus on the good?

Sadly it is as difficult to define the Good as it is to define God. One plus which may come from this reading of the Bible is that in studying Biblical ideas about God we shall also be studying ideas about the Good. We may be helped towards our definitions, though we shall probably never feel completely assured that we have got it right and we shall certainly never achieve unanimity.

However, with or without the Bible and with or without unanimity, we can always find enough agreement to carry us forward in life. Focusing on a minimum agreed definition of the Good would bring human society benefits beyond our wildest dreams.

Much of the book of Deuteronomy is powerfully written. After all these centuries its message comes across forcefully. But parts of it need to be rejected equally forcefully.

The concept of a chosen people is a dangerous and divisive one. Even religious people can't agree on who the chosen people are. Jews? Christians? Moslems? All too often that idea of a chosen people has led to racism, brutality, cruelty, human destruction and strife. In 7:16 and 23–24 for example, God is said to command:

'You shall destroy all the peoples that the Lord your God will give over to you, your eye shall not pity them. . .'

It is not enough that religious people reject that as a command of God. Along with a great deal of similar material, it actually needs to be removed from the body of 'holy writ'. As long as it continues to bear that name, it can be misused both by religious extremists and by the enemies of religion.

While reading chapter nine I found myself musing on the contrived artificiality of the New Testament story of Jesus. Here, there is a picture of the Jewish escape from Egypt; of Moses receiving the law on the mountain; and of the advance into the Promised Land after forty years in the wilderness.

In the gospels Jesus, the second Moses, comes out of Egypt and later goes into the desert place to prepare for his ministry – for forty days – before coming to lead his new chosen people into the promised land of the kingdom of God. How much is fact and how much is fiction? Can anybody say?

A similar comparison can be made between the Jewish Passover and the Christian Last Supper, the foundation of the central rite of Christian worship.

Returning to Deuteronomy: the second half of chapter ten contains a very powerful portrayal of the character of God which still stirs the hearts and minds of those who believe in him. It contains elements worth consideration by all those who are interested in the development of our human characters and society. God is depicted as 'not partial' (so no chosen people then?), 'taking no bribe', executing 'justice for the fatherless and the widow', caring for 'the sojourner' (the immigrant?), the visitor.

These are all qualities we look for and cultivate in any decent, civilised society and it does us no harm to be reminded of them.

In chapters 11 and 12 the relationship between God and his chosen people is spelt out. On their part complete obedience and single-minded faithfulness are required. On God's side there is the promise of care for the faithful and death and destruction for those who fail to keep their side of the bargain: a carrot and a pretty comprehensive stick. If I believed in God I wouldn't think much of a god who falls so far below the best human relationships.

46

Chapter 15 is about generosity to the poor and includes the law of release. It is an interesting one. At the end of every seven years debtors are to be released from their debts and slaves are to be given the opportunity of choosing freedom.

I don't imagine that these laws have ever been strictly adhered to, but what a transformation (and what havoc in the financial markets) if they were. The strong feeling among many that third world debts should be cancelled is not unrelated to this kind of idea, and is supported by some of the churches. Many of those debts are largely the result of the purchase of armaments over the years – purchases which have benefited countries like Britain, France and America with their huge armaments industries. If there is a cancellation, perhaps it should be linked to some sort of limitation on the sale and purchase of arms.

In chapter 16, in the midst of a mass of useless ritual law, there is a charge to judges. There was another in chapter one. Both of them are worth quoting:

> 'Judge righteously between a man and his brother or the alien that is with him. You shall not be partial in judgement; you shall hear the small and the great alike; you shall not be afraid in the face of man. . .' (1:16–17)

Similarly, judges. . .

> '. . .shall judge the people with righteous judgement. You shall not pervert justice; you shall not show partiality; and you shall not take a bribe, for a bribe blinds the eyes of the wise and subverts the cause of the righteous. Justice, and only justice, you shall follow.' (16:18b–20a)

Chapter 18 contains condemnation of 'anyone who practices divination, a soothsayer, or an augur, or a sorcerer, or a charmer, or a medium, or a wizard, or a necromancer.' The author is determined to leave no one out.

Where such people are taken seriously they can be dangerous. Psychiatrists will all have people on file who have needed treatment as a result of the damage they cause. But I would guess that there are far fewer of those than the many thousands slaughtered for witchcraft over the centuries. Is religion to blame or society? As we leave such things behind us, do we reject the Bible or Biblical religion as well? I come back to what I said earlier. Liberal Biblical scholarship with its 'pick and mix' mentality is not enough. 'Holy writ' needs to be shriven. All that is unholy needs cutting out.

It needs to be physically removed if atheists like me are to read the Bible and find it worthy of our best attention. In the meantime we shall feel that any gold is surrounded by far too much dross.

My Christian brother has taken me to task for this last paragraph. He writes:

'Holy writ cannot be tampered with. From a secular point of view it is a historical source book and must not be tampered with. What each of us make of it is a different story.

'Liberals may well say that the sections you admire may be God inspired and the rest man made. Since they don't accept verbal inspiration they are no more picking and mixing than you are.

'Deuteronomy is a bit like a museum of ancient art. We have so few pieces that we cannot bear to throw away anything at all. But some few pieces are inspired – well before their time. The rest is dross. Let's hold up the first and neglect the second. You are doing this. The liberals do this.

'YOU may do a rewrite and draw attention to all that's worthy but we must hold on to our source book, warts and all.'

He is absolutely right, of course. But perhaps religious people should produce abridged versions of their holy books for ordinary consumption. The trouble is, they would never be able to agree about what should go in and what should be left out.

Chapter 19 underlines that. It demands to be taken seriously, but it remains behind the level of the best of human thought and endeavour. It sees the criminal law as a law of retribution, even if it aims at fair retribution. The question 'why' is never asked. 'Why should we obey the law?' 'Why did the criminal commit this crime?' Nor is there any thought of rehabilitation or of reclaiming a criminal for a decent future life.

'Your eye shall not pity; it shall be life for life, eye for eye, tooth for tooth, hand for hand, foot for foot.' (19:21)

Those are memorable sentiments and many people never rise above them, but they hardly represent an ideal towards which we should move. And the death penalty is there for all sorts of trivial offences: a son who 'is stubborn and rebellious, a glutton and a drunkard.' (21:20) It makes you wonder how many of us would survive into adult life.

Many of the laws are ridiculous (eg 22:5 & 23:1) and many more are ruthless and harsh beyond belief – more criminal than the sexual offences with which they seek to deal.

Chapter 23:2 refers to illegitimate children and condemns them to suffer because of the behaviour of their parents. Why? Yet such a law was taken seriously enough to ensure that such children have suffered throughout western society well into the twentieth century.

Religion underpinned and gave blessing to such laws. Wherever human progress towards a decent and humanitarian society has been attempted, there you will find the dead weight or even the active hostility of religion holding things back. And this is still true. In those societies where Christianity or Islam still have power, the people suffer from inhuman laws and from their religions' obsession with sex.

And yet there are times when Deuteronomic law can be very humane. This is never true of sexual matters, where its devotion to detail would sometimes be funny if it were not so serious (25:11–12), but when dealing with such things as human possessions, wealth and poverty, then the law can be humane and kindly (24:10–15 & 17–22).

Chapter 28 tells the Jews the blessings of obedience to God's law and the punishments for disobedience. Needless to say, it is far more eloquent on punishment than on blessing. The chapter is powerfully written, but people will only believe such things if they are borne out in their daily experience. They are not. Human behaviour is not black and white and life is not just. We are neither rewarded for virtue nor punished for wrongdoing. If we

49

choose a path of virtue it must be for its own sake and not because of the promise of rewards or the threat of punishment. The Bible consistently gets this wrong.

Except for chapter 32:2 there is nothing else in Deuteronomy worth mentioning. It ends with the Jews poised to enter Palestine, their Promised Land, and with the death of Moses. But 32:2 expresses a wish and a hope which any teacher might echo:

> 'May my teaching drop as the rain,
> my speech distil as the dew,
> as the gentle rain upon the tender grass.

Deuteronomy has been a difficult book to study. It is full of so much that is good and so much that is bad. Whatever you think of its (often contradictory) teachings, it is a book which repays close study and I'm well aware that I have not done justice to it. I hope that by reducing my comments to bite-sized chunks, I have at least managed to make it accessible.

We have reached the end of the Torah, the Law. For Jews it is the most important part of scripture. But they would stress that it has to be read and understood in the light of Mishnah (c. 200 CE) and the Talmud (c. 55 CE). These define and demonstrate how to interpret and obey the law. Christians interpret it in the light of the New Testament, Moslems in the light of the Quran. I have simply taken it as it comes and that will be my approach throughout.

The Historical Books

For Jews the second section of the scriptures is the Nevi'im – the Prophets. These include most of the historical books: Joshua, Judges, 1 & 2 Samuel and 1 & 2 Kings.

Four other historical books (1 & 2 Chronicles, Ezra and Nehemiah) belong to the third Jewish grouping, the writings or Ketuvim.

The word historical should not be taken too seriously. There IS history here but the authors were far more concerned with God and religion than with historical accuracy.

For simplicity's sake, I shall follow the order of the Old Testament and take all the historical books together, plus the tiny book of Ruth.

Joshua

The book of Joshua can be ignored completely.

It tells the story of the invasion of Palestine by the Jews. Although the Bible is supposed to be God's book and God's truth we need not imagine that there is much connection between the story in Joshua and reality.

Modern archeology has demolished many of the 'facts' of

Joshua, but in fact, the Bible itself demolishes them. Unlike Thucydides the Greek, the Jews had little interest in factual history. Their only interest lay in demonstrating the power and glory of their God and of his Chosen People – a people who shared God's power as long as they were obedient to him.

The story begins excitingly enough with spies and a collaborator, continues with miracles and becomes an utterly boring tale of wholesale success and slaughter. It ends with the division of the country between different Jewish tribes and with the death of Joshua.

Later in Old Testament history the Jews divided into two separate kingdoms. Chapter 22 has a story pretending to date from Joshua's time. It aims to demonstrate that the two nations are one people.

In chapters 23 and 24 in Joshua's farewell speech he warns the people to preserve their racial purity because God doesn't approve of mixed marriages. The next book (Judges) will show us that that was a warning the Jews ignored.

Throughout the Old Testament we shall find a division between those who took Joshua's line and those who recognised that racial purity is a fiction. Even if it were desirable, as many of these Jews thought, it was not possible. It is not possible. One of the most serious failures of our time has been the failure to learn that any form of racism is intolerable.

But it is here, in these early pages of the Bible, that we find the first written evidence of racial intolerance and the beginning of the long sorry saga of religion supporting racism. It led with horrible irony to the holocaust, the doctrine of apartheid and the appalling 'ethnic cleansing' in East Europe. Racism continues to be a curse infecting the daily life of multitudes of ordinary human beings.

Judges

For anyone in a hurry, this is another book that can be skipped. The book of Judges corrects the historical picture painted in Joshua. In Joshua we are given the impression that conquest led to the complete extermination of the previous inhabitants of

Palestine (with the exception of the tribe of Gibeon). The invaders were painted as having overwhelming power, thanks to their god.

Judges makes it clear that the truth was rather different. For the tribe of Judah 'could not drive out the inhabitants of the plain because they had chariots' (1:19) and in Jerusalem of all places the tribe of Benjamin 'did not drive out the Jebusites . . . so the Jebusites have dwelt with the people of Benjamin in Jerusalem to this day.' (1:21)

It is clear that the Jewish tribes did not really *conquer* Palestine at all. They moved into the hill country and established themselves alongside the people already living there. Disputes broke out and sometimes the Jews won and sometimes they lost, but they did manage to establish themselves and they laid claim to wider areas than they actually managed to hold. They also intermingled with their predecessors. There was no such thing as purity of race or religion.

> 'The people of Israel dwelt among the Canaanites, the Hittites, the Amorites, the Perizzites, the Hivites and the Jebusites; and they took their daughters to themselves for wives, and their own daughters they gave to their sons; and they served their gods.'
> (3:5–6)

History in the book of Judges is recorded as a series of cycles:

The Jews worship the agricultural gods of their neighbours. Things go badly and they are oppressed. They cry out to their own god who had proved himself to be a god of war. He explains their oppression as the result of their worship of other gods. Then he calls out a leader, a 'judge', who conquers their enemies. They live in peace and plenty, turn to the agricultural gods for help with their farming, and the whole cycle begins again.

Their god is a jealous god who intends them to learn that the agricultural gods are not gods at all. He is the only god and he alone is to be worshipped.

Some of the stories in Judges make quite good reading but, with one exception, there is nothing actually *worth* reading. Many, such as the stories of Samson in chapters 13–16, are of about the same quality as the war stories in pictures that many boys love to read.

Samson was a great lout who couldn't resist a pretty woman. Each woman he fell for caused trouble and the last, Jezebel, caused both his own downfall and that of the Philistines. The stuff of sensational films, it has nothing to do with religion or anything else of value either.

The book ends with a horrible story almost identical to that in Genesis 19 which described the destruction of Sodom and Gomorrah. The horror leads to civil war between the eleven tribes and the twelfth, the tribe of Benjamin. So another book of 'holy scripture' draws to its close. The only story within its pages which might be considered worth reading is in chapter 11.

It tells the tragic story of Jephthah's vow and the sacrifice of his daughter. It is a story which still has power to move the heart. It was the inspiration for Handel's last great oratorio.

Only slowly did the Jews learn that human sacrifice is unacceptable and not until the Roman destruction of Jerusalem in the first century did they cease to sacrifice animals and birds to God. But in these things they were no worse than the rest of the human race.

These crimes are down to human superstition, ignorance and folly as much as to religion. As we rid ourselves of religion can we be sure that we shall also rid ourselves of superstition, irrational behaviour and cruelty? The evidence is not encouraging.

Ruth

It is a pleasure to turn from the things we have been reading to the book of Ruth.

This is a delightful little story full of romance, kindness and decency. It contains one of the most beautiful and moving declarations of love and fidelity that we shall ever meet and is one of the few books in the Old Testament that is really worth preserving.

The story begins in tragedy. Because of famine a man from Bethlehem takes his wife Naomi and his two sons to the neighbouring country of the Moabites.

The man dies. His two sons take Moabite wives (more mixed marriages) and then they both die. So Naomi is left in a foreign country with two foreign daughters-in-law to care for. She decides to go home.

She urges her daughters-in-law to return to their parents. 'May the Lord deal kindly with you, as you have dealt kindly with the dead and with me.'

There is genuine and deep affection between the women but eventually one of the girls goes home. This leaves Naomi with Ruth. But when Naomi points out to Ruth the wisdom of going back to her parents, Ruth says:

'Entreat me not to leave you or to return from following you; for where you go I will go, and where you lodge I will lodge; your people shall be my people, and your God my God; where you die I will die, and there will be buried.' (1:16–17)

So the two come to Bethlehem to a future which promises nothing but poverty and hardship.

After the reapers had cut the harvest, the poor were allowed to glean the leavings so Ruth went out to collect what she could, and proved to be a hard worker.

As it happens one of Naomi's in-laws is a well-to-do farmer (believe it or not, there have been such people). He sees Ruth working, has heard her story and ensures that she is treated well and with respect.

When Ruth reports on her day, Naomi smells romance and opportunity. She tells Ruth to offer herself to Boaz and Ruth does her bidding. It is all very modest and tasteful.

Boaz treats her with respect and kindness but points out that there is a man who has a prior claim to her according to the laws of kinship. The following day he invites the man to take up his claim. When he refuses, Boaz takes Ruth as his wife.

Why does the Bible contain this lovely story? Because the son of this mixed marriage was the grandfather of King David, the ideal king of Jewish romantic religious and historical memory.

When we come to Matthew's gospel we shall find that, in his genealogy of Jesus, Matthew makes great play of the fact that four of the women in the line of David were unsatisfactory to purist Jews. Ruth was one of them.

1 and 2 Samuel

The books of Samuel tell the story of the prophet/priest Samuel and of the first two kings of the Jews, Saul and David. They are composite books containing more than one tradition of some of the same stories.

There are some excellent stories, one of the best known being the story of David and Goliath, and the books are very popular with Christians for use with children.

Quite incidentally the first chapter gives an insight into one of the problems which can face women in a polygamous society. However, the intention of the early chapters is to describe how Samuel becomes the leading priest of the Jews. The story of the call of Samuel by God was always a great favourite in religious circles and rightly so for it is a very moving story and much of it is very lovely.

Throughout history there have been a host of such stories, stories of men and women who have felt that they had a direct call from God to become his servants. When candidates for the Methodist ministry were interviewed one of the things they always used to be asked was to describe their 'call to the ministry'. Even at the time, I felt that it was an artificial thing and presumptuous of us to suggest that we had been specially singled out by God for this work. But there are people, and there have always been people, who feel that they have had a direct call from God to serve him in some specific way.

Whilst I am now of the opinion that there is always a psychological explanation for these experiences, I don't think we should call them in question or mock them. They are very real to those who have them and often lead to significant lives.

From chapter eight onwards comes the story of how the Jewish tribes adopted monarchy as their form of government and of how Samuel anointed Saul as the first king.

Neither God nor Samuel were keen on the idea of monarchy. They both preferred a theocracy. When was religion ever willing to share power with a secular authority? Samuel warns the people of the monarchy but they still choose to 'be like other nations'.

So Saul became king and led the people into battles galore.

Right from the start there were tensions between Samuel and Saul. Saul consistently showed a measure of independence of spirit and acted on his own initiative. In his treatment of the vanquished and of the spoils of war he was more practical and less ruthless than God and his priest desired. And there were times, in the absence of Samuel, when he took on priestly functions.

In Sunday schools there was often a tendency to paint simplistic pictures of Samuel the man of God and Saul the king who was too big for his boots. But the book reveals a much more complex picture. A good psychological novel or play could be written about the relationship between Samuel and Saul on the one hand, and Saul and David (who has yet to appear) on the other.

It seems to me that it is largely the behaviour of Samuel towards this highly superstitious king that gradually broke him down and led to his depressive illness and his final destruction. Here was man with great potential, destroyed by a priest who has become too rigid and too powerful – a priest feared by the people. (16:4).

Chapter 16:7 is a very famous verse and worth a moment's thought:

'The Lord sees not as man sees; man looks on the outward appearance, but the Lord looks on the heart.'

16:12 promptly contradicts this and shows the Lord choosing a man who 'was ruddy, and had beautiful eyes, and was handsome', but the principle of verse 7 is a wise one. We all need to learn not to judge by outward appearances.

From 16:14ff we begin to see the signs of Saul's depressive illness – an illness which was regarded as being sent by God. David's music helped him to cope. Music is often a help to people suffering from illnesses of the mind.

The belief that such illnesses were sent by God hindered the development of a proper understanding of mental illnesses and of such things as epilepsy. How different was the approach of such people as Hippocrates and the members of his school. (See my book *Some Ancestors of Humanism*.)

Sadly it was the religious approach to illness which was to dominate thought in Europe for many centuries. Other approaches were suppressed by an all-powerful church. Although great strides have been made in the 20th century, there is still a long way to go and illnesses of the mind still receive far less attention (and far less money) than physical illness.

1 Samuel 17 contains the famous story of David and Goliath. Written with considerable skill and drama, it is a good read and demonstrates the supreme self-confidence of the young, in this case supported by absolute faith in God. As I write, football lovers will perhaps think of the precocious skills of teenaged young stars, and gymnasts have long been thrilled by the fearless abilities of fourteen/fifteen year old schoolchildren. As we grow older our self-confidence wanes and we grow more aware of all those other factors which combine to work against human achievement.

The story of David and Goliath is a superb story. It is probably not a true story. In Samuel 21:19 the credit for killing Goliath is given to Elthanan. That is probably the truth. Elthanan's glory was transferred to David, the ideal king, in some ancient image building.

Chapter 18 records David's growing success and popularity and the king's fits of jealousy and hostility. But the king's son Jonathan and David become bosom pals and David marries the king's second daughter Michal. The story of David and Jonathan is of a deep and genuine friendship. Jonathan comes across as a particularly genuine, straightforward and decent man.

But the king's suspicious hostility grows and David flees to become an outlaw, a sort of Robin Hood figure. There are stories of David having opportunities to kill the king and refusing to do so because the king is God's anointed. Some of these stories are very special and well worth reading.

Finally David seeks refuge among the Philistines and only avoids having to fight against his own people because the Philistines do not fully trust him. Saul's sons are killed in battle against the Philistines. Saul himself is wounded and dies rather than fall into enemy hands. There are two differing accounts of his death which carry us into the second book of Samuel.

The second book tells the story of David's reign as king. The division of the Jews between Judah and Benjamin and the ten tribes of Israel is already clear. Although they unite under David and his son Solomon, the fault line is already clear and division is never far away. In fact it is there from the beginning of Jewish history, dating from Jacob's time and experiences in Egypt which not all the tribes shared. In chapter 7 God promises David that his family will continue to be kings for ever: 'and your house and your kingdom shall be made sure for ever before me; your throne shall be established for ever.'

Religious people claim that 'God's promises never fail'. This one did.

In chapters 11 and 12 the story of David and Bathsheba is told. This story of forbidden love and the abuse of power is a must. It is worth reading for a variety of reasons, not least because it is a good story well told.

Although David has any number of wives and concubines, he falls for Bathsheba, the wife of Uriah. While Uriah is away serving in the army, David takes Bathsheba and makes her pregnant. He tries to cover his tracks by bringing Uriah home on leave. But Uriah has an incredible sense of justice and comradeship. He refuses to lie in comfort and delight with his wife while his comrades are in danger and discomfort at the front. So David arranges for Uriah to be killed in battle and then adds Bathsheba to his harem.

For the very first time God is displeased with David. He sends Nathan the prophet to denounce the king and announce his punishment. The story is full of drama. If it actually happened, then Nathan showed immense courage as well as the ability to tell a forceful parable. As I said earlier, *this story is a must.* There are not too many Nathans around, nor are there many in positions of power with the grace and integrity to accept such a condemnation.

The message is applicable to anybody with any kind of power. Power is not to be abused. The abuse of power may not bring the punishment of a god, but it will inevitably bring the decay and corruption of character. One of the values of genuine democracy is that power is held in check and can be taken away.

The second half of the chapter is interesting for David's approach to the sickness of his child and to grief. When people are ill and their illness leads to death, we fight as hard as we can for life, if we know that we are fighting a losing battle we often do a great deal of our grieving while they are still alive. Death may actually come as quite a relief. As Julius Caesar said, 'Death is a relief from troubles. . . it puts an end to all mortal ills.'

We turn from death to celebrate our loved ones as they were in the fullness of their powers, and we begin slowly to turn back to our own lives again.

Following the Bathsheba incident, the story of David the ideal king has peaked. The watershed has been reached and it is now downhill all the way from chapter 13 onwards. It all begins with the rape of his daughter Tamar by her half-brother Amnon which leads to the murder of Amnon by Tamar's brother Absalom. This leads to a split between the king and Absalom which seems to be patched up but ultimately leads to the rebellion of Absalom against his father.

The rebellion is crushed and (against David's express orders) Absalom is killed. This is followed by another rebellion in which the fault line between Judah and Israel is revealed again. The union of the twelve tribes is very fragile and it never takes much to bring division.

In chapter 22 there is a very powerful poem about God and his relationship to David.

It has value as poetry and also gives a picture of what is expected of a blameless and righteous man: loyalty, purity, honesty, straightforwardness and humility – a set of values we can all respect.

As poetry it has much to teach us about the power of words to hold and inspire. The Bible, the Quran, the Bhagavad Gita and old poems such as Beowulf and the Viking sagas, all contain passages which have immense power when read aloud. It is good to glory in their poetic force but dangerous to be seduced by them.

There is nothing more in 2 Samuel worth our attention.

(Note: I have been ticked off for saying that God wishes/ intends/does despicable things. I should only say that people believed this of him. It is a fair comment. But since this is what the Bible says over and over again – God said/God did, etc – I'm afraid that I shall ignore my critic and go on with Bible usage!)

1 and 2 Kings

1 Kings begins with the story of the reign of Solomon after a palace coup. Solomon was the son of David and Bathsheba. Solomon asked God for 'an understanding mind to govern thy people, that I may discern between good and evil.' He was immediately presented with the puzzle of two women claiming the same child. For those who don't know the story it is worth reading 3:16–28.

The rest of the story of Solomon is eminently skippable. It tells the story of the building of God's temple in Jerusalem (which took seven years) and the building of Solomon's palace (which took thirteen years – and heavy taxation).

Solomon was renowned for his wisdom, but it was such that it left his son facing a very rebellious people. His building works and his luxurious life-style had overtaxed the people. As soon as he was dead the ten tribes of the north rebelled against his son and set up a separate kingdom. For a long time to come there were to be two Jewish kingdoms: Israel in the north and Judah centred on Jerusalem. The story of the divided kingdom need not concern us. We can move forward to chapter seventeen and the stories which feature Elijah the prophet.

These stories are full of miracles and (particularly in chapter eighteen) full of drama too. For us the stories are important in two ways. They show how primitive belief in the gods still was, and they raise the question of the role of prophecy.

Belief in the gods

In chapter 20 we are told that when the Syrians lost a battle against the Israelites they assumed that it was because they had fought in the hills. 'Their gods are gods of the hills.' As a result they planned to fight the next battle on the plain.

From their point of view there was good evidence for this. When the Jews first invaded their promised land, they gained a foothold in the hills, but failed to conquer the cities of the plains where armies had chariots.

The Jews of the same period shared the Syrian belief in a large number of gods. What set them apart was their belief that their own god was not limited by geography. He was not a god of hills or rivers or valleys or trees or rocks. He was a national god and they were his chosen people. As a result, he was their god wherever they were. He travelled with them and was to be worshipped wherever they went.

As long as the ark of the covenant was kept in a tent, this belief was strengthened because the ark could travel with them if the need arose. It was a belief weakened when Solomon built the temple in Jerusalem and housed the ark of the covenant there. From that time onwards there were Jews who insisted that the worship of their god must be in Jerusalem. The results of that belief rumble on still.

It was a belief which Jesus was to deny (John 4:21) but he still believed that 'salvation is from the Jews'.

The gods believed in were pretty horrible. Those Jewish kings who are said to have done 'evil in the sight of the Lord' shared in the worship practices of their neighbours, practices which still included human sacrifice. But the god of the Jews was not much better. Some of the things attributed to his commands were foul. Nowhere is that clearer than in these boring chapters of wars, civil war and bloodshed in the name of God. If such a god were real, far from worshipping him, any decent human being would revile and denounce him.

However, towards the end of 2 Kings (chapter 19, vs.18 and 19) in the prayer of Hezekiah, there is a major step forward. He claims that gods other than the God of the Jews are 'not gods, but the work of men's hands, wood and stone.' 'Thou, O Lord, art God *alone*.' This is a major advance.

Many years ago I used to lecture to sixth forms and others on the historical progress from polytheism to monotheism. Even then I used to wonder why no listener ever suggested that perhaps the next stage in human history was progress from monotheism to atheism. In the course of time I was to take that final step into atheism and to find that there were plenty of others who shared my belief that there are no gods at all.

In the light of all that, let us return to Elijah and 1 Kings 18. There is a great contest on Mount Carmel between the prophets of Baal who worshipped gods of place and Elijah who worshipped the national god of the Jews. Elijah challenged his nation:

> 'How long will you go limping with two different opinions? If the
> Lord is God, follow him; but if Baal, then follow him.' (18:21)

The logic of belief in a national god is that, even if other gods
exist, they are not to be worshipped by Jews. The Jewish national
god is a jealous god who requires his chosen people to worship
him to the exclusion of all other gods.

But the atheist is bound to ask, what if there are no gods? Why
then we cease to be worshippers or followers. We work out our
own best path through life, willing to learn from both religious
and non-religious sources and testing what they have to say
against our own experience of life and our own thinking.

In 18:27, when Baal makes no response to his prophets'
prayers, Elijah mocks them: 'either he is musing, or he has gone
aside, or he is on a journey, or perhaps he is asleep and must be
awakened.'

But such mockery rebounds all too easily. As I write there is
famine in South Sudan caused partly by drought and partly by
civil war between the Moslem government and the Christian
south. As I write there is famine. As you read there will be
something else, for there is always something happening or
brewing somewhere in the world. And where is God in all of this?

Where is God in natural disasters? Where is God when
religious factions fight it out in the Sudan or the Balkans, in Iraq
or Israel/Palestine? Either he does not care, or he sleeps, or he is
powerless, or perhaps he does not exist at all.

There are many people who are not atheists but who still find
it hard to believe in a loving creator who has made such a hell of
a mess (I use the word hell advisedly) of the world and of the
humans who are supposed to be 'made in his image'.

Note on Prophecy

The stories of Elijah introduce us to the first of those who are
thought of as major prophets. What truth there is in any of the
stories about him is anybody's guess.

Just as Moses became the model law giver and David the
model king, so Elijah became the model prophet. Followers of
John the Baptist were to claim that he was a second Elijah and
followers of Jesus were to claim that he was a second Moses, a
son of David, and a greater prophet than Elijah.

The prophets seem originally to have been little more than dancing dervishes. Group hysteria was not understood. Dervishes were assumed to have divine or diabolical possession. They terrified some people but there were always others who were more cynical. When King David was caught up in prophetic frenzy his wife Michal despised him for it. (2 Samuel 6:16)

But there was always a more serious side to prophecy. The famous story of Nathan in 2 Samuel 12, to which we have already referred, makes this vividly clear. The prophets were regarded as the mouthpiece of God and the conscience of the nation. They called kings and people to account, summoning them to do what was right and passing judgement when they failed.

Inevitably they were also seen as people who could foretell the future but most Biblical foretelling is a sham. Centuries after events have taken place, writers put those events into the mouths of prophets as prophecies of the future. When Bible writers actually try to look into the future they prove to be no better with a crystal ball than the rest of us.

The best example of Biblical foretelling being a sham is the book of Daniel.

Much foretelling is not a sham but just plain wrong. As a result it 'had to be explained away. It was born of the conviction that God would not desert his people but would intervene' in history on their behalf. 'Most prophecies assume that intervention will come in the prophet's life-time or soon after' (this is also true of the prophecies of Jesus). 'The explaining away has to shift the intervention by a few hundred or a few thousand years. The Messiah foretold by Isaiah and Jeremiah was expected to deal with the threat to Judah from Assyria and then Babylon.' But no Messiah came.

The prophets as crystal ball merchants are unimportant. It is in their central role, when they call people to do what is right, that they are important. For what is right is important whether it is claimed that knowledge of it comes from a god or from human understanding. It may well be that we shall find that some of the prophets have valuable insights to share with us. Curiously enough, Elijah is not one of them. The stories about him may make good reading but they teach us nothing at all.

Elijah's end carries us into 2 Kings chapters 1 and 2. The story begins in mystery with Elijah being carried into heaven on a chariot of fire with horses of fire. It ends in extreme bathos. Elijah's successor is Elisha. Jeered at by small boys because he was bald, he used the power of God to summon wild bears out of the forest to maul them. If we pretend for a moment that these stories are true, both Elisha and God must take responsibility for a pretty horrific act. Earlier Elijah had caused two groups of fifty men sent to him by the king to be burned alive. Again both he and his god must accept responsibility.

It is such stories which must call into question the value of the Bible. Holy? Clearly not. God's word? If so, God is despicable. If not, let the Bible be judged in purely human terms and not surrounded with a false aura of supernatural significance.

The early chapters of 2 Kings, the stories of Elisha, have such close similarities with parts of the first three gospels that one can't help wondering how many of the 'miracles' of Jesus were simply inventions aimed at showing that Jesus was even greater than the Old Testament prophets.

The stories themselves make quite good reading. In chapter 4 Elisha fed 100 men with 20 loaves, but Jesus fed 5000 with 5. In chapter 5 Elisha heals a boy who was thought to be dead (notice that Elisha himself never says that the boy is dead). It is a story which has many similarities with the gospel story of Jesus raising the daughter of Jairus from the dead (notice that Jesus himself never says that she is dead, only that she 'sleeps'). In 2 Kings 5 Elisha cures leprosy. Jesus did the same.

I'm told that many Christian scholars would put this more strongly than I have done. They accept that it was 'surely very easy for a Jesus enthusiast to be sure that if Elisha could cure leprosy then Jesus obviously must have been able to.' So stories accrued and multiplied. This, according to these scholars, should make us hesitate to affirm the accuracy of the New Testament but 'doesn't lessen the importance of Jesus'.

Even if that is true, it surely makes it extremely difficult for ordinary people to assess what his importance really was. But we'll worry about that when we reach the New Testament.

The rest of 2 Kings is of almost no interest at all. It tells the story of good kings and bad kings through several centuries.

It is perhaps noteworthy that Manasseh, the king most renowned for wickedness, had the longest reign of all, fifty-five years. Since God failed to dislodge him, the punishment for

65

Manasseh's sins fell on a generation so far removed from him that only the historians would have had any knowledge of him at all. Such is the nature of divine justice apparently.

There are two noteworthy historical moments in these chapters. In 721 BCE the Assyrians under King Shalmaneser carried the people of the northern kingdom into exile and repopulated the land with exiles from other conquered countries. These were to become the 'Samaritans' so hated and despised on racial grounds by the pure blooded Jews of Judah with their pure worship in Jerusalem.

In chapters 18 and 19 the story is told of Sennacherib's abortive attack on Jerusalem. It looks as though some kind of epidemic swept through his encamped armies leading him to call off the siege. These are the chapters that lie behind Byron's poem:

> 'The Assyrian came down like a wolf on the fold
> and his cohorts were gleaming in purple and gold. . .'

Chapter 22 tells the story of the reforms of Josiah on the basis of the book of the law and the re-enactment of the Jewish passover festival. But in spite of these reforms, at the end of his reign the Jews came under the authority of the Pharaoh of Egypt. When he was conquered by the Babylonians it was not long before the Jews followed. This time (586 BCE) Jerusalem was destroyed and the leading Jews of Judah were taken into exile to Babylon. Thus miserably the tale ends.

I should perhaps add a comment or two about the reforms of Josiah in 621 BCE (chapter 22). They came about because of the 'discovery' of a book of law in the Temple. Whether it was an old book just discovered, as the story claims, or a book just written and conveniently 'found' is an open question. But it is widely believed to be the first actual book of Jewish sacred scripture. It probably comprised most of the present book of Deuteronomy (chapters 5 to 26 and chapter 28).

It is not so much 'law' as a preacher's reinterpretation of the law in the spirit of the reforming prophets. We shall turn our attention to these prophets in due course.

1 and 2 Chronicles

With the exception of 1 Chron. 16:5–34 which is a magnificent and exhilarating poem there is little point in reading either of these books. They tell the story already told in 1 and 2 Kings although this version has been censored. For example, there is no mention of David's misbehaviour with Bathsheba.

Belief in the gods is still thoroughly superstitious and worship is sacrificial. The gods are thought of as those who send natural disasters such as drought, pestilence and disease. These are punishments for wickedness.

In 1 Chronicles 5:22 there is a little comment about a battle that 'many were slain because the war was of God'. Is this a recognition that religion exacerbates human conflict? It does not, as it so often claims, bring peace and reconciliation.

Solomon's prayer in 2 Chronicles 6 perhaps marks a measure of advance in religious thinking. It specifically links forgiveness with penitence and blessing with walking in 'the good way'. It asks God, 'if they repent with all their mind and with all their heart . . . then maintain their cause and forgive.' (2 Chronicles 6:38–39)

These links are as important in human relationships and human justice as they are in the field of religion. It may be extraordinarily difficult to judge whether repentance is genuine, but a judicial system aimed at the reform of criminals and their reclamation for decent society is infinitely more worthwhile than one which is solely concerned with punishment and the security of those who obey the law.

In 2 Chronicles 16:12 there is a comment which may amuse. King Asa 'did not seek the Lord' in his final illness 'but sought help from physicians'. Needless to say, he died.

The story of Micaiah the prophet in 2 Chronicles 18 (already told in Kings) illustrates that most prophets were more concerned to tell people what they wanted to hear than to tell them the truth.

Finally in 2 Chronicles 25:4 there is a law to which I have already referred; 'The fathers shall not be put to death for the children, or the children be put to death for the fathers; but every man shall die for his own sin.'

This recognition of personal and individual responsibility is a major advance on the view that punishment should continue 'to the third and fourth generation'.

The history generally is a sad tale of the division of the Jewish tribes between Israel and Judah; of their periodic subjugation by their neighbours Syria, Egypt, Assyria and finally Babylon; of times when they worshipped their own god with a measure of faithfulness and of times when events convinced them that it would be wise to worship the gods of their stronger neighbours. Neither policy worked and, as we have seen, in the end the top people of Israel were carried into exile in Assyria and the top people of Judah to exile in Babylon.

Ezra

There are no good reasons for reading Ezra and a number of good reasons for not reading it. Although it records events of genuine historical significance it does so in the dullest possible manner. To make matters worse, it stands for much that is vile in the field of ethics and human relationships.

The exile of the Jews of Judah brought the first example of the incredible determination of the Jews to sustain themselves as a separate people with their own separate religion.

We may not think much of religion in general or of the religion of the Jews as we have seen it so far. However, their religion and their belief in themselves as the chosen people of their god were major factors in their survival as a nation.

The fact of their survival both then and since is one of the most amazing stories in all of world history. But there has been a high price to pay for Jewish separatism. Jews themselves have paid a high price, perhaps the highest. But there are many other peoples who have suffered severely both as a direct result of Jewish separatism, and indirectly through the racist ideas at the root of all such separatism.

Ezra begins with a decree of Cyrus, king of Persia, allowing the Jews to return home. Those few who become returned-exiles set about building a new temple in Jerusalem. The people already in Palestine offered to help 'for we worship your God as you do, and we have been sacrificing to him ever since the days of Esarhaddon king of Assyria who brought us here.' (4:2)

It was a wonderful opportunity. It may well have been the supreme opportunity for establishing true peace and happiness in Palestine. The returned Jews rejected it out of hand on the grounds of racial and religious purity.

Race and religion: two of the greatest divisive forces in the whole sad story of human history. Both are still at it in Palestine/ Israel; in the Balkans; Afghanistan; all over the world. Only the reduction of nationalism to the levels of cultural difference and sport, together with the destruction of the power of all kinds of religion; only these things and the development of secular internationalism can put an end to all these long standing hostilities.

This is why, in spite of all their faults and weaknesses, the United Nations Organisation and such smaller groupings as the European Union deserve our wholehearted support.

It is in Ezra that Jerusalem first really becomes regarded as the Jewish holy city, although the movement towards that idea was visible throughout the earlier historical books from the time of David onwards. But if Jews and Christians and to a lesser degree Moslems too, regard Jerusalem as a holy city, most of us will probably translate the view expressed in Ezra 4·12 as meaning that Jerusalem is a pain in the neck. Of all holy cities it has probably the worst record for causing trouble.

The first returned exiles gradually settled down and even began to intermarry with those who were already there. Work on the temple ground to a halt. Then a second small group of exiles returned led by Ezra. This was during the reign of Artaxerxes of Persia. The story reads a little like some of the early stories of settlers in the USA. This group was more puritanical than the first. Under Ezra mixed marriages were banned.

However wrong such a policy may be, it is just about defensible. What was indefensible was the destruction of those mixed marriages that had already taken place. The wives and children of mixed marriages were 'put away'. Only four men are recorded as having the courage to oppose this policy. They deserve to be remembered: 'Jonathan the son of Asahel and Jahzeiah the son of Tikvah, and Meshullam and Shabbethai the Levite supported them.' (10:15)

What sort of a god requires such evil? What sort of a religion is it that can write of such things with such approval? What sort of religions are they that can regard such books as holy scripture? The seeds of all the racist policies that have blighted human societies throughout much of the world are all to be found in the Bible. And in some branches of the Christian church (the Dutch Reformed Church in South Africa and the Southern Baptists of the USA to give but two examples) the seed has found fertile soil and flourished.

The fact that many religious people denounce racism as strongly as we do does not alter the fact that it is in their own holy books that the seeds of such evils are to be found. Although both sides of the debate about racial purity are to be found in the Old Testament, it was the racists who dominated. All the more credit is due to those who expressed the alternative and more tolerant view (which we have seen already in the book of Ruth).

Nehemiah

This is another book that is only really of interest to people wanting to know more about the ancient history of the Jews. It lacks the benefit of an interesting style. But in spite of these things, it is a book I have enjoyed reading.

Nehemiah was a cup bearer to King Artaxerxes of Persia. A report came to him of the poverty and hardship faced by the Jews in Palestine.

He obtained permission from Artaxerxes to go to Palestine as governor. He seems to have been both a truly good man and a genuinely capable and sensible leader – the first returnee of that calibre.

He organised the rebuilding of the walls of Jerusalem and their defence. In spite of the hostility and taunts of their neighbours, the work went ahead successfully and was completed.

Nehemiah had found a situation where a few of the wealthier Jews were exploiting their fellows and causing a good deal of their poverty. He set a good example himself, put an end to exploitation and restored justice.

He encouraged the people to celebrate the festival of booths.

The festival of booths was called the feast of tabernacles in the old Bibles. It was the Jewish festival of Sukkot instituted in Leviticus 23:33. It is a week-long festival of rejoicing combining harvest festival and a memory of the time the Jews wandered in the desert before entering their promised land. The name 'booths' comes from the temporary makeshift homes many Jews make to live in during the festival.

During the course of the festival Nehemiah had Ezra the priest engage in a series of public readings of the law of God. This includes a summary of the history of the Jews (chapter 9). It is a story of God's faithfulness and man's unfaithfulness. It is perhaps useful to have such a summary. It begins with Abram the shepherd leaving Babylonia to seek for the promised land and it ends with a group of exiles leaving Babylonia to return to the promised land.

Here is a reading of history which credits God with everything good that has happened and blames the people's unfaithfulness for all the bad things that have happened (bad things which God has caused to happen as punishments). There is no understanding of political reality or of their own insignificance on the world stage.

The story of Nehemiah ends on a pretty dismal note and shows that in spite of all his work, and in spite of all the religious reforms and the new covenant made between the people and their God, nothing has really changed. After returning to Artaxerxes, Nehemiah makes a second visit to Palestine and finds that the people have slipped right back into the way of life they followed before his reforms.

Yet, the rather dismal end to Nehemiah should not blind us to the long term facts. The Jews did manage to eke out a living and to slowly rebuild their nation, clinging on to their belief in their uniqueness as the chosen people of God. The combination of racial and religious exclusiveness proved to be powerful enough to enable them to survive – and to go on surviving. But whether that combination was for good or for evil is another question altogether – perhaps the jury is still out.

The picture of God in Nehemiah is one that does perhaps have some universal value. If it is true that we create the gods and make them what we want them to be, then the gods become a reflection of our own ideals. So these pictures of the Jewish God should be read as pictures of their ideal man and leader: noble in character, faithful, generous and kind, but also immensely powerful, jealous, stern and severe in punishment. Two verses which express a few of these things are:

God is 'ready to forgive, gracious and merciful, slow to anger and abounding in steadfast love.' (9:17) and He is 'the great and mighty and terrible God, who keepest covenant and steadfast love. . . who hast dealt faithfully. (9:32–33)

It is easy to understand the importance of the historical books of the Old Testament for the Jewish nation but it is not so easy to understand their value for religion.

God is often portrayed as ruthless, heartless and cruel although the picture of God in Nehemiah does achieve a level of nobility. Added to that, with few exceptions, the men of God are totally unacceptable as role models. They may be very real, and some of them may be full of fascination, but very few of them are genuinely good men. They are not men of virtue or quality of character. Many of them are not even likeable, and some are thoroughly unpleasant.

My own list of genuinely good men would include Abram, Nathan the prophet, Jonathan son of Saul and Nehemiah. David's character was seriously flawed but he had great virtues too. Saul seems to me to be a king deserving of far higher praise than is usually given to him. But the superstitious nature of his religion and his awe of Samuel enabled Samuel to destroy him. Saul is one of the genuinely tragic figures of Old Testament history. In my mind, I always see him as a Biblical King Lear.

I cannot see that these Biblical books are of value to those concerned with human ethics. There is little in them to help us to live our lives well unless we can learn from the frailties of other flawed human beings.

There is little to teach us about social compassion, justice or righteousness and there is plenty to lead us astray. These books are full of an unspoken male dominance (even if many of the women have learned how to get the better of their menfolk and to control them). There is an unthinking acceptance of slavery even if it was more compassionate in its ideals than slavery usually was. And there are the beginnings of racism and racial intolerance.

Nor is there anything to teach us the way to personal fulfilment and satisfaction or to such things as contentment, happiness and peace. Why these books are still regarded by so many people as holy writ is beyond understanding.

Section Three

The Ketuvim – The Writings

We have already looked at a number of books included in 'The Writings' by the Jews: Ruth, 1 & 2 Chronicles, Ezra and Nehemiah. In their Biblical order the rest of them are Esther, Job, Psalms, Proverbs, Ecclesiastes and the Song of Solomon.

They also include Lamentations and Daniel which are placed amongst the prophets in the Bible and will be dealt with there.

Within the Writings there are books that are known as part of the Wisdom literature of the Jews. It may be useful to introduce the Wisdom literature before moving on.

In the society depicted in the Old Testament there were three human sources of authoritative guidance.

The priests were responsible for worship in the Temple and for the Law, which was thought of as the Law of God.

The prophets included an incredible variety of people who all claimed to have direct access to God and the ability to communicate his word. Dancing dervishes like the most hysterical of modern pentecostalists were at one extreme, and men and women of real quality and ability who proclaimed a serious ethical message were at the other.

The third group comprised the wise men. These would have been at home in many an old ethical society and in the rationalist wing of the humanist movement – except for the fact that they believed that all wisdom comes from God. Thus they claim that 'the fear of the Lord is the beginning of wisdom.'

73

There are a number of books which contain the teaching of these 'wise men'. In the Old Testament they are the books of Job, Proverbs and Ecclesiastes. In the Apocrypha, which was a sort of Greek appendix to the Hebrew Old Testament, there are two more books: The Wisdom of Solomon and the Wisdom of Jesus the son of Sirach (also known as Ecclesiasticus). We shall examine each of these in due course.

Esther

Unless you like nasty horror stories of humans behaving badly to one another, don't bother to read this book. Although it tells quite a story, it need not detain us. From memory, I can't say whether the story has any basis in historical fact and it isn't important enough to make it worth checking.

The story is that Esther, an orphan looked after by her cousin Mordecai, became the queen of the Persian King Ahasuerus. The king's chief minister, Haman, had a grudge against Mordecai and obtained from the king permission to engage in an empire-wide pogrom against the Jews (because they insisted on being different). But Esther brought about the downfall of Haman, the pogrom was called off and the Jews engaged in their own orgy of bloodletting in revenge.

There is also a sub-plot involving Mordecai and Haman.

Nobody comes out of the story with any credit.

Job

It is often said that the book of Job is about the problem of pain. It tries to answer a question which gives religious people no end of trouble – not least because there is no satisfactory answer to it. In my own religious days it caused me more heart-searching than any other. The question is: Why is there pain and suffering in a world created and sustained by a good god?

That is a question that is quite irrelevant to an atheist. If there is no god, that particular problem does not exist. Pain and suffering present only three problems, all of them practical: how can we ease it; how can we end it; and how can we prevent it.

Does that mean that atheists should skip the book of Job? Far from it. There are a number of good reasons for reading this book. The most important one is the fact that it opens up a rather different question to the one about pain and suffering. It wrestles with a question which is of universal significance. Although its answers are religious answers, they also need to be examined.

The question is: 'Why choose virtue?'

Now that is a question which exercises ethical humanists just as much as anybody else. Like the best of religious people, we are concerned with finding how best to live our lives.

Religious people often say, 'if you are an atheist there is no reason for you to live a good life.' What they mean is that there is no divine imperative, no God to tell us what we must and must not do or how we should behave. That is quite true. We have to work things out for ourselves and come up with our own answers. If religious people can help us, so much the better. If the book of Job can help us, that will have made our study of it thoroughly worthwhile. It faces head on the question 'why choose virtue' and that is a question that concerns us all, religious and atheist alike.

The book begins with a story. It is the tale of a man who has everything anyone would wish to have: health, wealth, success, a loving family and the respect of his neighbours. He is a thoroughly good man.

Satan claims that Job is only righteous because God has rewarded him so well. So God gives Satan permission to test Job by taking everything from him including his health. Even his children are killed off.

It is a tale beautifully told. Indeed such is the quality of the language in the old Authorised Version that Sir Arthur Quiller Couch (better known as the novelist Q) used Job as the text book for an English literature course at Oxford.

After the story has been told, the rest of the book describes the way in which friends of Job try to help him. Although they all approach Job's situation in slightly different ways, they all assume that he or some member of his family must have been very wicked and that his troubles are a punishment for wickedness.

We know that they are wrong and so does Job. An impasse has

been reached and a problem posed: how can God be just if a good man can be made to suffer as much as Job. The problem is made worse by the fact that the Jews of the time shared the view of most modern atheists, that this is the only life we have. This may come as something of a surprise but amongst Jews, belief in a real life after death came much later. It is impossible to put an exact date to these things but it would be fair to say that belief in the resurrection of some kind of body was not widespread among the Jews until after the Maccabaean revolt in the 160s BCE.

If there is no life after death, and if there is no reward for virtue in this life, two questions follow: where is God's justice? and why choose virtue?

These questions offered a vivid challenge to the accepted wisdom of the time. The usual teaching was that God rewards the virtuous and punishes the wicked IN THIS LIFE.

The book of Job demonstrates that that is clearly not the case. The accepted wisdom was wrong. The wicked often prosper and live happily. The good often suffer. So how can God be just and why should people choose virtue?

Job himself comes up with one answer which I propose to leave for a while. But one of his friends, Zophar, comes up with another – still the classic Moslem answer to problems like this: God is great. It is not for puny little man to question his ways.

In the book of Job, God seems to agree with this. When he finally condescends to speak it is in order to display his greatness, majesty and power. Instead of affection, help, sympathy, the best that this all-powerful God can manage is:

> 'Shall a fault-finder contend with the Almighty?
> Will you even put me in the wrong?
> Will you condemn me that you may be justified?
> Have you an arm like God,
> and can you thunder with a voice like his?' (40:2, 8 & 9)

I don't think I need to comment further on that kind of answer. At the end of the book there is a sort of post-script which many scholars believe was added by a different author. It aims to show that the received wisdom was right after all. Job's sufferings were just a test, and having come through the test he is restored to his former position and given a very long life (140 years) in which to enjoy it. Because Job held on to his virtue he was rewarded handsomely.

But can a happy ending and a new set of children really compensate for all that Job has been through? Will it compensate for the children who were killed? Will Job not always grieve for them? This answer just will not do.

In another of the books of wisdom, 'the Wisdom of Solomon', the discussion is carried further. The author's suggestion is that although goodness is not necessarily rewarded in this life, we choose virtue because God rewards the virtuous with immortality. But what does he mean by 'immortality'?

One of the things he means is that a virtuous man is remembered by future generations: 'In the memory of virtue is immortality. . . The righteous man, though he die early, will be at rest' because his righteousness will be honoured by those who outlive him. (4:1 & 7) (In fact death is often God's way of protecting a good man from changing and becoming wicked in his old age!)

Virtuous people die in honour and are 'numbered among the sons of God'. This is their immortality. I am reminded of the famous speech of Pericles in which he says:

'This is good fortune – to end our lives with honour . . . One's sense of honour is the only thing that does not grow old, and the last pleasure, when we are worn out with age is . . . having the respect of our fellows.' (Thucydides, History of the Peloponnesian War)

Shakespeare turns this on its head and sums it all up perfectly – (*Julius Caesar* Act 3, Scene 2):

'The evil that men do lives after them;
The good is oft interred with their bones'.

Unfortunately that is true. Hitler must be one of the best remembered people of the twentieth century. And if any one of us were to make a list of the people we remember from history, there would be very few saints among them.

There is a kind of immortality of the memory but it has nothing to do with virtue or vice, nothing to do with God's rewards or punishments, and no value for the person who is dead. When we are dead, if this is the only life there is, we have no knowledge of the fact that people remember us. I think it was Achilles who said that he would rather be a living slave than dead. Most of life is better than just being a memory. And whilst it is better to be remembered by people who are thankful that we have lived, that is not why we choose virtue.

However, the word 'immortal' has another meaning. Scholars are not sure whether the Wisdom of Solomon (written some time after 100 BCE) carries that meaning. But there is no doubt that some of his words *can be* interpreted in such a way as to speak of a real life after death. Christians certainly use them with that meaning in mind and they are so beautiful that they are worth reading anyway.

> 'The souls of the righteous are in the hand of God,
> and no torment will ever touch them.
> In the eyes of the foolish they seemed to have died,
> and their departure was thought to be an affliction,
> and their going from us to be their destruction;
> but they are in peace.
> For though in the sight of men they were punished,
> their hope is full of immortality.' (3:1–4)

> 'The righteous live for ever,
> and their reward is with the Lord;
> and the Most High takes care of them.
> Therefore they will receive a glorious crown
> and a beautiful diadem from the Lord,
> because with his right hand he will cover them,
> and with his arm he will shield them.' (5:15–16)

Whether these words refer to the kind of immortality of the memory of which we have already written, or to a new life after death is not altogether clear. But there is no doubt that they can be interpreted as looking to a new life and they may well have helped the Jews to make the great leap of faith to belief in another life.

It is a belief which the Hasidim, the forerunners of the Pharisees, stressed. It has been taken up enthusiastically by both Christians and Moslems. For all of them it is the final proof that God is just and the final reason for choosing virtue. Virtue is worthwhile because in the end it is rewarded. In another life beyond the grave all the wrongs of this life are put right and the virtuous are compensated for any suffering and injustice they have suffered here.

There are two major problems with this line of argument. First of all, there is no concrete evidence that there is a life after this one. Most religious people would agree with the assumption that when anything else in the natural world dies, it is dead. Why should they imagine that we are any different?

But even if there is another life in which virtue is rewarded and the virtuous are compensated for the ills of this life, we have already seen that compensation never really compensates. It cannot undo what has already been suffered.

Let me sum up the arguments thus far:

We choose virtue because it is rewarded by God in this life.
We choose virtue because we shall be remembered for it.
We choose virtue because God rewards it in the next life.
We choose virtue because God demands it.

Whilst most of us would like to be remembered for good reasons, I wonder just how many people choose virtue for any of the reasons put forward so far?

Job himself – yes it is high time that we returned to Job – points us in a completely different direction. It is a direction which has nothing to do with rewards or punishments, nothing to do with dreams of immortality or hopes of a life after death. And although Job himself is not aware of it, it is a direction which has nothing to do with any god either.

If it is true, and we have seen that it is true, that the wicked can do very well for themselves, then there can only be one real reason for trying to be a good, decent and honourable human being. This is how Job puts it:

'My lips will not speak falsehood,
and my tongue will not utter deceit. . .
Till I die I will not put away my integrity from me.
I hold fast my righteousness, and will not let it go;
my heart does not reproach me for any of my days.' (27:4, 5b & 6)

The only reason for choosing virtue is that that is what we wish to choose because that is the way to self-respect. 'My heart will not reproach me.' Without self-respect there is no true happiness.

Before one of his Wimbledon matches Tim Henman said, 'I do not go out to play for the crowd or for England. I play for myself.'

Similarly, we do not choose virtue to please a god or to win honours or plaudits. We make that choice for ourselves, for our own self-respect and for satisfaction with our lives, for that contentment which is true happiness. We want to be able to say with Job, 'my heart does not reproach me for any of my days.'

I wonder how many can say that? Some of us fall so far short of the ideals that we set ourselves that we lose our self-respect entirely and our hearts reproach us pretty forcibly. In those circumstances there is nothing for it but to begin all over again. Fortunately it is never too late. It is never too late to rebuild our lives, to recover a measure of self-respect and to find contentment and peace of mind again.

All this can be achieved by ordinary human beings operating on the purely human level. There is no need for the kind of salvation offered by the various religions. In fact, I would go so far as to say that they are a hindrance rather than a help. But 'salvation' and salvation theology is a major subject and needs to be treated on its own. It has no place in this particular study.

This study has been about the question why choose virtue? The answer we have arrived at is very simple. We choose virtue for its own sake. We believe that the path of virtue offers the best hope for lives that are fulfilled, satisfying and contented. It is a path which enables us to be happy with ourselves.

Religion and the gods are quite irrelevant. The choice is a simple human one which any of us can make or refuse to make. It is the book of Job which was one of the earliest demonstrations of that fact. It makes it a book deserving our careful attention.

Psalms

A fair number of my poems have been published in anthologies and poetry magazines. When the publications arrive, I read all the poems by other people. Every so often one of them stands out as a poem I would like to read again, either to enjoy its use of language or because of the quality of its thought. The psalms are like that. There are 150 of them but only a few make you feel that you want to read them again.

These are worth reading for their quality as literature and also because they sometimes express religious sentiment at its finest. They are hymns, poems, expressions of faith and prayers.

Prayer can be meditative and a refreshing stimulus to both thought and action. But all too often it is a substitute for both. It is often the cry of the helpless and the hopeless to their god to do something, to act for them because they either cannot or will not act for themselves. That is the tone of many of the psalms and of a great deal of prayer in worship. Since there are no gods, that kind of prayer leads nowhere. Nothing is done.

Faced with intractable human problems we only find solutions by getting up off our knees and working together with other people. When I was a boy I had a habit of disappearing. On one occasion a girl was sent to tell my grandmother – a very devout and also a very practical Christian. The girl said, 'Oh Mrs Hammond, Leslie's lost. Let us pray.'

My grandmother replied, 'First go and tell the police. Then you can pray.'

Difficult problems need human solutions and human co-operation. When we have to work with people whose back-ground, culture and hopes are quite different from our own, special qualities of determination and courage are required. But no problem is incapable of solution. There have been moments of hope in Palestine, though these seem to be at a low ebb as I write. In Northern Ireland, on the other hand, there seems to be real hope, even though so many people still seem to have a trench mentality.

Whether on the grand scale or the international stage or in our personal lives, prayer provides no answers. In some cases it even seems to make matters worse. We have to work things out for ourselves and find our own solutions to our problems.

I have digressed. If we return to the psalms we shall find that they rest on the belief that their writers are the chosen people of God and that insofar as they do his will God will (or should) bless them. Goodness is to be rewarded in this life 'for in death there is no remembrance of thee; in Sheol who can give thee praise?' (6:5)

Many of them are political in the sense that they are asking for God's blessing on the nation and for his power and his punishments to be felt by their enemies who are, by definition, evil.

But what are good and evil? Most of the time the good are those who worship the god of the Jews. The wicked are those who do not. Not a very satisfactory pair of definitions, but there are others for those who will look for them. For example, the good man is defined in Psalm 1:2–3.

> 'His delight is in the law of the Lord, and on his law he meditates day and night. He is like a tree planted by streams of water, that yields its fruit in its season, and its leaf does not wither. In all that he does he prospers.'

It is a lovely picture, but goodness is not defined by material prosperity. However it *is* good to find joy in life and to be able to lie down and sleep in peace (4:7–8). It is good to have integrity, to be upright and righteous – to do what is right (7:8–10). And the tiny little psalm 15 gives more ideas of what is meant by goodness.

As always it is easier to describe badness. It is bad to be boastful, deceitful, a liar or a flatterer. It is bad to be bloodthirsty or violent, which implies that many of the psalmists and many of the Old Testament writers and characters (most recently Esther and Mordecai) are bad. It is bad to requite friendship with evil or to plunder 'my enemy without cause'. (Psalms 5 and 7) But the psalms are full of imprecations on the bad. There is no need for me to multiply examples.

However, some of the psalms are of great beauty and power. Sadly that sometimes makes their teaching all the more dangerous. Psalm 8 is one such psalm. The first four verses underline human insignificance but then verses 5–8 sing of human glory. Where is the danger in that?

It teaches human dominion or lordship or authority over all other living things, a teaching we first met in the creation stories in Genesis. THAT teaching is dangerous both for us and for all living things – as many of those now extinct could have testified.

We exercise lordship in the world at our peril. There is an

interrelationship and an interdependence between all living things which demands a much more humble, sensitive and respectful approach to the world than the Bible approach. If we do not learn to live in harmony with the world instead of always assuming that it is there for us and for our benefit, we shall bring disaster upon ourselves and a great many more creatures.

The opening psalms have given us a fairly diverse set of thoughts by way of introduction. As we skim through the rest, we shall find continuing diversity. For example: There are elements of interest for atheists in psalm 10. It is clear evidence that there were atheists in such a religion-dominated society as that of the Jews. (10:4 – All his thoughts are, 'There is no god.') There is more such evidence elsewhere (eg: psalm 14).

This psalm trots out all the typical religious accusations and assumptions that are still bandied about by some religious people concerning atheism. It is a totally false assumption that if you don't believe in God you must be wicked, just as it is a totally false assumption that if you do, you must be good.

Virtue and vice have no necessary connection with religion at all. Although religion is usually on the side of virtue that is not always the case. And when it is not it is often thoroughly vicious and evil

Psalm 18 deserves a mention. Unlike many of the psalms it is a confident assertion that faith in God is justified. Verses 7–15 are a tremendous picture of the power of God revealed in nature. Verses 20–24 show that the author's faith is built on his confidence in his own goodness and his confidence in God's faithfulness.

This is the kind of psalm that strengthens the faith of religious people. By the power of its writing and its sure confidence it can make them feel good – inspired even. As a result, the kind of questions it raises about this kind of religion are lost and the fundamental question of whether there is any justification for religious faith at all is one which never surfaces.

There are many of the psalms that my re-reading has made me feel I never want to see again. One exception is psalm 19. It is very beautiful and verses 7–10 express the feelings of religious people concerning their faith in a very concise, impressive and lovely way. Faced with this kind of religion (and there is plenty of it about), the atheist will neither mock nor argue. Quality is admirable in any field. Just as we can admire a painting without liking it; so we can admire genuine piety without believing in the gods. We have no religious faith, but we share the quest of the best of religious people for quality and depth of life and goodness.

Psalm 22 has a special meaning for many *Christians*. The first words, 'My God, my God, why hast thou forsaken me' are words attributed to Jesus when he was dying on the cross.

When we come to read the New Testament we shall find that verses 16 and 18 were also applied to the crucifixion:

> 'They have pierced my hands and feet – they divide my garments among them, and for my raiment they cast lots.'

It makes you wonder just how much of the crucifixion story is factual.

The psalm ends triumphantly. As a result many Christians (though by no means all), suggest that when Jesus quoted from it, he was deliberately inviting his disciples to make the connection and to believe in his triumph. But given the other connections one has to ask whether Jesus actually spoke the words at all.

If those Christians are right it was an incredible expression of faith. Those Christians who still believe in the resurrection believe that it was justified. It is an immense source of strength for their own faith. It means so much to so many people and used to mean so much to me, that I find it difficult to express my present and much more sceptical view, but it must be done.

I now believe that much of the detail of the gospel story is simply fiction. The early Jewish-Christian preachers knew of the crucifixion and believed in the resurrection. Even though they may not have seen the death of Jesus, they may well have seen other crucifixions just as many of our forefathers saw hangings.

In preaching the story of the crucifixion they elaborated and dramatised. These things became part of the accepted narrative before it was written down. Consciously or unconsciously links were made with this old psalm, links which have such power for Christians today.

Psalm 23 ('The Lord is my shepherd') is probably the best known of all psalms. Our familiarity with it can dim its perfection both as a poem and as an expression of religious faith. Psalm 24 is another of similar quality. But atheists are not looking for a shepherd or any other kind of leader. We feel that it is time to grow beyond the childhood of humanity. We should take charge of our own lives and work out our own destiny.

The next psalm on which I wish to comment is number 37. Only those who love poetry enough and those who are curious to discover how religious people pray or prayed will read the ones in between. Those who do will find an occasional verse of great beauty but nothing which demands attention.

37 is a clear expression of the accepted view that the righteous prosper and that any prosperity enjoyed by wicked people is temporary and doomed. But this psalm also includes one verse which may be the source of one of the beatitudes of Jesus:

'The meek shall possess the land,
and delight themselves in abundant prosperity.' (v. 11)

If this were true we might have rather more righteousness and rather less wickedness, but the book of Job has already demonstrated pretty forcibly the fact that it is not true.

38 is the cry of a man who has done serious wrong, knows it and is sorry. Think of such a man and what might happen to him.

If he comes from outside the religious community to temple or church or mosque in a spirit of genuine penitence, he will be welcomed and helped. He may even be paraded as an example of what God can do to reclaim fallen lives. And he may find himself able to sing psalm 40:1–10, the song of a grateful worshipper.

But if he is within the religious community when he commits some form of serious wrong, heaven help him for the community won't. There will be no help forthcoming either from his god or from god's people. He will be virtually on his own and will have to get beyond the lamenting stage and begin to pull himself together. He is the one who will have to put his house in order. No one else will do it for him. But as he begins others will begin to step forward to help with their friendship and often in practical ways too.

I mentioned psalm 40 above. It shows that people are moving beyond belief in a god requiring sacrifices in a temple to a god whose demand was for obedience to his will. The early verses are a splendid expression of the religious frame of mind but in 11–17 the psalmist falls back into the usual cries for help and confusion to his enemies. How on earth did these people manage to make so many enemies?

Psalm 39 speaks of the brevity of life and has one curious and amusing verse. The psalmist asks God to 'look away from me, that I may know gladness before I depart and be no more.' (v. 13)

Psalm 41:1 is similar to a beatitude of Jesus. Is that beatitude a misremembering of these words 'Blessed is he who considers the poor' or is it a deliberate alteration?

Here the idea is that it is a part of the path of virtue to seek the welfare of 'the poor'. But when the psalmist speaks of the poor is he thinking of himself – as he is in the rest of the psalm?

Psalms 42 and 43 belong together. From the depths of his despair the psalmist hopes against hope that he will one day join the throng again as they go 'in procession to the house of God, with glad shouts and songs of thanksgiving, a multitude keeping festival.'

We do not know the cause of his despair or whether he has grounds for hope, but there is none of the whining and complaining that fill so many of the psalms and there are none of the cries for vengeance on enemies. These two psalms are a very beautiful and moving poem. The fact that we believe that his hope in God is misplaced does not alter that.

86

44 is unusual. It was assumed that if the Jews were faithful to their God he would protect the nation. If troubles came upon the nation, they were due to unfaithfulness (wickedness).

This psalmist is honest enough to admit that in spite of their faithfulness, God has not protected them. Verses 9–22 are a pretty comprehensive indictment of their God and his complete failure to look after his people. The psalm ends with the psalmist telling God to get his finger out!

45 is not a religious psalm at all. The first half praises the king. The second tells one of the princesses in his harem to prepare herself for the privilege of serving the royal stud and giving him sons. Curiously the editors of the Common Bible call this 'a love song'. It is certainly not that. Compare this with the story in the book of Esther – love does not enter into the equation, nor the feelings of the woman. The king is a bull and the members of his harem his cows – I do not use the word in the modern insulting way – perhaps people would be happier with the image of stag and hinds.

Psalms 46–48 are songs of faith, praise and pride in God and in Jerusalem. They are a welcome change from some of their whining predecessors.

Number 49 warns against jealousy towards the rich 'though while he lives he counts himself happy.' We should not be jealous because there is nothing for him after death. (Compare psalm 73.)

The psalmist seems to believe that for the rich death is the end or there is some sort of Greek style shadow existence in Sheol, the place of the dead. But for the psalmist there is something different, though what is unclear: 'God will ransom my soul from the power of Sheol, for he will receive me.'

Such ideas were new to the Jews but were to be developed by the Pharisees and later by Christians and Moslems. Humanists, who believe that we are simply one species among many in the world of nature, assume that this is the only life we have. We live our lives accordingly.

Psalm 50 is a call from God for sincerity and integrity, things which are far more important than temple sacrifices.

Apart from the last two verses, probably added by a temple priest, psalm 51 is a lovely psalm asking for forgiveness, purity of heart and a right spirit.

Atheists do not share the religion but we can appreciate the beauty of the psalm and the sincerity of the desire for forgiveness, cleansing and renewal. We consider that the religious concentration on sin and guilt is unhealthy but there are times when we all need and desire human forgiveness; times when we need to turn over a new leaf and begin again.

It is the steadiness of that renewal which will demonstrate our 'clean heart and new spirit' and show that we are worthy of forgiveness.

This 'fool' finds psalm 53 a source of amusement. Here is further evidence that there have always been plenty of other fools saying 'There is no God'. If we are 'in terror' it doesn't seem to show.

55 is the source of the song 'O for the wings, for the wings of a dove' but it is a miserable psalm. The psalms seem so often to give the impression that there were an awful lot of dreadful and nasty people about, but are the godly any better? Just look at 58, v. 10: 'The righteous will rejoice when he sees the vengeance; he will bathe his feet in the blood of the wicked.'

The more I read these psalms the more I feel that many of them are sick – sick in their obsession with evil and treachery and plots. Here is the source of the violence of thought and language of the Ian Paisleys of this world and of the besieged fortress mentality of modern Israel. If this is the voice of religion, we are better off without it. There is no picture of normal humanity here.

Sadly for religious people, there are all too few of the psalms which are fit to be used as prayers. Most of them have their elements of hate and violence. One of the exceptions is 72 which is a long prayer for good things. And there are occasional verses which would make this god worth knowing if they were true (eg 67:5–6).

Prosperity and wickedness are often equated in the Bible. If we bear that in mind, we shall find psalm 73 a very honest, and in its way, a very brave psalm.

The psalmist speaks honestly of his envy towards those who are healthy and prosperous. He sees no sign that their prosperity will be taken from them, or that he himself will become prosperous and healthy. The most he will say is that they could 'fall to ruin' and they will certainly die one day and be 'like a dream'.

So what about him? He recognises that envy and bitterness are 'stupid and ignorant' and that, if he has nothing else, he still has his faith. He wakes up to the fact that that is enough (just as Job realised that the important thing was that he should hold on to his integrity). So for this psalmist, his faith is all he needs and after death it leads to 'glory'.

This psalm marks a number of advances even if it has not reached the point where a man can genuinely be glad for another if the other is healthy and prosperous. The psalmist still needs to believe that their roles will be reversed after death. Yet in his discovery that his faith is enough he is inching towards the discovery that life is not about health and prosperity, no matter how important those two things may be. As Jesus was to say, 'Life is more than raiment'.

Life is about peace of mind, contentment within ourselves, satisfaction with the way we live our lives, the things we do, the way we behave, our relationship with others and our treatment of them. For some, this is all bound up with their religious faith, for others with a non-religious philosophy of life. It doesn't seem to matter much which it is as long as the end result is good. It certainly has nothing at all to do with belief in life after death.

74 demonstrates the human ability to go on hoping when hope should be dead – but we are back with psalms we can happily ignore.

84 is justly popular in religious circles. It describes the house of God as a place of refuge and refreshment for man and bird alike; a place where the upright find themselves strengthened for virtue. Thanks to Mendelssohn some of its words are very well known

89

indeed. For example:

'How lovely is thy dwelling place,
O Lord of hosts.
My soul longs, yea faints,
for the courts of the Lord;
my heart and flesh sing for joy to the living God.

Even the sparrow finds a home,
and the swallow a nest for herself,
where she may lay her young,
etc.

There are plenty of people with no particular dogmatic religious beliefs who go to places of worship precisely because they find them to be places of refuge from the turmoil of life; places where they find refreshment of heart and mind, a source of strength for the lives of virtue they desire to live.

Where places of worship really do help people in these ways they are offering a valuable service to the community. Even though we do not share their religious beliefs, we can recognise and understand the value of such things. Here we reach beyond dogmatic disputation – beyond religion too – to the depths of human psychology and to human appetites that can be fed and nurtured by things like music, peace and quiet, a sense of belonging to a community and to a community that reaches over the centuries. None of these things is necessarily religious, but they are often associated with religion at its best.

In psalm 91 there are two verses quoted in the New Testament by Satan during the period Jesus spent preparing for his ministry and in other psalms there are occasional well-known verses such as 'the years of our life are three score and ten, or even by reason of strength four score.' How things are changing. A reporter on TV news tonight suggested that on our eightieth birthday we are 'entering old age'. But nothing demands our attention before psalm 94 – and then we find ourselves back on familiar territory.

The psalmists begin from the assumption that God rewards virtue and punishes evil. As a result they ask ad infinitum 'why doesn't it happen?' Only very rarely is the question pushed further.

Very little has changed. Unthinking religious people still make the same assumption. In the face of all the evidence. When things go wrong they still ask, 'Why should this happen to me?'

Why shouldn't it? Why should they be immune to life's sufferings? There are those religious thinkers who would even argue that it is a privilege to suffer. 'Whom the Lord loves he also chastens.'

It is amazing how rarely people actually sit down and work out rationally why particular things have happened. Yet it is often when we do so that we begin to be able to make sense of life, the bad as well as the good. And if we cannot make sense of things we still do not need to fall back on religious solutions. So many people brought up within the Judaic/Christian/Moslem traditions fail to look for rational answers to life's injustices so they have to fall back on the hope that things will be put right after death. That is a hope for which there is no concrete evidence at all.

In the psalms from the late 90s and from 103 there are a number of confident ones full of praise for God. Occasionally the psalmist spoils everything: 101 begins with fine words and aspirations and ends brutally.

Psalm 104 is a wonderful celebration of God as the creator and sustainer of the natural world – worth reading and re-reading even for those of us with no belief in a creator.

106 tells Jewish history more accurately than the old Testament sometimes does. In the process it destroys myths of racial and religious purity (vvs. 35–37). But neither this nor the following psalms need detain us.

118 is perhaps only remembered today for verse 22, which Christians applied to Jesus: 'The stone which the builders rejected has become the head of the corner.' But I have good reason to remember psalm 119. It is the longest of the psalms. At my Christian boarding school we were often punished. One punishment given in preference to 'one hundred lines' was 'copy out psalm 119 by tomorrow morning's assembly, boy.'

Both staff and prefects loved to inflict it on us. Perhaps it was not entirely unsuitable: 'How can a young man keep his way pure?' etc (v. 9). But I suspect that we preferred verse 99: 'I have more understanding than all my teachers' and by the time we arrived at verse 134 we must have echoed 'Redeem me from man's oppression.' But we still had quite a way to go.

There must be many people all over the world who could echo 120:6–7 and 133:1: 'Too long have I had my dwelling among those who hate peace; but when I speak, they are for war.' 'Behold, how good and pleasant it is when brothers dwell in unity.'

Psalms 121 and 139 are both great favourites in religious circles and deservedly so. 121 is a beautiful little poem. 139 expresses belief in the fact that God is ever-present, all-seeing and all-knowing. It does so in a thoroughly attractive way. We can see the attraction without sharing the belief. We can also see how such a belief was often perverted to make children afraid of this all-seeing God. It used to happen all too often. Does it still?

My approval of the psalm does not include verses 19–22 which degenerate into an all too common hatred. The same is true of the famous psalm of exile at number 137. See how horribly it ends.

144:12–15a represent the hopes and wishes of a nation of farmers.

146 tells us not to put our trust 'in a son of man, in whom there is no help'. (v. 3) 'Son of man' is one of the favourite titles of Jesus in the gospels. Perhaps we should take note.

The book ends with a few psalms of praise. For a change there is no whining, no self-centred moaner feeling sorry for himself, and no hatred or pleas for violent punishment of enemies. They are all praise and as a result make quite pleasant reading.

In my Christian days I used to read several chapters of the Bible every day as part of my daily devotions. The book of Psalms was regarded as one of the literary and devotional high-spots of the Bible. Nowadays, instead of reading the Bible I read poetry. There is none of the sheer nastiness and brutality of many of the psalms and there is often beauty, thoughtfulness and inspiration to match the very best the psalms contain.

Proverbs

At the beginning of section three I wrote briefly of the 'Wisdom Literature' of the Bible. We turn now to two of the Wisdom books, Proverbs and Ecclesiastes.

The purpose of these books is defined at the beginning of Proverbs (1:2–6):

'That men may know wisdom and instruction,
understand words of insight,
receive instruction in wise dealing,
righteousness, justice and equity;
that prudence may be given to the simple,
knowledge and discretion to the youth –

the wise man also may hear and increase in learning,
and the man of understanding acquire skill,
to understand a proverb and a figure,
the words of the wise and their riddles.'

In his book *The Alternative Tradition* James Thrower tells us that these wise men 'have little or nothing to say about the institution of religion nor of the special relationship between God and his people. Rather they address . . . the individual man in his individuality and social relationships, and so constitute the nearest thing that we have to humanism in Israel.'

'The wise men do not appeal to revelation but to experience. Their counsel has to do with how men ought to act in the work-a-day world, with personal character and with a way of life that is good because coherent, meaningful and valuable.

'Their authority lies in their own and the past communities' experience of life, taken together with a trained intelligence. Their method is that of instruction and, at a later stage of development, of persuasion and argument.' (*The Alternative Tradition* by James Thrower. Mouton Publishers, 1980.)

The books of Proverbs and the two Wisdom books of the Apocrypha consist largely of loose collections of 'wise' and sometimes memorable sayings on a number of mostly mundane subjects. In my Christian days it always intrigued me that these books seemed to be particularly popular with women, as bedside books, yet they were written by men for men and are thoroughly sexist.

As we turn to the text of Proverbs we find the author calling his 'son' to reject the invitation of sinners. He puts forward a secular idea which is completely new to the Old Testament.

In 1:8–19 he claims that evil is to be avoided because it is self-destructive. There is nothing here about God or God's rewards and punishments.

This is simple, human (parental) teaching. Unlike the accepted religious wisdom we have met so far, this human teaching hits the nail on the head at once. We follow virtuous teachings because they enhance our lives like 'a fair garland for your head, and pendants for your neck.' We avoid evil because 'it takes away the life of its possessors' – it is self-destructive.

Chapter 2 shows us that the author believes that wisdom originated from God but it almost takes on an independent life of its own. This is beautifully described in 3:13–18 and also in 8:22–31. As a result it is very easy for an atheist to adapt its message:

> 'My son, if you receive my words
> and treasure up my commandments with you,
> making your ear attentive to wisdom
> and inclining your heart to understanding;
> yes, if you cry out for insight
> and raise your voice for understanding,
> if you seek it like silver
> and search for it as for hidden treasures; . . .
> Then you will understand righteousness and justice
> and equity, every good path;
> for wisdom will come into your heart,
> and knowledge will be pleasant to your soul;
> discretion will watch over you;
> understanding will guard you. . .'
>
> (2:1–4 and 9–12a)

This is the same message as the shorter messages of Jesus, 'Seek and you shall find.' 'Blessed are those who hunger and thirst for righteousness, for they shall be satisfied.'

All that is really being said is that, if we choose the right goals and pursue them, we shall achieve them. Similarly if we choose the wrong goals and pursue them, we shall achieve them. It is therefore of vital importance that we should choose the right goals, put them first and pursue them with single-minded dedication. These are things which are true whether we are religious or not.

But chapter 3 assumes that religion is necessary. The author bids us 'Trust in the Lord with all your heart, and do not rely on your own insight. In all your ways acknowledge him, and he will make straight your paths.' (3:5–6)

Here we part company with religious seekers after virtue. Although we would agree that we should not rely on our own insight or wisdom, in the end we do have to form our own human judgements and make our own human decisions. Together with other seekers, we study the insight and wisdom of others through the ages and then we come to our own conclusions and live life accordingly.

The Buddha, Moses, Confucius, Socrates, Epicurus, Jesus, Muhammad and a host of others may be of assistance to us, but in the end we have to mark out our own path and follow it. No one else can do it for us.

But it is not so much for its depiction of wisdom that Proverbs has traditionally been valued. It has been valued more for those occasional passages of hard-hitting, down to earth, practical teaching:

> 'Bind loyalty and faithfulness about your neck,
> write them on the tablet of your heart.' (3:3)

> 'Do not withhold good from those to whom it is due,
> when it is in your power to do it.' (3:27 and also 29–31)

Chapter 5 urges the discipline of chastity as a matter of common wisdom, sometimes in picturesque and memorable words:

> 13: Drink water from your own cistern.
> 18–19: 'rejoice in the wife of your youth,
> Let her affection fill you at all times with delight.'

Even those of us who have not managed to follow such teaching will see both its sound sense and its value as an ideal. If we do not succeed the first time round we shall still keep the ideal before us if we try again.

6:26–33 and the whole of 7 continues the theme. 6 makes an interesting distinction between using a prostitute which only costs a loaf of bread and committing adultery which brings disaster: 26–29 and 32–33.

Chapter 6:6 speaks of the virtue of hard work in words that have become famous: 'Go to the ant, O sluggard; consider her ways and be wise.'

6:16–17 lists seven vices.

In chapter after chapter the good and the evil are compared. Only occasionally is there anything more than the simple recital that good brings good and evil brings evil. But here and there and particularly in chapter 15, there are sayings for which Proverbs has been popular in the past. Here are a few:

15:1: A soft answer turns away wrath.
   4: A gentle tongue is a tree of life.
  13: A glad heart makes a cheerful countenance.
15:17: Better is a dinner of herbs where love is
         than a fatted ox and hatred with it.
17:1: Better is a dry morsel with quiet
         than a house full of feasting with strife.
15:20: A wise son makes a glad father.
  32: He who heeds admonition gains understanding.
16:18: Pride goes before destruction
         and a haughty spirit before a fall.
  24: Pleasant words are like a honeycomb,
         sweetness to the soul and health to the body.
17:6: Grandchildren are the crown of the aged.
  17: A friend loves at all times,
         and a brother is born for adversity.
  22: A cheerful heart is a good medicine.
22:6: Train up a child in the way he should go,
         and when he is old he will not depart from it.

This is rather more attractive than the frequent encouragement to beat children: 'Spare the rod and spoil the child'.

At the end of chapter 23 there is a famous passage about the dangers of alcohol which temperance organisations used to quote ad infinitum and which Bernard Miles used in one of his marvellous dialect monologues. 31:6–7 restores the balance slightly by pointing out that alcohol has its uses for 'him who is perishing, and . . . those in bitter distress.'

Inevitably a great deal of this is less than compulsive reading, although passages like 26:20 keep on tempting the reader to press on: 'For lack of wood the fire goes out; and where there is no whisperer, quarrelling ceases.'

Proverbs is beginning to move beyond the simplistic teaching that virtue is rewarded with wealth. 28:6: 'Better is a poor man who walks in his integrity than a rich man who is perverse in his ways.'

The books ends with a famous description of a good wife (31:10–31). It is interesting that the Bible has no such description of a good husband. Perhaps there is no such thing.

Ecclesiastes

My Old Testament tutor at theological college dismissed the book of Ecclesiastes in a sentence or two because it is one of the least religious books in the whole of the Bible and its teaching is clean contrary to the spirit of a great deal of religious teaching. It advocates a responsible hedonism. As always with hedonistic teaching its responsibility is either overlooked or ignored.

The author looks at the accepted belief that God rewards the righteous and punishes the wicked in this life and states bluntly that it isn't true. He has looked at life and discovered that it is nothing but 'vanity and a striving after wind'.

'What does man gain by all' his 'toil? . . .
A generation goes, and a generation comes, . . .
The sun rises and the sun goes down, . . .
What has been is what will be,
and what has been done is what will be done;
and there is nothing new under the sun.
Is there a thing of which it is said,

97

'See, this is new'?
It has been already, in the ages before us. . .
All is vanity and a striving after wind.' (from 1:3–14)

The author is totally fatalistic. His fatalism underlies the beautiful passage which is so often used and so little understood:

'For everything there is a season,
and a time for every matter under heaven:
a time to be born, and a time to die;
a time to plant, and a time to pluck up what is planted;
a time to kill, and a time to heal;
a time to break down, and a time to build up;
a time to weep, and a time to laugh;
a time to mourn, and a time to dance;
a time to cast away stones, and a time to gather stones together;
a time to embrace, and a time to refrain from embracing;
a time to seek, and a time to lose;
a time to keep, and a time to cast away;
a time to rend, and a time to sew;
a time to keep silence, and a time to speak;
a time to love, and a time to hate;
a time for war, and a time for peace.'

and then the sentence that everyone omits:

'What gain has the worker from his toil?'

What Ecclesiastes is really saying is that everything has its time and it all ends in death. We cannot change the eternal plan of God. It is all fixed and unalterable so the only thing for us to decide is how best to make use of the life we have.

'For the fate of the sons of men
and the fate of beasts is the same;
as one dies so dies the other.
Man has no advantage over the beasts
for all is vanity.
All go to one place;
all are from the dust,
and all turn to dust again.'

The author looks at some of the things people strive after and comes to the conclusion that all their striving is pointless. He says, to take but one example, don't put your faith in wealth, or power or the wealthy and powerful:

'He who loves money will not be satisfied with money; nor he who loves wealth, with gain.' But he will be surrounded by scroungers. 'When goods increase, they increase who eat them.' And the wealthy man will go to the grave as naked as he was born. 'What gain has he that he toiled for the wind, and spent all his days in darkness and grief, in much vexation and sickness and resentment?'

It doesn't matter who we are or how much or little we have, if we have no capacity for enjoyment we have nothing. If we cannot enjoy life's good things there is no point in being alive.

But if we have that capacity, if we can eat and drink and find enjoyment in our work; if we can find happiness and satisfaction in our ordinary, everyday lives; then we won't give much thought to the futility of life or to death.

This does not mean being frivolous or trivial or spending our lives in the company of fools. If we really want to enjoy life we should follow the path of wisdom because we can never master all the knowledge there is. There is always more to learn and discover and the quest is very satisfying.

'A man's wisdom makes his face shine,
and the hardness of his countenance is changed.'

So the best way to enjoy life is to take it seriously, to seek wisdom and the company of the wise, and to try to find the middle way (how Aristotle and the Greeks would have cheered to read this):

'Surely there is not a righteous man on earth
who does good and never sins.' So
'Be not righteous overmuch,
and do not make yourself otherwise;
why should you destroy yourself?' But also
'Be not wicked overmuch,
neither be a fool;
why should you die before your time?'

Remembering that life takes no account of righteousness or wickedness; that the righteous are not rewarded and the wicked art not punished: remembering that 'one fate comes to all', to the righteous and the wicked, to the good and to the evil, to the clean and to the unclean, to those who offer worship and to those who do not; make the most of life while you have it for 'the living know that they will die but the dead know nothing.'

The best way to live is to obey the authorities because that saves a lot of trouble, and within the bounds of what is possible, simply to enjoy life. 'For man has no good thing under the sun except to eat and drink and enjoy himself, for this will go with him in his toil through the days of life which God gives him under the sun.'

'Be clean and well dressed and enjoy life with the wife whom you love. . . Whatever your hand finds to do, do it with your might.' The author has no concept of leisure.

What he advocates then is a responsible hedonism. He believes that we should find enjoyment in the lives we have, not in striving after something other that is beyond our reach. If we keep our self-respect; if we use our hands and our minds to the best of our ability; if we make the most of the good things with which we are surrounded we shan't be unduly troubled by the fact that sooner or later it is all going to come to an end.

Like all hedonistic teaching this was very swiftly condemned. It is astonishing that so few religious thinkers are ever able to see the seriousness and responsibility underlying the best hedonistic teaching. They fail to see that 'eat, drink and be merry' is a motto for life that can live happily in harmony with the very highest ethical and social standards.

One of the first condemnations of the teaching of Ecclesiastes comes in the wisdom literature itself – in the Wisdom of Solomon, which seems to me quite cynically to mis-state the teaching of Ecclesiastes before denouncing it. Others were to do exactly the same with the teaching of Epicurus.

After misrepresenting the teaching of Ecclesiastes he claims that hedonistic teaching is wicked, that hedonism implies selfishness and that hedonists hate righteous people. These claims are still frequently made by religious people. No one would deny that there are hedonists who are wicked and selfish just as there are religious people who arc wicked and selfish. The history of the church is littered with them. But hedonistic teaching whether in Ecclesiastes or in the teaching of Epicurus is sensible, moderate, responsible and decent. And in some respects the teaching of Epicurus is *still* in advance of Christianity.

What is significant here is the fact that at the heart of one of the most theocratic societies of all time, and enshrined in the corpus of its holy books, there is a this-worldly philosophy which has so much in common both with the ancient Epicureans and with modern atheistic humanism.

It lacks a social dimension however. There is nothing of the outreaching or warmly embracing friendship of the Epicureans and there is none of modern humanism's social conscience or concern for the well-being of others. But it is a start, and given the society from which it came, it is a very significant start.

The Song of Songs
or The Song of Solomon

Now here *is* a book which can be dismissed.

How this book found its way into a library (which is what the Bible is) of supposedly holy books, only the ancient Jews can explain.

If you have a taste for erotic oriental poetry, read it. If not, skip it.

Section Four

The Nevi'im – The Prophets

The Jews include a number of the historical books among the prophets: Joshua, Judges, Samuel and Kings. We have already looked at these in section two.

From Isaiah until the end of the Old Testament all the books with two exceptions belong to 'the Prophets'. The two exceptions are Lamentations and Daniel which belong to 'the Writings'.

As I have done thus far, I shall simply follow the Old Testament order and include these in section four. For a general comment on prophecy, there is a note at the end of 1 Kings.

Isaiah

With Isaiah we come to the first of the major prophets. Scholars divide the book (particularly at chapter 40) seeing it as a composite containing more than one voice. For our purposes scholarly study has little relevance. Our only concern is to ask, what do the prophetic books say and to follow that with a second question. Is what they say worth reading? Has it any continuing relevance or importance for people seeking how best to live their lives now?

Isaiah 1:1 sets the book in its historical context and then, from verse 2, gets down to work.

The nation is sinful and God is sick of its animal sacrifices. 'Even though you make many prayers, I will not listen; your hands are full of blood.'

Verses 16–20 make it clear that God requires clean, virtuous lives. Given these things God will pardon all past sin and bless his people. Without them there will come destruction. It is no use trusting to their status as God's chosen people because God distinguishes between the good and the bad. He redeems the good and punishes the bad.

It is a powerful message for those who believe in this god. For those who do not, its only value lies in its depiction of a god whose values we share. He bids us 'seek justice, correct oppression; defend the fatherless, plead for the widow.' (1:17)

Chapter 2 has a vision of Jerusalem as a city of peace to which 'all the nations shall flow' to learn the ways of their god. It continues with a comprehensive condemnation of all other kinds of worship and the warning of judgement. This kind of condemnation continues in the following chapters. It is sad that Jerusalem has never managed to become a city of peace.

These chapters are powerfully written but they rest on false assumptions. The first is the assumption that there is a god, a personal god who rules over history. But the assumption which runs right through the Old Testament story is that some generations are virtuous and others are not. It is similar to the claim of old people of every generation that the past was better than the present and that they 'don't know what young people are coming to these days.'

My own view is that while society changes from generation to generation, people do not change. There have been a number of evil men in positions of power in my lifetime. They have caused terrible things to be done. In doing so they have degraded and dehumanised some of their own followers. (A European thinks immediately of Stalin and Hitler but there have been others elsewhere in the world.)

Yet it is quite clear that in general, the people of Russia and Germany at the time of Stalin and Hitler were neither better nor worse than the people of those two countries at any other period of their history. Nor were they either better or worse than the people of other countries including our own.

Evil certainly always needs to be denounced and evil men and women need to be curbed and controlled. But it is never the case that whole societies deserve condemnation.

In good times and in bad times most people just get on with their lives, keeping their heads down when it is necessary. They make the most of their families and friends, they keep out of trouble and they do their bit for society. In that phrase that I hear again and again as a funeral celebrant: 'He/she would never do anybody any harm.' And again, 'He/she was always willing to help.' That is a reasonable description of most people of any period of history and any country. Is that so reprehensible?

7:14 and 9:2–7 have a special importance for Christians because they apply them (and other passages in Isaiah) to Jesus. They are passages of great literary power and beauty.

Anyone who is reading the whole of Isaiah will find 9:2–7 like a shaft of sunlight in a gap between closed curtains. The book has been virtually all darkness and gloom and judgement because of the view that 'every one is godless and an evil doer' (9:17). Now in the midst of it all comes this glorious poem promising light, a kingdom 'with justice and with righteousness from this time forth and for evermore.' (9:7)

It was during Isaiah's time that the Assyrians destroyed the northern kingdom of the Jews carrying the leading people into exile. Their army came to Jerusalem and then some epidemic, perhaps the plague, decimated its ranks and the siege of Jerusalem was called off.

All this was seen as the protective work of God. This is what chapters 10 and 11 are about, the saving of Jerusalem and hope for the future that the exiles will return home. All the triumphs of Assyria prior to the epidemic are also seen as the work of God. God claims that Assyria is 'the rod of my anger, the staff of my fury.'

Sadly such primitive ideas are not dead. Perhaps we should ask those who hold them what sort of a god it is who can approve such destruction and distress. If he existed he would be unworthy of our worship for he has less common decency and compassion than all but the worst of us.

The vision of peace in chapter 11 is both beautiful and famous. Once again Christians purloin it and associate it with Jesus. If the coming of Jesus had brought such peace we would probably all become his followers but, in his own words, he did not come 'to bring peace but a sword'. And the history of Christianity has been bound up with the sword at least as much as with a gospel of peace.

But the prophet cannot sustain his message of peace for long. He is soon back wallowing in blood and horror (13:15–16). But now we have jumped one hundred and fifty years and power is with Babylon instead of Assyria. Then in chapter 14 we return to Assyria. It doesn't much matter. The main message is that all nations are in the hand of God. Their times of ascendancy are a part of his plan and their destruction is also part of his plan. He is Lord over all.

Religious people hear the message that God is Lord over all. They fail to recognise that if this were true, he would deserve to be despised and hated rather than worshipped.

After chapters of utter desolation, at the end of chapter 19 (verses 23–25) there is a prophetic promise that Assyria and Egypt will one day worship the god of the Jews and the Jewish kingdom will be ranked on a par with these two powerful neighbours. It is a prophecy that was never fulfilled. (Although modern Israel has fulfilled part two of the prophecy.)

The gloom and misery continues with barely a hint of joy (24:14–16a) and even that is swiftly doused (16b). After so much misery chapter 25 comes as a complete surprise. Yet there is no evidence that verse 4 is true:

'Thou hast been a stronghold to the poor, a stronghold to the needy in distress, a shelter from the storm and a shade from the heat.'

In all the tales of destruction *everybody* has suffered. It is always so, but perhaps the poor suffer most of all because they have no possibility of escape – no camel or private jet; no foreign bank accounts, no moveable wealth; and no friends in high places.

As we look at the tides of refugees it is the poor we are looking at. The rich have escaped to new lives abroad. The gods have never been a stronghold to the poor and needy or a shelter from the storm. The most that can ever be said for religion is that it often inspires worshippers to join with other humanitarian agencies in sending relief after the event, but is that the inspiration of the gods or just plain human compassion?

Even when Isaiah is promising better days (25:6ff) he still has it in for the Moabites. And of what value will these better days be to all the innocent victims of the times of judgement? When prophecy begins to be questioned, the gods do not come out of the examination very well.

26:3 is a lovely and popular verse amongst religious people.

'Thou dost keep him in perfect peace,
whose mind is stayed on thee.'

We have seen that belief in life after death was rare in Old Testament times, but there is one verse pointing that way in 26:19.

A great deal of the reputation of the prophets lies in their stand for 'moral values' (the mantra of politicians here at the end of the 20th century). In 28:5–20 Isaiah lives up to that reputation. Yet he actually teaches very little. He stands for justice and righteousness but has nothing to say about these things except that they become second nature to those who are 'instructed aright' (v. 26). We are not told what right instruction actually is.

The chapter ends with a fine parable which is largely lost on 20th century urban populations. It speaks of a farmer's work; of how he does the right things at the right times of year, and of how he treats different seeds in different ways that are appropriate to their nature. We are left to work out for ourselves the message or moral for us.

In 29:13–24 we have a warning against hypocrisy followed by a utopian dream promising hearing to the deaf and sight to the blind, joy to the meek and poor. But the dream remained a dream until *human* technology began to find ways of turning it into reality for some of the deaf and the blind.

Fearful of the Assyrians, the Jews looked to Egypt for a defensive alliance. Isaiah warns them that Egypt will prove unreliable and tells them to put their trust quietly in God (30:15 & 18–26). Whether this was prophecy before or after the event, it proved to be true. The Egyptians were no match for the Assyrians, but when the Assyrians came to besiege Jerusalem an epidemic decimated their ranks and they went home. There, Sennacherib was murdered by his sons and the threat to Jerusalem passed. Chapter after chapter is devoted to the twin themes of God's judgement and his kindness towards Jerusalem. None of it requires our time or attention.

34:8–17 is of interest however. It describes the results of God's vengeance against Edom. The land returns to nature and a wide variety of birds and animals is mentioned. It would be interesting to compare that list with the wild-life of the area today. I suspect that it would show pretty vividly the devastating effect our species has had on the rest of the natural world.

We do not need the Bible to teach us such lessons. We only have to walk in meadows owned by organisations such as 'Plantlife' and then in some of the 'improved' meadows all around us to see what we have destroyed.

35 offers a happier, better future for the Jews. Idealists of modern Israel believed that they were bringing this vision into being – a human, not a divine achievement. Sadly, few can still hold such a naive and lovely dream.

I have mentioned the arrival of Sennacherib's army at the gates of Jerusalem several times. Chapters 36 to 39 tell the story. The whole of the first 39 chapters of Isaiah have been dominated by this one event. What happened must have been very impressive to the Jews of Jerusalem at the time – as significant to them as the victory at Marathon was to the Greeks and the escape at Dunkirk was to us. And we can understand a fairly primitive people giving their god the credit.

These chapters 36–39 speak of the faith of Isaiah that God would protect Jerusalem and also of the faith of Hezekiah the king. But another story is told which prepares us for events still to come. Visitors came from the king of Babylon and Hezekiah showed them his treasures. Isaiah warns that one day the Babylonians will destroy the city and take the treasures for themselves. This raises the question, why did God save Jerusalem from the Assyrians if he was going to allow its downfall later? Scholars see chapter 39 as the end of Isaiah, with chapter 40 as the beginning of *Second Isaiah*. They also believe that there is more than one author involved in Isaiah 40–66. Their studies and debates need not concern us.

Isaiah chapter 40 is magnificent.

It has been worth trawling through all that is irrelevant just to come to this – just as every so often in a book of poetry we find one that cries out to be read again and again.

If we want to understand the enduring power of religion we need do no more than read this chapter. It speaks of the majesty, glory and eternity of God and his word and of our insignificance together with the brevity of life.

In my Christian days I preached from this chapter. If I were a Jew, Christian or Moslem now, I think I would just read it aloud without comment, and allow it to make its own impact.

Taken literally (and many religious people no longer take it literally), even this is open to criticism. The warfare of Jerusalem is still not ended, and the world would be a very dull place if verse 4 were fulfilled. Nor are most of us willing to be likened to a flock of sheep. But these are trivialities compared with the glory of this as a piece of religious literature.

I no longer believe in the god or the message – no atheist does – but this does not detract from my enjoyment of the passage or my appreciation of its greatness.

No one could expect such quality to be sustained but there is a marked difference in tone between these chapters and 1–39. Chapters 42 and 43 would be of comfort to all who believe themselves to be the specially chosen people of God. There is a new confidence and assurance in God himself, which is perhaps because this prophet believes so firmly that his god is the only god, God over all.

His monotheism is far more clear cut than anything that has gone before. An atheist will enjoy his mockery of idol-worshippers in chapter 44:9–20. After two and a half thousand years it is still not altogether without relevance. But perhaps it is useful to bear in mind the comment made by James Thrower in his book *The Alternative Tradition* (Mouton Publishers, 1980). The Hebraic prohibition against 'graven images' forbids us from worshipping anything made by ourselves:

'It is because the ancient Hebrews believed in an utterly transcendent God that they were led to denigrate and relativise all human values and their representations. An utterly transcendent God, however, . . . has the uncanny knack of becoming so utterly transcendent as to be no God at all – a situation which leaves man free to explore and experiment with the world, including the structure of human society, without any reference at all to divine interference.'

There have been a fair number of Christian theologians of late whose god has become that transcendent.

In chapter 45 we have leaped forward in time to the period of Cyrus, ruler of Babylon's empire. These chapters purport to be addressed to him. Why would Israel's god speak to Cyrus?

First because he claims to be God over all, the only God, the creator who speaks the truth and declares what is right.

Secondly for historical reasons. The two Jewish kingdoms no longer existed. The Assyrians had destroyed the northern kingdom Israel in 721 BCE. The Babylonians under Nebucha-drezzar had destroyed Judah and Jerusalem in 586 BCE. On each occasion the leading people had been carried away into exile.

It was Cyrus who gave permission for some of them to return, to rebuild Jerusalem and the temple. In spite of this act of generosity chapters 46 and 47 promise judgement on Babylon and salvation for the Jews. And this (48) in spite of the fact that God doesn't think much of the Jews. 'I know that you are obstinate, and your neck is an iron sinew and your head brass.' (v. 4) 'You have never heard, you have never known, from of old your ear has not been opened. For I knew that you would deal very treacherously, and that from birth you were called a rebel.' (v. 7)

Yet he has chosen them and will redeem them and by verse 20 he is telling them to 'go forth from Babylon with a shout of joy.'

49: This 'despised' people, 'abhorred by the nations' has been chosen to demonstrate what God can do; chosen to be 'a light to the nations, that my salvation may reach to the end of the earth.' (vvs. 7 and 6)

Chapter 53 is very important to Christians. It is about the 'suffering servant'. This has been taken by Christians and applied to Jesus. Passages in the New Testament probably owe their phrasing to this chapter.

For Christians believe that the sufferings and death of Jesus as 'an offering for sin' achieve forgiveness and the opportunity of a new life as children of God for those who trust in him.

An immense salvation theology has grown up in an attempt to explain how the sufferings and death of one man can bring salvation to the rest of us. Some of the more primitive sacrificial ideas are pretty repulsive, but there are also highly sophisticated and noble ideas. Some branches of the church pay far more attention to salvation theology than others. Mine was one of them. As a result I spent a great deal of time and effort wrestling with these ideas. Although there was a good deal that was attractive in some of them, none of them was ultimately fully satisfying.

As with the problem of pain and the doctrine of divine providence, so with salvation theology, it failed to answer the questions it raised and sought to address.

For atheists it is all pretty irrelevant. We feel that human beings must stand on their own feet. We shall be assisted by other people – and we are wise to take all the help we can get – but in the end we are on our own.

If we feel that we have blotted our copybooks badly enough to need forgiveness we have to earn the right to forgiveness. We have to learn how to begin again and how to rebuild our lives, and then we actually have to get on with doing it. Even if we arrive at the point where we deserve forgiveness, we may never receive it from those we have wronged. But the crucial question is not whether they can forgive us, but whether we can forgive ourselves.

Moral failure leads us to lose our self-respect. By the quality of the lives we lead and the new ideals and standards we set ourselves and reach towards, we can recover our self-respect. It takes time, but we can achieve it.

None of this has anything to do with a suffering servant or a sacrifice or a saviour or a god. It has everything to do with human choice, human ideals and the will and determination to pursue them.

The best of men and women may provide us with examples and with inspiration. And sometimes we shall need the special skills and help of professionals. But in the end it is always down to us.

Returning to the text: the dominant feature of these chapters is the kindness God is going to show his people in the future. This makes them much pleasanter reading than all the chapters of judgement, but it doesn't make them any more relevant.

For religious people chapter 55 is another favourite. It is full of promises to those who 'seek the Lord while he may be found.' (v. 6) It brings comfort to those who believe it. But it also demonstrates why it is impossible to hold a proper debate with religious people. Whenever they are in a corner they claim a superior knowledge and a superior wisdom outside human experience. (55:8–9)

In chapter 56 there is one brief, significant advance. Just as weakened churches begin to remember the prayer of Jesus 'that they may all be one' and seek comfort and strength through union, so a weakened 'chosen people' began to look beyond its national boundaries (56:3–8). 'These' (the foreigners who join themselves to the Lord) 'I will bring to my holy mountain, and make them joyful in my house of prayer for my house shall be called a house of prayer for all peoples.' (56:7)

Sadly the inclusiveness of this passage was never to become wholehearted either in Judaism or in Christianity or Islam. Christians might join Isaiah in welcoming 'the eunuch', 'the dry tree', but a recent vote of Anglican bishops still shows them unable to welcome practising homosexuals and lesbians into the family of their god.

57 condemns idolatry in the language of a jealous husband or wife. But it ends with the promise that the humble and contrite will be healed, led and comforted.

For believers verses 14–21 are a genuine source of comfort, but only for believers.

It is from verses like 16 that the Christian doctrine of God the Holy Spirit, the third person of the trinity, has been formulated: 'from me proceeds the spirit, and I have made the breath of life.'

In chapter 57 we learn that God desires worshippers 'of a contrite and humble spirit' (v. 15) and in 58 the path of virtue is spelled out in some detail. Here at last is something for an atheist to get his teeth into.

Acts of religious devotion, no matter how frequent or sincere or thoroughgoing, are meaningless without the right spirit (verses 1–5). God's worshippers are required to be people who strive against oppression and injustice, who care for the poor, the hungry and the homeless, and who avoid gossip and scandal and passing judgement on others. They also honour God's sabbath as his holy day 'not going your own ways, or seeking your own pleasure, or talking idly.' (verses 6–14)

There is a great deal of common ground here between what is required of worshippers and the ideals any decent human being will strive for. To read such a passage is to be reminded of our ordinary human responsibilities and to be challenged to go beyond what is suggested here – to work towards an end to poverty, hunger and homelessness for example.

Chapters 59 and 60 to 62 are vividly written and offer a complete contrast to one another. 59 speaks of the universal wickedness of the nation and 60–62 paints a picture of a future golden age. All golden ages are either long past or far in the future. This one is no exception. It is as distant today as it ever was.

Nor is the prophecy even true. 62:8b promises that there will be no future desolation. But the worst desolation was still to come in Roman times.

However, I'm told that it is unfair to criticise the prophets for getting the future wrong. 'The words of a prophet are either of the "keeper of the King's conscience" kind' perfectly expressed in the story of Nathan and David 'or of the Martin Luther King "I have a dream" variety. The idea that a prophet foretold the future is a fundamentalist notion which took hold when the church was fundamentalist and it takes a lot of shaking off.'

Part of what my critic says is absolutely true so that I would agree with him when he continues: 'The Messianic passages are of the "I have a dream" variety and only in an extremely tenuous way refer to Jesus.' But of course they don't actually refer to Jesus at all. It is Christians who have applied them to Jesus and that is a very different matter.

Where I would disagree with my critic is over the question of prophets attempting to foretell the future. There is no doubt that sometimes they did, and when they did, inevitably they were more often wrong than right.

But we must return to the text of chapter 62.

Note verse 6: 'They shall bring gold and frankincense' – is this the source of two of the gifts supposed to have been brought by wise men to the baby Jesus?

63:1–6 describes God as stained with the life-blood of the nations. Rarely can there have been a more accurate picture. I write after a weekend of violence in Northern Ireland and bombings elsewhere. Of the first, the news correspondent spoke of the hatred of Catholics and Protestants for one another and of what little hope there is for peace when people are brought up to such hatred. Some bombings elsewhere are thought to have been the work of Moslem extremists. Even though that may be unfair, they are certainly capable of such things. All three groups believe

112

that they are *exclusively* the people of God. In semi-quotation of Isaiah: the lifeblood of the nations stains their garments and their god is a god drenched in blood.

Yet, while living out this horrible truth, they can go on immediately and join the prophet in speaking of the 'steadfast love of the Lord' (v. 7) without any thought of the contradiction between these two extremes. The rest of the chapter shows that even such 'steadfast love' failed to keep the Jews faithful. As a result, Isaiah wails 'we have become like those over whom thou hast never ruled, like those who are not called by thy name.' (v.19)

The prophet prays to God to take action on behalf of his chosen people. He obviously believes that they have been punished long enough and he *almost* hints that God himself is responsible if they do not come up to scratch:

'Yet, O Lord, thou art our Father;
we are the clay, and thou art our potter;
we are all the work of thy hand.' (v. 8)

He doesn't quite reach the point of asking why God hasn't made a better job of his pottery, but many people do. Many who are far from being atheists wonder how it is, if God is as wonderful as he is supposed to be, that he has made such a rotten job both of the world (full of natural disasters); and of religion (divided, schismatic and mutually exclusive and hostile); and supremely of people (whose vices seem to be both natural and endless and whose virtues seem to be achieved only with great difficulty).

In chapter 65 God justifies himself (verses 1–2) but fails to answer the question I have just raised. In 66 he tries to answer that question by suggesting that all man's sufferings before the golden age are like the sufferings of a woman in labour. They have to be endured before the joy arrives, but are worth it for the joy.

There are many, many women who would find this an unsatisfactory answer. Why could a creator-god not have made giving birth free from pain? And why should endless generations suffer just to provide a golden age for some other generation in the far distant future?

The questions do not go away. If there is a god he has too much to answer for. He is not worthy of our 'humble and contrite'

113

worship, nor do we tremble at his word. (66: 2)

Returning to 65, after condemning the wicked once more he goes on to promise that famous, elusive golden age once more (verses 17–25). It is a lovely vision, the kind of vision or ideal that is worth keeping before us and striving for. But it is no use looking to a god to 'create new heavens and a new earth' for us. Two and a half thousand years after Isaiah the world still waits. If there is ever to be a golden age we shall have to fashion it for ourselves. In the meantime we do well to establish what paradise we can within the framework of our present lives for who knows what tomorrow may bring.

Chapter 66 begins with a condemnation of sacrificial worship but the Jews never gave it up until the Romans destroyed Jerusalem and its temple centuries after Isaiah.

The book ends with another picture of future glory when God will come 'to gather all nations and tongues; and they shall come and see my glory.' And what is his glory? Part of it lies in the very last words of the book. Let Isaiah speak and let the rest of us make of it what we will:

> 'And they' [the nations who have come to worship the Lord] 'shall go forth and look on the dead bodies of the men that have rebelled against me; for their worm shall not die, their fire shall not be quenched, and they shall be an abhorrence to all flesh.' (66:4)

Such a god is not fit to be worshipped.

Jeremiah

Jeremiah is the second of the major prophets. Chapter 1 sets him firmly in his historical context and describes his call to be a prophet.

The historical period of the book is the period of the conquest of Judah, the southern kingdom of the Jews by King Nebuchadrezzar of Babylon. Jerusalem fell in 586 BCE.

But the book is not sequential. It hops about looking forward, looking backward, prophecies in one reign set cheek by jowl with prophecies from another. None of this matters very much except to ancient historians. What matters is the message and the question whether it has any relevance for the present.

There are two main messages. The first is that the Jews have been a faithless people and have failed to give their exclusive worship and service to their god. This failure means that they are condemned as evil and their punishment is the destruction of their state and of Jerusalem and exile in Babylon for their leading people. The second is that their god will bring them back after a considerable period in exile and will re-establish a Jewish state centred on Jerusalem and ruled by kings of the Davidic line with priests from the ancient priestly family of Aaron.

Jeremiah is a gentler prophet than most. Because his prophecies of doom came at a particularly sensitive time, they required considerable courage from him. Although he suffered periods of imprisonment and personal danger, it is remarkable that the authorities were as tolerant with him as they proved to be.

Chapters 2 to 3 condemn the Jews for deserting their god and for putting their trust in alliances with Egypt and Assyria and in the worship of idols.

God speaks sadly. He cannot understand why his people have turned from him. He pleads as a loving husband might plead with a faithless wife.

Chapter 4 foretells the invasion of Judah and the disasters and human suffering it will bring. But although this is the judgement of God, this is a god who grieves for his people. There is none of the blood lust that has marked some other parts of the Old Testament.

Through chapters 5 and 6 God demonstrates how patient he has been. But the faithlessness of Judah runs right through society. As a result he feels justified in bringing disaster 'from the north country'.

Their faithlessness has been of long-standing and in spite of the prophets. Yet he still offers them a chance:

'For if you amend your ways and your doings, if you truly execute justice one with another, if you do not oppress the alien, the fatherless or the widow, or shed innocent blood in this place, and if you do not go after other gods to your own hurt, then I will let you dwell in this place, in the land that I gave of old to your fathers for ever.' (7:5–7)

115

Here is a concern not just for religion, but for just dealings and common decency. What is more, Jeremiah's god is a god who actually cares about what he does. It grieves him to punish his people. (c. 8) But 'what else can I do' (9:7). Here is a god with feelings like ours. This is not the remote, awe-inspiring, all-powerful god who commands worship by his majesty. This is a god who only punishes because he feels that he must. He can see no alternative.

In 9:23–24 he spells out the nature of true religion. The irreligious can respect such a god without believing in him. And we can stand side by side with religious people who care about such things as 'steadfast love, justice, and righteousness in the earth'.

In chapters 10–12 the condemnation of the Jews continues. Their worship of idols is particularly singled out. They must have been a particularly bad people to have merited so many pages of condemnation from one prophet after another. Yet if the truth be told, they will have been no different from any other generation anywhere else in the world – just the usual mix of good, bad and indifferent.

Chapter 13 begins with a parable and contains the famous line 'Can the leopard change his spots?' (v. 23). There are actually two lines but the other is politically incorrect so of course I couldn't possibly quote it – and why would an Ethiopian want to 'change his skin' anyway?

Chapter 14: drought is seen as part of God's punishment. God's condemnation of the Jews goes on and on and becomes thoroughly wearisome reading. Jeremiah's message is utterly uncompromising even though it leads to him being put in the stocks. He claims that he would prefer to be silent but 'there is in my heart as it were a burning fire shut up in my bones, and I am weary with holding it in, and I cannot.' (20:9)

But in 23:3–8 he does offer future hope, a return from exile, a 'righteous Branch' of the house of David for king and security in the land. 23:9 condemns his fellow prophets as false.

In 24 we find Jerusalem fallen to Babylon. The exiles and those belonging to the puppet regime left in Jerusalem are separated. The exiles are to be God's chosen ones and those remaining in the land will be rejected. No reason is given. One group of people is wholly praiseworthy, the other wholly evil.

Frankly, that is nonsense.

Jeremiah's prophecies of doom and judgement are widened in chapter 25 to include the whole world. Needless to say this made him very unpopular and there were those who wished to put him to death (c. 26). We can admire his courage but I can't help feeling that reading all this doom and gloom or constantly hearing it could easily give people a pretty jaundiced view of humanity.

In spite of defeat, all the surviving nations are considering an alliance and resistance to Nebuchadrezzar. In chapter 27 Jeremiah warns them and tells them to live quietly under their yoke. He also writes to those in exile and tells them to settle down. 'Build houses. . . plant gardens. . . Take wives. . .' (29:5–6). The exile will be long but not permanent. 'For I know the plans I have for you, says the Lord, plans for welfare and not evil, to give you a future and a hope.' (29:11)

Amidst all the prophetic voices all claiming to speak in the name of God, it must have been impossible for people to know who to believe. But Jeremiah has been proved right so far and now in chapters 30 and 31 he promises an ultimate return from exile and the rebuilding of Jerusalem. 31 is a particularly optimistic and attractive one. Verses 29–30 mark a change in belief concerning moral responsibility.

Moral responsibility had always been thought of as tribal to the third and fourth generations – in other words, an ongoing responsibility carried from generation to generation. Here it is thought of as individual: 'Everyone shall die for his own sin.'

The question of moral responsibility is of huge and permanent importance. That we are responsible for our own actions is, or should be, clear. But how far do we share in the responsibility of society as a whole and for how long? This is a question faced by the grandchildren of Germans responsible for the holocaust; of Japanese responsible for the maltreatment of prisoners of war; of the British looking back at the centuries of imperialism and of the misgovernment of Ireland but not of these countries alone. Almost any country has episodes in its history of which it should be ashamed – and the shame goes on.

In shameful times do we stand up to be counted and take the consequences, or do we keep our heads down and keep our own lives as clean and blameless as possible? John Donne was right when he said that 'no man is an island'. We are interdependent and this involves us in the life and decisions of others whether we like it or not. The question of our social responsibility has no easy answers, but it is a question we can be sure that we shall always have to face.

31:31–34 is very important for Christians and particularly for Protestant Christians because they apply it to themselves. The old covenant was to the tribes which made up the Jewish nation. The new covenant is individualistic and is written in people's hearts. There will be no need for priests and prophets as teachers for 'they shall all know me, from the least of them to the greatest, says the Lord'. (v. 34)

Thus Jeremiah breaks free from the legalism and ritual of the old covenant and its priesthood. He brings the individual face to face with his god and requires generosity of spirit and caring for others.

This was one of the major breakthroughs achieved by the Old Testament prophets and it was taken up by Jesus and emphasised constantly by him. 'The sabbath was made for man not man for the sabbath.' That cut a swathe through Jewish sabbath ritual and regulation and by implication through all ritual and dependence upon the priesthood.

Jeremiah broke free and so did Jesus but religion did not. Ritual is easier than personal responsibility. 'Go to Mass, cut out chocolate for Lent, pray for the poor and needy.' It is so much easier to pray for the widow and orphan than to look after them. All the praying in the world is worthless unless it leads praying people into social action.

So Jeremiah was a trail blazer. But, as always with trail blazers, he swings the pendulum too far. There will always be a need for codes of social conduct to be expressed in laws. And there will always be a need for moral teaching and therefore for moral teachers.

There is no necessary connection between religion and moral teaching. Much of the best moral teaching is not religious at all. But, if religion is to have any continuing value it will be in this field. But it will only be of value if its teaching is relevant, human and appropriate to its own social period. Our understanding of what is right and what is wrong changes from generation to generation. So does our understanding of what is important and what is unimportant. Religion must keep in tune with society if its moral teaching is to have any value. This does not mean following every latest whim or dropping its standards. But it does mean keeping in touch and offering a teaching relevant to today, a teaching of value to society rather than a divisive and harmful teaching. Moral teaching has always to be tested against those very few principles which seem to be both fundamental and permanent.

However, Jeremiah is right when he insists that ultimately moral values are inward things. Until and unless we make them our own, they will have no influence on our behaviour. In that sense Jeremiah is wholly right. If we are to become people of virtue or excellence, our values have to be written upon our hearts.

Placed under house arrest during the siege of Jerusalem (chapter 32), Jeremiah buys a field as an act of faith in the future. It is a remarkable gesture, a simple act which demonstrates the genuine sincerity and integrity of this prophet. His twin messages continue: Jerusalem will fall because the people have been unfaithful to their god and therefore evil. But a new day will dawn when Jerusalem and the Jewish state will be restored. Both Jeremiah and his god seem to believe that future generations will be different from past. For a creator, this shows little understanding of his creation.

Chapter 35 speaks of the faithfulness of the teetotal Rechabites. But they have made the mistake of leaving their tents to come to Jerusalem to escape Nebuchadrezzar. There can have been little comfort in Jeremiah's promise that some of the family would survive the siege.

In 36 we are told that Jeremiah used Baruch the scribe to write his words down and read them in the temple. He used other scribes. Books have begun to take on a new importance. It probably began with Josiah's reforms following the finding of a book of the law in the temple. When Jeremiah's scroll was read to the king, he cut it up and burned it, but Jeremiah had another scroll written. I doubt if this king was the first to try to stifle unwelcome ideas. He was certainly not the last – both rulers and religions have followed his example and shared his failure.

As I mentioned earlier, historically the book is somewhat confusing because it keeps hopping forward and backward through various reigns. But we never wander far from the siege and fall of Jerusalem. In 37 the Babylonians leave the siege to deal with a threat from the Egyptian army. There was immense relief in Jerusalem but Jeremiah warns that the Babylonians will be back. Then he set out to visit his new field and to take possession of it. He was arrested, charged with desertion, beaten and imprisoned. The king reduced his punishment.

Jeremiah continued his prophecies of doom and his advice to the people to surrender. It may have been sensible advice and very brave, but it was hardly calculated to make him very popular with the authorities. Four of the defenders put him down in a dry cistern and left him to die of starvation. But Ebedmelech, an Ethiopian eunuch in the service of the king, obtained permission to save his life. (c. 38)

Jeremiah stood by his message. Chapter 39 tells the story of the fall of the city. Gedaliah was appointed governor and Jeremiah was given the freedom to choose between exile and life in a devastated Judah. He chose to stay.

Gedaliah refused to believe warnings that Ishmael was out to murder him. When he died, Johanan (who had warned him) attacked the murderers but Ishmael escaped. Afraid to face the reaction of the Babylonians, Johanan and his companions decided to take refuge in Egypt. Jeremiah warned them not to go: God will bless them if they stay and punish them if they go. They ignored his message and took him with them. In Egypt Jeremiah prophesied that Nebuchadrezzar would come and conquer Egypt but his messages were ignored. The Jews in Egypt, and especially the women, insisted that they would worship the Egyptian goddess 'the queen of heaven' (ch. 40–44).

Most of the rest of the book consists of prophecies of the judgement of God on nation after nation: Egypt, the Philistines, Moab, the Ammonites, Edom, Syria and finally in chapters 50 and 51, Babylon itself. Then the exiles will be restored to their homeland and there will be no iniquity or sin. How can anyone with any knowledge of human nature promise such a thing.

The Lamentations of Jeremiah

This book is one of 'the Writings' even though it appears in the middle of 'the Prophets'. I have written of these sub-divisions of the Biblical books elsewhere.

The Lamentations begins with a very moving lament for Jerusalem including the famous words: 'Is it nothing to you, all you who pass by? Look and see if there is any sorrow like my sorrow.' (1:12)

As we read chapter 2 we can imagine the author drifting aimlessly through the city after its destruction as so many have walked through their blitzed and battered towns and villages in the 20th century overwhelmed by the scenes of destruction.

Just as self-pity is beginning to make chapter 3 tedious, there comes a remarkable expression of either faith or a clinging to the shreds of faith in God's 'steadfast love' and a reminder that God requires justice. It is worth reading in full (chapter 3:21–42a) but here are a few samples:

'The steadfast love of the Lord never ceases,
his mercies never come to an end;
they are new every morning;
great is thy faithfulness.' (22–23)

The Lord is good to those who wait for him,
to the soul that seeks him.
It is good that one should wait quietly
for the salvation of the Lord. (25–26)

For the Lord will not cast off for ever,
but, though he cause grief, he will have compassion
according to the abundance of his steadfast love;
for he does not willingly afflict
or grieve the sons of men. (31–33)

It is not necessary to believe these things to find them very moving. And it is good in the midst of all this misery and desolation to find a reassertion of the importance of justice:

To crush under foot all the prisoners of the earth,
to turn aside the right of a man
in the presence of the Most High,
to subvert a man in his cause,
the Lord does not approve. (34–36)

After this the lamentation continues to the end. The book is short. As a lament and as a very human picture of a man battling against despair, clinging to and fighting for hope, it is worth anybody's time.

But the humanist would have to say to anyone in such despair that it is no use placing hope in a god. When we are at rock bottom we have to pick ourselves up and find our own way back to life. I have tried to express this in one of my poems:

> *Not from a god came the resource*
> *I needed in that day*
> *but deep within myself*
> *I found the human victory way.*
> *Slowly and painfully at first*
> *the upward road was climbed. . .*

And that is what we would want to say to despair. The upward road can be climbed 'to freedom and to happiness, which you could also find'. (*The Sunlight Glances Through* p. 71)

Ezekiel

Ezekiel is the last of the major prophets.

He was a priest, one of the exiles in Babylon, a man of vivid and colourful imagination. His imagination sometimes makes for interesting reading regardless of his messages but I can't recommend anything before chapter 18.

The strange pictures in chapter one are designed to depict 'the appearance of the likeness of the glory of the Lord.' (1:28) Closely examined it is a picture which gives a very clear idea of Ezekiel's concept of the characteristics of his god – a god of power, movement, single mindedness, creative force, and enough humanity to enable humans to relate to him and worship him.

God calls Ezekiel 'son of man' which was one of the favourite titles used by Jesus. Perhaps Jesus saw himself as one of the prophets. Other people certainly did.

God has little respect for his own 'stubborn' and 'rebellious' people but he gives Ezekiel a scroll to eat, words which he will speak and which he is to 'receive in his heart and hear with his ears.' (3:11)

Ezekiel paints vivid pictures of God's punishment of both Jewish kingdoms and he acts out parables of that punishment. According to his figures, the northern Jews carried off by the Assyrians in 721 BCE would be free to return in 431. The Jews of the southern kingdom of Judah carried off to Babylon in 586 would be free to return in 546.

While there was an organised return from exile from Babylon in 539, there was no such organised return from Assyria.

In chapters 6 and 7 Ezekiel's god is revealed as a god of fury, harsh judgement and cruel punishment. As far as one can make out the only real crime of the people has been their worship of other gods. For all his power, Ezekiel's god has always been unable to inspire or persuade his people to remain faithful and to worship him in splendid monotheistic isolation. Does the fault lie with the people or their god? In chapters 8 and 9 he proves to be even more ruthless and merciless than Ezekiel can stomach.

In 10 Ezekiel's vivid imagination comes into play again as he tries to describe his vision of the presence and the glory of his god. 11 and 12 continue the theme of the punishment of Jerusalem but there is also a renewed promise of a restoration that will not be long delayed.

13 and 14 condemns false prophets and idol worshippers and singles out Noah, Job and Daniel as righteous men from the past. At least two of these are fictional characters. Is it only in fiction that we find true righteousness? And what is this righteousness? Noah's reaction to escape from the flood was to get gloriously drunk – very human but very righteous?

In chapter 16 Jerusalem is painted as the bride of God, a bride who has played the harlot. This raises the question again: why would a bride play the harlot if her husband was all that she desired?

The chapter insults neighbouring peoples but has an interesting account of Sodom's sin. In Genesis this is depicted purely in sexual terms. That is included at the end here but it is more important to Ezekiel that 'she and her daughters had pride, surfeit of food, and prosperous ease, but did not aid the poor and needy.' (16:49) A message for our time perhaps?

After all her punishments Jerusalem and the neighbouring nations will be restored. Chapter 17 agrees with Jeremiah in condemning the puppet government of Jerusalem installed by

Babylon. It is condemned for breaking faith with Babylon and turning to Egypt for military support.

18 takes up another theme raised by Jeremiah. It is the first chapter so far that I could commend to fellow atheists as worth their time. There are two subjects worth looking at here: the question of responsibility; and the ideal of righteousness.

Ezekiel begins with the old proverb: 'The fathers have eaten sour grapes, and the children's teeth are set on edge.' (18:2) Ezekiel challenges that view. He says 'The soul that sins shall die. The son shall not suffer for the iniquity of the father, nor the father suffer for the iniquity of the son; the righteousness of the righteous shall be upon himself, and the wickedness of the wicked shall be upon himself.' (18:20)

It is clear that this was a subject still under debate. Even more debatable in his time was his further claim that 'if a wicked man turns away from all his sins. . . and does what is lawful and right, he shall surely live; he shall not die. None of the transgressions which he has committed shall be remembered against him; for the righteousness which he has done he shall live. Have I any pleasure in the death of the wicked, says the Lord God, and not rather that he should turn from his way and live?' (18:21–23)

The converse is also true. If a righteous man turns to wickedness, he will also be judged accordingly. So God calls on his people to 'repent. . . Cast away from you all the transgressions which you have committed against me, and get yourselves a new heart and a new spirit. . . I have no pleasure in the death of anyone, says the Lord God; so turn and live.' (18:30–32)

In all of this there is no sign of the need for a Saviour. Each individual is able to make his or her own choices and has the responsibility for doing so.

If we remove god from the equation, all this is perfectly acceptable to a humanist. We also believe in personal responsibility and in judging people by their present behaviour rather than by their past.

But this chapter is also interesting for its delineation of what is lawful and right and what is not. The good man does not worship idols; does not commit adultery; treats his wife with consideration; does not oppress anyone financially; avoids usury; commits no robbery; feeds the hungry and clothes the naked; executes true justice and obeys God's law. (18:5–9)

124

That offers a standard of right behaviour worthy of any human being. We shall do well if we manage to live up to it.

Sadly, that passage is almost the only one in Ezekiel worthy of our attention. Chapter 19 is a lament and 20 is a history of Jewish worship of idols and of their god's wrath and punishments. Vividly and vigorously the recital of sin and punishment goes on in the following chapters. It is likened to adultery or harlotry. The supreme evil of idolatry is child sacrifice.

Even the death of Ezekiel's wife 'the delight of his eyes' is used as a sign of God's judgement and punishment. (24:15ff)

Chapters 25 to 28 widen the judgements to include all the neighbours of the Jewish kingdoms with a special lament for Tyre. 29–31 go on to include even Egypt.

At the end of 31 (15–18) there is a picture of Sheol, the nether world, 'the Pit', the place of the dead. It envisages some kind of continuing life for the dead and 'all the trees of Eden, the choice and best of Lebanon, all that drink water, will be comforted in the nether world' because water will be transferred from the rivers above ground down to Sheol.

This leads on to a picture of all the peoples whose dead are to be found in the nether world and of reminders of widespread ancient beliefs. 'The fallen men of old went down to Sheol with their weapons of war, whose swords were laid under their heads, and whose shields are upon their bones.' (32:27)

33 repeats an earlier message about the justice of God, namely that the righteous shall live. But if he turns from his righteousness he will die and if the wicked man turns from wickedness to righteousness he will live.

But what is this 'life'? It seems to be no more than old age and there is no evidence to support the idea that the righteous live longer than the unrighteous. On Ezekiel's view, critics say that 'the way of the Lord is not just.' (33:17) If there were a God, they would be absolutely right.

33:30–33 paints a picture of a prophet as a singer whose love songs people come to hear and enjoy, but whose message they ignore.

34 spells out the failure of the shepherds or leaders of the people and promises to gather the people and bring them safely home to 'their own land' where God will 'feed them on the mountains . . . with good pastures.' (34:13–14)

This message is filled out and continued to the end of the chapter. It makes a welcome change but in chapters 35 and 36 we return to the theme of judgement. And then God suddenly realises that all this destruction is being misinterpreted. (God is clearly a slow learner.) People are assuming that God's people have suffered, not because of their unrighteousness, but because of the weakness of their god and his inability to protect them. God feels insulted. His honour has been besmirched and so he is going to act. 'It is not for your sake, O house of Israel that I am about to act, but for the sake of my holy name.' (36:22) How pathetic!

The picture that follows has God cleansing and restoring his people. 'I will put my spirit within you, and cause you to walk in my statutes and be careful to observe my ordinances.' (36:27) He will also make life good for them so that their desolate land becomes 'like the garden of Eden'. (36:35) Against all the evidence that these things never happened, some people still manage to believe in them and in the god who made these promises.

37:1–14 is one of the most famous passages in the Old Testament. It is Ezekiel's vision of the valley of dry bones restored to life. It has been immortalised in what we used to be allowed to call a Negro Spiritual. Was it the inspiration for Saint Saens' '*Danse Macabre*'? or Gilbert and Sullivan's song of the ancestors in *Ruddigore*? I always think of it when I play Gounod's '*Marionette's funeral march*' on my piano. It is worth reading just for the fun of it.

It is followed by the parable of the two sticks (the two kingdoms of the Jews) bound together to make one nation again. (37:15–28)

The story of the dry bones is to convince sceptics that their god can restore the nation, and the parable of the sticks is to demonstrate the fact that the Jewish future lies in a restored unity.

In 38 to 39 we are back with the theme of judgement. The land of the Jews has been repopulated by people who live quiet, successful lives but have no protection. Their enemies will invade, expecting easy pickings but God will destroy them by the power of his (selective) natural forces – earthquake and volcano by the sound of it. The birds and beasts will have a field day on the carcases of the dead, God's sacrificial feast. The people in Israel will take years to gather up all the loot and to bury the dead, and God will restore his people.

All this talk of judgement and slaughter is hardly calculated to make anyone want to worship such a god. It might be possible to fear him but not to worship him. He deserves to be denounced.

Ezekiel's vision of the (restored/rebuilt) temple in Jerusalem (chapters 40 to 42) is a complete bore to anyone except perhaps an architect. He dates his vision from the 25th year of exile and the 14th after the city was conquered or devastated. This is a useful historical reminder that there was a puppet government for a few years. When it united with Egypt and rebelled, Jerusalem was destroyed.

In 43 Ezekiel describes how 'the glory of the Lord filled the temple' (43:5) and the temple became God's dwelling place. Animal sacrifice is to begin all over again. Clearly priestly religion has learned nothing during the period of exile. Such sacrifices continued until the destruction of Jerusalem by the Romans in about 132 CE.

In chapters 44 to 46 Ezekiel's rules for the restored temple are nationalistic and divisive. The materialistic zeal for the purity of the priests is petty and laughable. 'The difference between the holy and the common . . . the unclean and the clean' (44:23) is primitive. These ideas linger on in the food laws of Jews, Moslems and in Hinduism. But these ideas also linger in some of the theology of ordination and consecration and in Catholic ideas of the sacrifice of the Mass.

The simple truth is that there is no mystique surrounding religious things, and that priests are simply human beings working in their own choice of profession. It is in their interest to try to create an aura of mystery and separateness and people are still superstitious and gullible enough to swallow it.

Protestantism at its best offered people direct access to their god with no need for any priestly intermediary. That was a real advance but it still left the mystique and mystery and magic of a majestic god. The death of the gods restores us to our proper place simply as creatures of the natural world finding our own way through from birth to death.

Chapter 47 speaks of the boundaries of the new land of the Jews and allows for the continuing place of 'the aliens who reside among you.' (47:22) The majority of the returned exiles were not to be so considerate.

The boundaries and the division of the land were no more than wishful thinking. They make thoroughly dull and pointless reading.

Daniel

This is the last of the 'Writings'. Daniel is one of those authors who pretends that he lived long, long ago and then foretells the future with fair accuracy until he arrives at his own time.

When Alexander the Great died in 323 BCE his empire was divided into four quarters. Palestine was part of the Syrian quarter ruled by King Seleucus and then by his son Antiochus.

Within the empire the chief cement binding it all together was a Hellenising of the way of life. Thus Jason (a puppet ruler in Jerusalem appointed by Antiochus) introduced a gym to Jerusalem where men performed in the nude.

To have naked men celebrating the human body in sport was bad enough but many Jews supported Hellenisation. Society was split until Antiochus Epiphanes carried things to extremes and attacked the heart of Jewish religion. He banned circumcision and the keeping of the Sabbath. And on December 15th, 168 BCE he set up a heathen altar in the temple and sacrificed a pig (abhorrent to Jews). This became known as 'the abomination of desolation' in prophetic books.

Jews led by Mattathias and his five sons rose in revolt and were ultimately completely successful. The books of the Maccabees tell the historical story. Daniel was a tract for the times, propaganda aimed at showing the courage of the faithful and the wonderful, protecting power of their god. Hence the stories of Shadrach, Meshach and Abednego in the fiery furnace and Daniel in the lions' den. The book was written to assure the Jews that their sufferings would end in triumph.

Through his image of the beast he pointed out that other empires had come and gone: Gold represented Babylon, Silver represented Persia, bronze was for Alexander the Great, Iron and Clay for the Seleucids.

The saying about people having 'feet of clay' originates here.

Parts of Daniel are worth reading for the stories. The famous story of Shadrach, Meshach and Abednego in the fiery furnace is one. And it is also of slight musical historical interest as it includes a reference to the instruments in use at the time: 'horn, pipe, lyre, trigon (a triangle), harp and bagpipe.' (3:5)

Daniel is an interpreter of dreams (although at the end of the book he proves unable to interpret his own). He interprets one of Nebuchadrezzar. The king will lose his reason for seven years and then be restored to the throne when he has learned that the god of the Jews is the true ruler of men.

In chapter 5 we jump to the rule of his son Belshazzar and the famous story which has given us the phrase 'the writing on the wall'. The writing depicts Belshazzar's inadequacy and downfall and the end of the Babylonian empire. It will be conquered by Darius the Mede.

Chapter six gives us yet another phrase which is perhaps going out of common usage: 'the law of the Medes and Persians' meaning something that cannot be changed. The chapter tells the story of Daniel thrown into the lions' den because he was faithful to his god, giving him precedence over royal decrees.

God preserved him and he came out alive, to be replaced by his accusers and also their innocent wives and children who were all eaten alive. The cruelty and injustice of this does not appear to have concerned the Biblical author.

The decree telling people throughout the empire of Darius to worship the god of the Jews is fictional of course.

In chapter 7 we bounce back to the first year of Belshazzar. Now it is Daniel rather than the king who has visions and dreams. Towards the end of chapter 8 it is made clear that these refer to the Persian empire, to the conquests of Alexander the Great and to the division of his empire at his death.

Daniel purports to be seeing these things in the future but is actually writing after the events he describes.

The vision of God in 7:9–11 has similarities with Ezekiel.

Christians associated verses 13–14 with Jesus, 'one like a son of man', and with the kingdom of heaven.

Chapter 9 shows Daniel beginning to think that it is time for the exile to come to an end. He prays, not 'on the ground of our righteousness, but out of thy great mercy.' (9:18)

Slowly the Jews began to learn that the blessing of God does not depend on human righteousness since 'there is none that is righteous, no not one'. It depends on God's generosity and mercy. Hosea will demonstrate this more fully. In terms of religious thinking, this is a real advance.

9:10–13 are full of visions of the future history of the Middle East up to the time of Antiochus Epiphanes, the Seleucid king who defiled the second temple, the one built after the exiles returned. This cut off point suggests that that is the period when all these 'future' visions were actually written. There is nothing in them to make us want to read them.

Hosea

With Hosea we move back in historic time to a period before the exile. The book begins with Hosea believing that his god wants him to marry a prostitute called Gomer. He marries her and three children follow. The first is his own. The second is a daughter called 'Not Pitied' and the third is a son called 'Not my people' presumably because it was not Hosea's child.

Gomer went back to prostitution and ended up having to sell herself into slavery. But Hosea heard that she was up for sale and went to the market. He bought her and restored her as his wife. It is a lovely story.

Hosea extrapolates from all this the story of his god's relationship with the Jews. Their god loves them but they play the harlot with other gods. They go downhill and end up in the 'slavery' of exile. Their god brings them back and restores them so that they live in peace with man and beast. (2:18)

2:18–20 is as beautiful a pledge of love as can be found anywhere. It is God's pledge to his people:

'I will betroth you to me in righteousness and in justice, in steadfast love and in mercy. I will betroth you to me in faithfulness; and you shall know the Lord.'

4:6 places the blame for the wickedness of the Jews firmly on the priests and prophets: 'My people are destroyed for lack of knowledge', not because they are inherently wicked. This is a new idea and has been the foundation idea of a great deal of modern education and criminal reform.

In 6:6 Hosea expresses the heart of true religion:

'For I desire steadfast love and not sacrifice,
the knowledge of God, rather than burnt offerings.'

We saw in Daniel that many Biblical expressions have passed into common use. There is such a couplet in Hosea 8:7:

'For they sow the wind, and they shall reap the whirlwind.'

Throughout these chapters God speaks, and there is a complete contradiction in what he says. On the one hand he says that in spite of their wickedness he cannot bring himself to harm them 'for I am God and no man' (11:8–9). But this is an isolated statement. Most of the time he is telling them how terrible their punishments will be: 'They shall fall by the sword, their little ones shall be dashed in pieces, and their pregnant women ripped open'. (13:16)

There is a couplet in 13:14 which is worth examination, and very familiar but not in the form found in Hosea. Here are words of judgement and destruction. God will not ransom the wicked from Death. He calls on Death to inflict plagues and destruction:

'O Death, where are your plagues?
O Sheol,' [the place of the dead] 'where is your destruction?
Compassion is hid from my eyes.'

Compare that with Paul in 1 Corinthians 15:54–55. In a complex chapter expressing Paul's theology of resurrection, he turns Hosea's words upside down. From a desolate cry of destruction, they become a glorious cry of triumph. This expresses the transformation Christian faith brings to the old gloomy ideas of death common in the ancient world:

'Death is swallowed up in victory.
O death where is thy victory?
O death where is thy sting?'

For those who really believe in the Christian doctrine of resurrection, it is a powerful source of comfort when death comes. But it is a belief which depends entirely on faith. It has no basis in factual evidence. You either believe it or you do not.

Humanists offer a different kind of transformation from those gloomy ancient ideas. For us, death is simply the natural end of a natural life. We see ourselves as creatures of the natural world. Dying may be difficult or easy, but death itself is a non-event. It is just the snuffing out of life's 'brief candle'. There is nothing after that: no gloom, no joy, and no punishment either. Death is really and simply the end of life.

Different people will find their comfort in different ways. For me, the simplicity and finality of the humanist viewpoint is the most comforting of all. Faith in any kind of life after death leads to a host of questions and complexities. Faith is content to leave them open. It has to do so because the human mind has been quite unable to find satisfactory answers.

The book ends in charming and positive style with a plea to the people to return to their god and a new promise from that god: 'I will heal their faithlessness.' If they can't do it for themselves, he will do it for them. 'I will love them freely, for my anger has turned from them'. (14:4)

Is this, I wonder, an echo of Hosea's marital experience with Gomer?

There is another line worth recording which appears for no apparent reason. 'in thee the orphan finds mercy.' (14:3) There it is. Just that statement. There is nothing leading up to it and nothing leading from it. One wonders why it is there unless it has some connection in Hosea's mind with his own children. It is a useful reminder that the orphan needs to be cared for.

Joel

The three chapters of the book of Joel were written with tremendous power. They were inspired by a plague of locusts described in forceful, vivid and vigorous language. The plague was seen as a judgement of God, and leads to a portrayal of God's judgement on the nations and the blessings he will pour on his own people.

2:12–14 express the hope that true repentance will lead to blessing but they don't seem very sure.

Certainty comes with writing about God's blessing and leads to the promise of God's spirit for all (2:28–29). This is a promise which Christians claim has been fulfilled. They say that God's spirit is available to all who believe in Jesus and surrender their lives to him. Looking at Christians, there doesn't seem to be much evidence to support their claim.

The ferocious, wrathful, avenging god of Joel 3 is not a god I would wish to believe in or to worship.

Amos

Amos was a herdsman. His prophecies date from around the tine of the Assyrian invasion and the exile of the northern Jewish people (Israel) in the eighth century BCE.

He was the first of the prophets to have his message preserved in writing. His book's theme is one of judgement – judgement on the nations and on the Jews. They are judged supremely for injustice, for failing the poor and for immoral behaviour. Injustice towards the poor is a constant theme.

Amos' god is a rural god. He is not impressed by the magnificence of the temple and its ritual and sacrificial worship, no matter how faithfully it is performed by the priests. Nor has he any time for the luxury of civilised town life.

When I look at the extravagance of many churches and remember that they were built in times when much of the population lived in extreme poverty, I feel as Amos did. Amos' sole concern was for social justice. 'Let justice roll down like waters, and righteousness like an ever flowing stream.' (5:24)

The theme of judgement, destruction and desolation goes on and on. Though the writing has great vigour and colour, it grows wearisome. It often seems to me that the prophets (of all ages) spend so much time condemning evil that they develop a thoroughly lop-sided and jaundiced idea of human nature.

No one who has lived through the twentieth century can doubt man's capacity for evil. But all the time, alongside all that has been foul and wicked, the mass of human beings have been quietly getting on with their lives, helping others where they can and carefully making sure that they harm no one.

These often suffer abominably, whether as a result of human wickedness or of natural disaster. With incredible patience courage and determination, they pick up what is left of their lives and set about the task of rebuilding and making good. They often do so from a point of extreme poverty.

No one can doubt Amos' courage or passionate sincerity. His demand for social justice and righteousness is one that is always needed. He deserves our admiration. But how I wish that prophets and preachers were better at recognising the fundamental goodness and decency at the heart of most ordinary human life.

Obadiah

Obadiah is not worth reading at all.

It is an expression of hatred towards Edom. Edom was the tribe which traced its ancestry back to Esau the twin brother of Jacob.

The capacity for hatred and hostility between these tribes would beggar belief if we had not seen so much of it in our own time – in the middle east, in Northern Ireland and in the Balkans.

To misquote the old Marlene Dietrich song: 'when will we ever learn? When will we ever learn?'

Jonah

The story of Jonah and the 'whale' (actually a 'big fish') is well known. It is a good story, vividly told.

In chapter one neither Jonah nor his god come out with any credit, but the seamen do. Superstitious, frightened, angry, they may be. But their humanity is such that they are prepared to pit their puny strength against the power of Jonah's god in a vain attempt to save him. They display a courage and nobility often found at sea. Their quality puts both Jonah and his god to shame.

After Jonah's prayer in chapter two, the big fish has a bilious attack and throws up leaving Jonah safely returned to dry land. He has tried to run away from god and from the task god has assigned to him, and has failed.

Now that task is given back to him. He has to go to Nineveh, the capital city of Assyria to pronounce his god's judgement on the city.

He doesn't want to go because he knows that the king of Nineveh will listen to god's message, will repent and be forgiven. And Jonah doesn't want Assyria to find forgiveness. But, grumbling and complaining all the way, he fulfils his god-given task and it all turns out just as he expected.

The king hears and believes the message. This is one of the very few times in the Old Testament when anybody takes any notice of the prophets – but then, this is fiction. He calls the people to repentance. God is so pleased that he revokes his judgement.

Jonah is angry. He has been made to look a fool. He knew this would happen. 'I knew that thou art a gracious God and merciful, slow to anger and abounding in steadfast love.' (4:2) He goes into a massive sulk.

But if all that were true, surely God would not have threatened destruction in the first place. He justifies himself at the end of the story and we find ourselves sympathising with Jonah and agreeing with God.

But the door has been opened wide. If God pities Nineveh and all its people and cattle, why have we seen him so completely ruthless in his treatment of people after people in book after book from his treatment of the Egyptians in Exodus to his promised treatment of Edom in Obadiah? The whole of the Old Testament is an indictment of this jealous, wrathful, violent, god.

On the other hand, this book can be seen as a major advance on all that has gone before. If God can be so forgiving towards the Assyrians, he can forgive *anyone*. Such a god is not just a god for the chosen people. He is a universal god.

Micah

There is rather more in Micah than in some of the prophets, but it is still a book full of denunciation. Micah claims that his words 'do good to him who walks uprightly . . . the peaceful and those who pass by trustingly with no thought of war.' (2:7–8)

In the early twentieth century there was a Punch cartoon of parents watching marching soldiers and a doting mother crying, 'Look, our Fred is the only one in step.'

Micah claims that he is the only one 'filled with the power, with the Spirit, of the Lord, and with justice and might.' All the other prophets 'lead my people astray'. (3:8 and 3:5).

I am always suspicious of those who believe themselves right and all other people wrong. I once had a long conversation with someone about Christianity. Every time I offered any criticism of Christians the answer was the same, 'Ah well, they are not really Christians are they?'

By the end of the conversation I wondered if there was anybody left – other than the person I was talking to of course.

4:1–5 paints a lovely utopian dream of the nations living in peace by the rule of law and of individuals living in peace and security without fear.

But Micah cannot sustain his dream. By the end of the chapter we are back to the old story of peoples being dashed into pieces.

Christians take 5:2–4 out of context and apply them to Jesus because in their story he came from Bethlehem to be king of kings. Placed back in context these verses are part of yet another horrible series of judgements and prophecies. It is astonishing that after so much destruction, brutality and bloodshed we can suddenly come on a passage such as 6:8:

'He has showed you, O man, what is good;
and what does the Lord require of you
but to do justice, and to love kindness,
and to walk humbly with your God.'

Why is it then that book after book of the prophets has portrayed generation after generation of the Jews living by corruption, injustice, callous indifference to the poor and false worship? Book after book portrays man at his worst.

My century has seen so much of that, that reading the prophets becomes sickening. Images from the trenches of the First World War to the concentration camps of Nazism, to Pol Pot and on to the Balkans in the late 1990s rise up. We have to face up to these things and to seek an end to them.

But I do not feel that there is any benefit to be derived from constantly focussing on them and I have no desire to go on with this stuff. It is surely better to focus on what is good and decent and true (as Paul says in one of his New Testament letters). It is as well that there is plenty that is decent about.

Micah ends on a bright note for the Jews and speaks of the compassion of his god. I don't find him compassionate. True compassion, like any other virtue, is a permanent element in character. It is not something to be switched on like an electric light after long periods of treading people down 'like the mire of the streets'.

Nahum

Nahum celebrates the end of the Assyrian empire through a mixture of natural disaster (volcano) and war.

As a piece of writing this is magnificent, vigorous and vivid. Try 3:1–4. But it has no other claim on our attention.

1:15 expresses the relief felt in Jerusalem that Assyrian might is broken. There is no realisation yet that an even more powerful invader is soon to follow. Christians use the verse of Jesus.

Habakkuk

Habakkuk is a man full of questions. Why is there no peace? Why is there no justice? Why doesn't God do something? Why indeed. If there is a compassionate and loving god, why does he leave everything in such a constant mess?

Belonging to a small nation constantly overwhelmed by stronger neighbours, the Jews clearly felt that a powerful god was their only hope. And the poor, insignificant people in a land where the rich paid no regard to justice, also felt that a powerful god was their only hope.

Prophet after prophet cried out against evil. But none of them seemed to wake up to the fact that, if it is humans who are responsible for injustice it is also humans who must put things right. The prophets, however, had no programme of reform and created no reform movement. They simply inveighed against evil and called on their god to judge the wicked and save the righteous. Their god, of course, did nothing for he didn't exist.

The language is vivid but the message never gets anywhere.

Habakkuk 2:4 includes words which became fundamental to Protestant Christianity 'the righteous shall live by faith.'

Religion really is a matter of faith. You either believe it or not. You either take it or leave it. There is no in-between. Religion cannot be proved. There is no knowledge in any normal sense of the word. That will not do for me.

To the man of faith Habakkuk 3:17–18 sounds noble:

'Though the fig tree do not blossom,
nor fruit be on the vines,
the produce of the olive fail
and the fields yield no food,
the flock be cut off from the fold
and there be no herd in the stalls,
yet I will rejoice in the Lord,
I will joy in the God of my salvation.'

This hoping against hope may be very brave but it achieves nothing and if there is no god of his salvation it is worse than useless. I am reminded of the old Scout claim, 'the scout smiles and whistles in all difficulties'. But the scout was also expected to do something about those difficulties, not just to whistle in the dark. I want to say to Habakkuk, 'Never mind rejoicing in the Lord, what are you going to do about your problems? How are you going to put things right or turn things around?'

There is one more verse in this book which is a great favourite in religious circles:

'For the earth will be filled
with the knowledge of the glory of the Lord,
as the waters cover the sea.' (2:14)

It is a prophecy that has been unfulfilled for rather a long time.

Zephaniah

Here is another book full of prophecies of doom. Part of 1:12 caught my attention: 'I will punish . . . those who say in their hearts, "The Lord will not do good, nor will he do ill." '

That is precisely what I have been saying throughout this

commentary. People who say such things have one of two beliefs. Either we do not believe in the gods at all, which is my position. Or we believe that the gods take no active part in human affairs. It is interesting to find another acknowledgement of our existence in so religion dominated a country.

One Christian, famous in his time, wrote:

> 'I could barely find in the three chapters of this book a single sentence of comfort for my heart or food for my soul or light for my mind. We can pass on from this outburst of gloom and despondency, this prophecy of apostacy and slaughter, as having little or no message for us today.' (*A Christian Agnostic* by Leslie Weatherhead.)

Did he not read the happy ending, the promise of better days to come? Then the people will be 'humble and lowly' and honest; the lame and the outcast will have new lives: 'I will change their shame into praise and renown' (3:19). Everyone 'shall pasture and lie down and none shall make them afraid' (3:13).

It is a nice dream but it takes human will and determination to bring these things about. As we said at the outset, 'The Lord will do no good.' (1:12)

Haggai

Haggai has the virtue of being different from any of the previous prophets. That is probably its only virtue. It belongs to the period after people have returned from exile in Babylon.

Haggai criticises the people for having their priorities *right*. They have been busy building their houses instead of re-building the temple. So now they rebuild the temple but it isn't a patch on the old one. No wonder. They didn't have Solomon's wealth (a wealth raised by grinding taxation).

God said that this poor edifice would do and promised that, having denied the people decent crops, he would now bless them.

It never ceases to amaze me that, when people have been living in hovels in grinding poverty, their rulers poured limitless sums of money and energy into building temples and churches. In the year 2009 we are still doing it, building football stadia in South Africa for the 2010 World Cup. But to return to churches: how is it that people like Jesus and Francis of Assisi are remembered with such gross extravagance? I remember with approval the comment of a Scottish lady on the builder of a cathedral in rural South India (and of a house for himself that looked rather like an old Lancashire cotton mill): 'When the divil came to Charles Posnett he came in the forrrm of brrricks and morrrtar.'

Zechariah

It is a peculiar book and I don't pretend to have understood it all. Those who like strange and colourful visions will like it. Most of Zechariah's visions are for the people who have returned from exile in Babylon. I am quite sure that there are scholars who have enjoyed working out in detail what each vision means.

No doubt there are also preachers who come up with lurid interpretations for the present day. I can imagine someone suggesting that 5:5–11 refers to the disposal of nuclear waste.

Our imaginations can run riot when we let them, but the basic message of this book is the same as all the rest: that Jerusalem will be blessed with the glory of God; that his people must live godly lives and that the wicked will be punished. Unlike many of the prophets, Zechariah does spell out what he means by godly lives.

'Thus says the Lord of hosts,
"Render true judgements,
show kindness and mercy each to his brother,
do not oppress the widow, the fatherless, the sojourner, or the poor;
and let none of you devise evil against his brother in your
heart." '(7:9–10)

And again in 8:16–17:

'These are the things that you shall do: Speak the truth to one another, render in your gates judgements that are true and make for peace, do not devise evil in your hearts against one another, and love no false oath.'

Whether these words are of 'the Lord' or Zechariah is irrelevant. Anyone concerned with living life properly would endorse them wholeheartedly. This is religion at its best. Scrap the first line and it is human ethics at its best too.

Chapter 8 presents another utopian dream for Jerusalem and its people and then comes a change. The oracles in chapters 9–14 come from a different historical period as the reference to the Greeks in 9:13 makes clear. These oracles are chiefly of interest because of the use made of them by Christians and the questions that use raises.

9:9–10 is used of Jesus riding into Jerusalem a few days before his death (celebrated on Palm Sunday). Did Jesus actually do this and thus claim to be king of the Jews? According to the gospels he was charged with making that claim. Or is the whole thing fiction?

And then again, 11:12–13 is used in the story of Judas Iscariot and his betrayal of Jesus. The way it is used suggests a complete misunderstanding of this part of the oracle. It could also suggest that the detail of the Judas story is pure fiction, whether the betrayal was fact or not.

A third such question arises from the very last verse of the book (14:21): 'There shall no longer be a trader in the house of the Lord of hosts on that day.' Jesus or the gospel writers have made so much use of Zechariah that one wonders whether this is the source of the story of Jesus driving out the merchants and traders from the temple. Is that also fiction?

And if these things or some of them are fiction, how do we know what parts of the gospels are fact and what are fiction? Too much comes straight from the Old Testament for us to be convinced that the gospel story is wholly factual.

These closing oracles of Zechariah are very confusing. Sometimes they are all about the way in which their god is going to bless and glorify the Jews in Jerusalem. Sometimes there seems to be a complete reversal. It doesn't really matter because they have nothing to say to us today.

Zechariah's god accompanies blessing on Jerusalem with such horrible things for everyone and everything else that, if we believed him we would wish he kept out of human affairs. We are quite capable of making life unbearable for one another and for the rest of the natural world without any help from a god.

Malachi

Zechariah had said that the days of the prophets were numbered. 'I will remove from the land the prophets', etc. Zechariah 13:2. But (if we ignore John the Baptist, Jesus and Muhammad) there is just one left, the last book in the Old Testament.

One has to ask the question 'why'? Has God no more to say to us than has been said already? Is the Old Testament God's final word?

The Jews didn't think so, nor did the Christians and the Moslems didn't either – nor did the Mormons, the Christian Scientists, the Jehovah's Witnesses. The list goes on and on – they all have God's final truth.

God's concept of love is very strange. He shows his love to Israel by hating the tribe derived from Jacob's twin brother Esau.

According to Malachi he is a god who requires animal sacrifices and who is only satisfied with the very best animals from the flocks and herds.

There is a great deal in this short book which is both unpleasant and unacceptable but there are some good things too. Any teacher or preacher would surely be proud if the following words could truthfully be spoken at his retirement: 'True instruction was in his mouth, and no wrong was found on his lips. He walked . . . in peace and uprightness, and he turned many from iniquity.' (2:6)

In 2:10 Malachi asks, 'Have we not all one Father? Has not one God created us?' We may no longer believe that one God created us but in evolutionary terms the first question still receives an affirmative answer. There is no more important question for human beings. Only when we learn to answer properly will we learn to treat one another properly as members of the same human family.

Malachi speaks of the things his god hates and in doing so he gives a clear picture of some of the things of which he approves. His message is virtually the same as that of Zechariah and others among the prophets:

God hates divorce and faithlessness. This does not mean that there can be no divorce for men, but that it is only acceptable as a last resort. The ideal is lifelong faithfulness within marriage.

Sadly few of us achieve it. (2:15–16)

God is opposed to sorcerers, adulterers, those who swear falsely, those who oppress the wage-earner, the widow, the orphan and the sojourner (the visitor or the immigrant). (3:5)

It follows that he approves, as does anyone with any humanity or decency, those who live faithful human lives; fair and generous employers; those who strive for a fair deal for the needy and the underprivileged.

The opening of chapter 3 (1–3) and the last verse of chapter 4, the very last verse of the Old Testament, have both been applied to Jesus. Malachi 4:5 has also been applied to John the Baptist. Handel's '*Messiah*' is perhaps the most memorable of all such applications.

On the whole I have found the Old Testament a disappointment. It has rarely deserved the attention it has been given over the centuries. But there *are* good lessons within its pages, and there are many good stories full of psychological insight. There is also some magnificent literature. Anything that can inspire a Handel to write such wonderful music must have something to be said in its favour.

Speaking of the Old Testament, my brother Aubs said to me, 'we were very lucky to be brought up on such a feast of stories.' He was thinking in particular of the stories of Genesis. At my council school I was also brought up on the stories of Homer's Aenead and Odyssey. And somewhere along the line I also came into contact with Hans Christian Andersen. All of these combined to provide a rich heritage for which I am grateful, but I now find no need for the religion that goes with the stories of the Old Testament.

Part Two

THE
APOCRYPHA

Introduction

During our reading of the Old Testament we found the Jews being carried away into exile. Some were taken by the Assyrians, some by the Babylonians and some fled to Egypt.

When exiles returned to their homeland, they were probably always a minority. The rest settled in their new countries, made new lives and spread throughout the world in what became known as the Diaspora.

Many of these simply merged with their hosts and disappeared from view losing all sense or knowledge of their Jewishness. But there were also many who sought to retain their sense of national and religious identity. They achieved this by obedience to the Law (as we found it in the first five books of the Bible and supremely in Deuteronomy). And also by the development of the synagogue as a focus for Jewish life. Some synagogues are very ancient indeed. Here Jews could meet for worship, read the Law and teach the young. They were also places where visiting Jews could find a welcome and the hospitality of like-minded people. They became far more important than the Temple in Jerusalem. It is not too much to say that they became the universal focus of Jewish life.

For Christians, churches, and for Moslems, mosques, fulfil much the same purpose and have much the same value.

As we have seen, the Jews in Palestine wrote books, many of which became a part of today's Old Testament.

The Jews of the dispersion often lost their Hebrew. So Hebrew books were translated into Greek and new books were written in Greek, the common language of much of the mediterranean world. Their books continued the historical story told in the Old Testament. They became very important but they never achieved the status of the books of the Old Testament.

The early Christians treated them with perhaps more respect than did the Jews. They included them in their Bibles. But at the Reformation, when the great Catholic/Protestant divide took place, the more extreme Protestants left the Apocrypha out of their Bibles, and it became widely neglected.

As the churches in Europe have grown weaker in the twentieth century, they have tended to move closer together to comfort themselves and give themselves an added sense of strength. As a part of that growing together, their scholars have worked on a translation of the Bible acceptable to all of them, and the Apocrypha has been restored. But it is regarded as of lesser importance. It lacks the authority of the Old and New Testaments. It is simply regarded as being 'useful for edification'.

The majority of Christians have probably never read these books – but then, the majority of Christians have probably never read the *whole* of the Old and New Testaments either.

The Apocrypha poses one additional problem. With both the Old and New Testaments, authoritative decisions were taken about which books should be included and which should be excluded. It was a long time before anyone did the same with the Apocrypha. Eventually at the end of the 4th century CE the Christian Councils of Africa finally took decisions which the wider church accepted – more or less! They left out I and 2 Esdras and also the Prayer of Manasseh which were all quite popular, and they also left out 3 and 4 Maccabees. The last two stayed out, but because of their popularity the other three were often included, and they are included in the Common Bible which I am using as the basis for this study.

Tobit

Tobit seems to be a compilation from two main sources. The first purports to be the autobiography of Tobit. He was a man carried into exile to Nineveh by the Assyrians. He is married to Anna and has one son, Tobias who marries Sarah (seven times a widow before her marriage to Tobias).

There is no mock modesty about Tobit. He tells us from the beginning 'I, Tobit, walked in the ways of truth and righteousness all the days of my life, and I performed many acts of charity to my brethren and countrymen. (1:3)

From Tobit we glean a picture of exiles who merge with their host nation and of others, of whom Tobit is one, who are determined to be faithful to their god and to preserve their nationality through marriage exclusively with other Jews.

The autobiographical part of the book is chiefly of interest when Tobit's idea of 'truth and righteousness' is spelt out in his charge to his son (4:12–21). Much of it is of permanent validity. Tobit begins:

'Beware, my son, of all immorality. First of all take a wife from among the descendants of your fathers and do not marry a foreign woman.' (4:12)

I'm sure that my parents' generation would have echoed that. Would my children? There is probably still a strong desire that marriage should be (for want of a better phrase) within the tribe. But as societies become more mixed, mixed marriages become ever more common. Marriage is an immensely demanding relationship, and there are plenty of pitfalls. Those who enter into a mixed marriage need all the support and love their families can give.

Tobit continues: Avoid pride and shiftlessness 'because shiftlessness is the mother of famine.'

'Do not hold over until the next day the wages of any man who works for you, but pay him at once'.
'Be disciplined in all your conduct. And what you hate, do not

do to anyone' [an interesting negative form of the golden rule].

'Do not drink wine to excess. . . Give of your bread to the hungry, and of your clothing to the naked. Give *all* [my italicising] your surplus to charity, and do not let your eye begrudge the gift when you make it.' [But charity is only to be given to the righteous, not to 'sinners'.] (4:13–16)

Few of us are likely to be so generous. And that makes it difficult to criticise such a passage. But the needs of today's poor are so overwhelming that charity is not enough. Our surplus needs to be given wisely to those who are trying to create conditions in which people will no longer live out their lives in poverty. And it needs to be allied to pressure on political parties to make a genuine commitment to ending world poverty. Given the will, that is not beyond achievement. Of course, we do not have to leave these things to others. There is nothing to stop us becoming involved ourselves.

Tobit ends by urging his son to 'Seek advice from every wise man,' and not to 'despise any useful counsel.' And then he bids him 'Bless the Lord God on every occasion.' Although I don't believe in gods, there is a nobility and quality about 4:21 which is worth repeating. Tobit has become blind and lost his wealth as a result. He has some money 'banked' in the land of the Medes and is about to send Tobias to fetch it, so he is not poverty stricken, but his circumstances have certainly taken a dive. It is in that context that we find him saying:

'Do not be afraid my son, because we have become poor. You have great wealth if you fear God and refrain from every sin and do what is pleasing in his sight.'

Chapter 5 begins what seems to be a second source. It takes the story of Tobias, Tobit's son. His journey to fetch his father's money is turned into a kind of fairy story. It has an angel and an evil spirit and a little bit of magic. It has a bride, seven times widowed by the evil spirit before any of her marriages was consummated. And it has Tobias the bridegroom conquering the evil spirit, thanks to the guidance of the angel who enables him to make magic smoke from the heart and liver of a fish.

What a romantic bridal chamber that must have been. With such a stink it is a wonder that the bride remained, let alone the evil spirit. But she must have been pretty desperate by the time

Tobias came along.

So the story has a happy wedding; a happy reunion of a man and his money and so the restoration of a man from his poverty; and finally it has the restoration of his sight. And everyone 'lived happily ever after'.

But only because Tobias took his father's advice and moved from Nineveh, the capital of a dying empire, to Ecbatana in the land of the Medes whose imperial star was rising.

The fairy story has been retold in children's books and in drama and makes for a pleasant read. It is interesting to see that the exiles in Assyria now have complete freedom of life and movement. It is also interesting to see that Tobit and his son had the wisdom not to go back to Palestine, but to go instead to Media or Babylonia.

I also found it interesting to see the addition of angels, spirits and magic to a religion that had managed without them. That addition is made without a hint of criticism. Away from the homeland religious ideas are less puritanical and more lax.

Judith

Is the book of Judith based on a genuine historical episode or is it fiction? The history in the book is hopelessly confused and scholars suggest that the book is fiction. It is thoroughly unpleasant and there is no good reason to read it.

The author speaks of the Assyrians as the people with international power. The Assyrians conquered northern Israel in 721 BCE and carried off the leading people into exile. But they failed to conquer Jerusalem.

The author speaks of the king of this empire as Nebuchadnezzar. Nebuchadnezzar was the ruler over the *Babylonian* empire when Jerusalem was conquered in 586 BCE.

The author speaks of the Jews as an independent people and of Simeon as both the father of Judith and as one who sustained Jews against invaders. From the time of the Assyrians to the time of the Maccabees (well after Alexander the Great 356–323 BCE) there was no period when the Jews were independent. One of the Maccabaean leaders under whom the Jews achieved independence was called Simeon. But they achieved their independence from Antiochus Epiphanes. He was one of the Seleucid kings and ruled over one of the quarters into which Alexander's empire had been divided after his death. It only matters if the book purports to be history. It probably doesn't. For my purposes it doesn't matter anyway.

According to the story, the Jews are independent and their life centres around the temple in Jerusalem.

Nebuchadnezzar, said to be of Assyria, claims overlordship and presumably an annual payment of tribute. The Jews reject the claim and Nebuchadnezzar determines to bring them to heel. His army under its general Holofernes camps near to the unknown Jewish town of Bethuliah. Holofernes seizes the town's water supply and waits for the inevitable surrender.

Inside the town things look hopeless. But Judith, a devout widow, promises that their god will save them. She prays for success and then goes to the Assyrian camp. She manages to deceive Holofernes into trusting her, cuts off his head and returns home with it. In doing so she shows herself to be devout and diligent in prayer and fasting, but also shameless in her flattery as well as a bold-faced liar and a ruthless assassin who gloats in her triumph.

Holofernes' death leads to panic in the Assyrian camp. The army flees and the Jews cut the fleeing troops down. They all plunder the Assyrian camp and Judith gives her share to the service of her god after singing a song of triumph.

If this story was true it would have been no wonder that the Jews celebrated 'for three months'. It is probably fiction based on two historic incidents: the murder of Sisera by Jael; and the unexplained retreat of an Assyrian besieging army from Jerusalem in 721 BCE.

Women often feature strongly in Jewish history and folklore. This is one of those occasions. It is a story that would have been good for morale on any of those occasions when the Jews were threatened with invasion. But I can't see that it has any value at all certainly not for our 'edification'.

Esther

The historical setting of this book is clear. This is set during the reign of king Ahasuerus of Babylon while the leaders of the Jews were in exile in Babylon (after 586 BCE).

The text of the book has come down to us in a pretty chaotic state. This is reflected in the way in which it is printed in the Common Bible. Of concern to scholars, this has no importance for the ordinary reader.

The book tells the story of Mordecai the Jew and his adopted daughter Esther. Esther was an orphan. She grew to be Mordecai's pride and joy.

She was taken into the King's harem and became the king's favourite, ending up as queen.

It came to the notice of Haman, the prime minister, that Mordecai refused to do obeisance to him. We are told later that Mordecai refused because he believed that his god was the only one to whom obeisance should be done. When Haman looked into the matter, he found that what was true of Mordecai was true of all Jews. They followed their own religion and its laws and customs.

Haman persuaded the king to sign a decree ordering the extermination of all Jews throughout the 'one hundred and twenty seven satrapies' 'from India to Ethiopia' for the sake of the unity and peace of the whole.

In days when government, religion and law were all part of one whole, unity of religion was perhaps more important than it is today. It was certainly regarded as one of the forces binding society together – not the only cement but one of the most important. Jews and (later) Christians often suffered persecution for their insistence on following their own religion and their own laws.

Both religions take pride in their sufferings and martyrs. Neither can take any pride at all in their behaviour when power has rested in their hands. Christians have been responsible for some of the most ghastly cruelties of all, many of them inflicted on dissidents within their own ranks. And Jews? Read this book of Esther.

Faced with Haman's decree, Mordecai and Esther went into mourning and said their prayers. Then Esther went to the king.

In a story full of irony, Mordecai was favoured by the king for services previously rendered. And then Esther secured the overturning of the decree. So far so wonderful.

But then Mordecai, Esther and the Jews as a whole, spoiled everything. They proved to be as bloodthirsty and vengeful as their enemies. Not only was Haman hanged on the gallows he had prepared for Mordecai, but his whole family was also put to death. That surely was more than enough. Far from it. The Jews smote all their enemies with the sword, slaughtering, and destroying them, and did as they pleased to those who hated them. (9:5) According to the story they killed 800 people in Susa and a further 75,000 elsewhere in the empire. (9:16)

The modern state of Israel seems to have taken Esther and Mordecai as role models for its own behaviour.

The Jews established the annual feast of Purim to remember these things. If the story is true, the Jews should remember it with shame. They read it aloud in the synagogue every year at the time of the festival of Purim. It demonstrates that Jews are as capable of inflicting violence as anybody else. Neither their religion nor their god have any power to make them more civilised or peaceable people. The same can be said of other religions and their gods. So what value does religion have?

The Wisdom of Solomon

The author pretends to be offering the wisdom of the king reputed to have been supremely wise, but his thought belongs to a period centuries later than Solomon as will become clear. The author assumes that you cannot have righteousness without religion. He is not alone. Yet there are plenty of irreligious people who could agree wholeheartedly with 1:5:

> '. . .a holy and disciplined spirit will flee from deceit, and will rise and depart from foolish thoughts, and will be ashamed at the approach of unrighteousness.'

154

Verses 6–15 show that religious thinking has moved on since Old Testament times, and there has also been a development in the concept of 'Wisdom' first seen in Proverbs.

'Wisdom' is a divine quality which sometimes seems to have an independent life of its own. Although 'Wisdom is a kindly spirit' it 'will not free a blasphemer from the guilt of his words.' It is interesting that the New Testament claims that blasphemy against the Holy Spirit (which no one seems able to define) is the only unforgiveable sin.

In England there is still a crime of blasphemy against the teachings of the Church of England on the statute books. A number of people have been punished under that law even in recent years. As it stands it is a law that is unfair to almost everybody, religious and irreligious alike. It should be repealed. It never was just.

This passage in the Wisdom of Solomon goes on to speak of 'the Spirit of the Lord'. Again this aspect of divinity sometimes seems to take on a life of its own, so much so that Christians defined the Holy Spirit as the third person of their Trinity. Here the Spirit represents the omnipresence of God, that all-seeing aspect that was sometimes used by nannies to try to frighten children into good behaviour in days gone by. The Spirit also represents the judgement of God but the concept of judgement shows a major advance on Old Testament thinking. While it is the Spirit who/which convicts us, we are the ones who actually bring judgement upon ourselves:

'Do not invite death by the error of your life, nor bring on destruction by the works of your hands; because God did not make death, and he does not delight in the death of the living. For he created all things that they might exist, and the generative forces of the world are wholesome, and there is no destructive poison in them; and the dominion of Hades is not on earth. For righteousness is immortal. But ungodly men by their words and deeds summoned death.' (1:12–16a)

These are new and fascinating ideas and they link with chapter 3:1–9 where there is a clear expression of a belief in immortality for the righteous. The author's view is expressed and developed in greater (and more complex) detail by Paul in 1 Corinthians 15. The Wisdom of Soloman's view is that God created life with

155

the intention that it should live and live. But humans 'created' destructive forces by their ungodliness. So human wickedness is the cause of death. However, death is not necessarily the end of life. Righteous people can escape death because God can give them immortality.

These ideas, first developed by the Hasidim (the precursors of the Pharisees) are new to the Bible. They are the beginnings of all Jewish, Christian and Moslem theology concerning life after death. Their expression is sometimes very beautiful (as in the early verses of chapter 3) and to those who believe them they can give great comfort.

But they are ideas, thoughts, hopes. They have no basis in known fact. They are not based on real knowledge of any kind. Christians might dispute this from their 'knowledge' of the resurrection of Jesus and of his miracles, but in doing so they are using the word knowledge in a way which is different from any normal definition of it.

Non-religious people prefer to base their lives on certainties. We know that we have one life and that is all that we know. Therefore we will live that one life as fully and as well as we can.

But like many religious people, this author cannot accept that. He associates rationalism with ungodliness. In doing so, he defines rationalism with some care and without intending to do so, he makes it very clear that it was a force to be reckoned with all those centuries ago.

It was probably easier for Jews outside Palestine/Israel to be open and honest in their thinking than it was for those in the homeland. There are certainly plenty of secular and even atheistic Jews in today's world.

To the author, rationalists reason 'unsoundly'. He makes no attempt to show how their reasoning is unsound. He simply states it as if it were a fact. As a result of that reasoning they assumed that this life is the only one we have.

'We are born by mere chance, and hereafter we shall be as though we had never been.' Therefore 'let us enjoy the good things that exist.'

The author assumes that means that rationalists believe that life should be one long riotous and irresponsible revel. He is wrong of course. We do enjoy a bit of revelry and we do believe in making the most of life and its joys. We could happily echo most of what he says in 2:6–9. But that does not make us irresponsible.

It is amazing how often the simple enjoyment of life is assumed to be irresponsible. We believe that saying 'yes' to life, to its opportunities and its joys, is the only sensible way to approach it. But that does not mean that we fail to take it seriously.

Joy and happiness can live perfectly well with a thoughtful and serious approach to moral and ethical problems. We may not believe in a divine imperative or in divine judgement (I suspect that few religious people in England take divine judgement very seriously any more). Our imperative comes from within us.

We take ethical matters seriously because we believe that is the best way to approach life – that the good life is the most fulfilled and happy life.

And it is precisely here that the author of the Wisdom of Solomon goes astray as do so many religious critics still. He assumes that righteousness is only to be found amongst religious people. He also assumes that irreligious people want to make life hard and miserable for the righteous. Both assumptions are wrong.

He comforts himself with his belief in the immortality of the righteous and also with his belief that rationalists will be punished for their rationalism.

He even believed that God would punish the innocent 'children of adulterers' and 'of an unlawful union.' How sad that anyone could believe such a thing. And how much worse that people holding such beliefs could impose them on society and make life harsher for such children (as they still did well into my adult life).

The religious condemnation of rationalism has not changed in over two thousand years. It is based on ignorance and assertion, not on fact.

Chapter 4:1–5 offers a message which is the precise opposite of Shakespeare's lines:

> 'The evil that men do lives after them,
> the good is oft interred with their bones.'

Shakespeare was too cynical, but the Wisdom of Solomon is too optimistic. Both good and evil send out ripples which continue to influence the world's life long after their perpetrators are gone.

In 4:7–19 the author tries to deal with the problem of the death of those who, in spite of their righteousness, die young. Given the beliefs of the time, people would tend to ask 'why didn't God give him old age?' Two answers are suggested:

1. Old age is not measured in years but in quality time. A righteous young man is older than an unrighteous old man.

I don't think many people would buy that idea as it stands, but they might be willing to accept that there is a measure of truth in Montaigne's words:

> 'The profit of life consists not in the space, but in the use.
> Some have lived long who have lived but a short while.'

Montaigne goes on to urge us to:

> Make use of life while you have it. Whether you have lived enough depends upon yourself, not on the number of your years.'

2. The second argument is even less convincing. *The righteous young man is taken early to preserve him from temptation 'lest evil change his understanding or guile deceive his soul.'* (v. 11)

So the only way God can save us from evil is by putting us to death. Surely, if the young man was genuinely righteous, he would be incorruptible.

In 4:18b–5:14 we are shown unrighteous people waking up to the emptiness of their lives.

5:15–16 is another favourite passage of comfort for religious people hoping for life after death (and further evidence that this 'wisdom' does not date from Solomon's time).

The crucial word relating to these passages is the word 'hope'. Religious ideas about life after death are all built on the desire some people have for such a life, and the hope that their desires will be fulfilled. Desire and hope but not knowledge. Nobody knows. In the absence of knowledge it is perhaps better to focus on this life and the best way to use it.

5:17–23 is a thoroughly confused passage in which God and Creation combine to set about the destruction of the unrighteous. They end up creating utter chaos and anarchy.

6:1–11 calls the rulers of the nations to holiness. It will remind

Christians of a sentence of Jesus 'to whom much is given, much will be expected'. This passage claims that more is expected of the great than the lowly 'for the lowliest man may be pardoned in mercy, but mighty men will be mightily tested.'

6:12–8:1. This long passage depicts and personalises 'Wisdom' and the pursuit of Wisdom.

Wisdom is feminine. In a man's world that perhaps makes her all the more worth pursuit! She is the source of all knowledge and understanding and of all goodness and contentment. The author pulls out all the stops in his picture of Wisdom. He uses every conceivable adjective and goes into great detail. Wisdom here has a good deal in common with Aristotle's goal in his Ethics of intellectual contemplation.

6:25–26 describes the relationship of Wisdom with God:

> 'a breath of the power of God,
> a pure emanation of the glory of the Almighty;
> a reflection of eternal light,
> a spotless mirror of the working of God,
> and an image of his goodness.

Even for an unbeliever, this passage in praise of Wisdom is of interest and value. It gives a clear picture of the kinds of scientific interest and study that were prevalent. It shows a sublime (and misplaced) confidence in the knowledge of the time and so demonstrates that nothing changes: 'it is he who gave me unerring knowledge of what exists.' (v. 17)

We are often too cocky about the level of our knowledge. But if we believe that our knowledge comes from a god, there is the added danger of imagining that it is complete, perfect and infallible.

Perhaps the greatest wisdom is that of Socrates – of knowing how little we know about anything. But that knowledge of our ignorance always needs to be allied with a hunger and a determination to know more.

In chapter eight the author sets out his stall as if he were Solomon the wise. The facts about Solomon paint a different picture, but never mind.

As Solomon he claims that he loved Wisdom 'and sought her from my youth, and I desired to take her for my bride.' (8:2)

The whole chapter describes his determination to live with

159

Wisdom and the value in doing so.

In verses 19 and 20 there is one curious little expression of a part of his belief:

'As a child I was by nature well endowed,
and a good soul fell to my lot;
or rather, being good, I entered an undefiled body.' [My italicising.]

It looks as though he believes that God has a limitless stock of souls waiting to enter human bodies when they become available and 'a good soul' will be given 'an undefiled body'.

Chapter 9 onwards reminds God of all that he has achieved by Wisdom throughout history for the Jews.

In 11:21–12:2 he expresses his belief not only in the power of his god but also in his love and mercy. Chapter twelve develops this theme. It is interesting for its evidence that people were asking the question I asked during my reading of Old Testament history: a question about God's destruction of whole peoples. This author wrote 'who will accuse thee for the destruction of nations which thou didst make? Or who will come before thee to plead as an advocate for unrighteous men?' (12:12)

The very fact that he asks is evidence that such questions were asked. One has the feeling that he is not altogether happy with his own answers:

1. His god is far superior to the false gods of 'those who dwelt of old in thy holy land'.
2. His god is almighty so he can do what he wills and no mere man should question his doings.
3. But his god is also righteous and merciful, teaching us that 'the righteous man must be kind, and thou hast filled thy sons with good hope, because thou givest repentance for sins.' (12:19) (It is hard to repent after you have been slaughtered.)
4. Yes, he did destroy whole nations 'but judging them little by little thou gavest them a chance to repent.' (12:10) So they only had themselves to blame if they were slaughtered.
5. However, this god still makes a distinction between his chosen people and their enemies: 'while chastening us thou scourgest our enemies ten thousand times more, so that we may meditate upon thy goodness when we judge, and when

we are judged we may expect mercy.' (12:22)

Thus if people are punished/slaughtered/judged it is their own fault. The arguments are unsatisfactory, but at least the questions are beginning to be asked.

13:1–15, 17 shows the author having some sympathy with people who worship nature or the wonders and beauties of the natural world. But he points beyond them to their creator as the one to be worshipped. Would modern evolutionary theory have altered his teaching? Non-religious people have abandoned the idea of a creator. But some religious people have shown themselves able to take on board evolutionary theory, adapting their concept of a creator without rejecting it.

The author has no sympathy at all with idolaters who worship gods made by humans. He both mocks and castigates them. Does he also misrepresent the best of them? 13:13–19: does the idolater worship the piece of wood or the spirit of the wood?

Nor has he any time for Emperor worship, the deifying of rulers and the pretence that they are gods.

Non religious people share all this mockery, but go on to deny the existence of any gods at all.

15:18–16:29. The author is so concerned to show that his god is merciful, that I find myself wondering if he shares my own revulsion at some of the Old Testament pictures of God. He claims that the purpose of God's punishments is to turn people to faith. They are directed at those who do not worship him. Meanwhile his miraculous blessings are bestowed on those who trust him. There are times when that claim leads him into teaching which could be dangerous or harmful if it were accepted: 16:12: 'for neither herb nor poultice cured them, but it was thy word, O Lord, which heals all men.'

This attitude was strengthened by the healing miracles of the New Testament. It has given naive Christians a great deal of grief over the centuries as they have asked the question disciples of Jesus asked: 'Why could we not heal?' It also deflected people from scientific medicine and research and contributed to the centuries-long delay in medical advance as the church set its face against such things.

The same kind of teaching occurs in 16:26: 'It is not the production of crops that feeds man, but . . . thy word preserves

161

those who trust in thee.' So the only reason for getting up early is to pray, not to tend the land. This kind of do-nothing pietism lives on. Fortunately most farmers are immune to it.

The final chapters of the book depict the Exodus from Egypt under Moses in a highly imaginative way. Their only value is as a reminder of how deeply ingrained the events and myths of the Exodus had become in the Jewish national psyche.

Ecclesiasticus *or* the Wisdom of Jesus the son of Sirach

The title is a reminder of how common the name Jesus was before the birth of Jesus of Nazareth. The author claims that he is simply translating his grandfather's work for a wider readership. As he speaks of the problems of translation he sounds very modern.

The first chapter speaks of Wisdom and chapter two of what it means to serve God with single-minded consistency and determination. These two chapters contain an ethical religious approach to life of the highest quality.

3:1–16 is a call to honour your father and mother. Fortunately most of us have good reasons for doing so. But this author gives one reason which is universal:

> 'Remember that through your parents you were born; and what can you give back to them that equals their gift to you.' (7:28)

Chapter three goes on to speak of the dangers of pride and stubbornness and the need to be humble and teachable.

4:1–10 speaks of the importance of caring for the poor and ends with words that could very easily be misinterpreted:

> 'Be like a father to orphans, and *instead of a husband* to their mother.'

4:11–19 returns to the praise of Wisdom.

4:20–6:4: It is difficult to summarise what often becomes almost a series of proverbs. They are all aimed at guiding us into a sensible, decent and righteous way of life. Almost every verse has something in it worthy of consideration. Unfortunately it all makes pretty negative and dull reading.

6:5–17 speaks of false and true friendship.

6:18–37 returns to Wisdom and the importance of seeking her and living by her.

7:1–8:19 offers more good advice. Most of it is applicable to anyone – anyone who wishes to live a dull, safe, no risks, virtuous life. It is a pity that his work comes across in this way. Life does not have to be dull and unadventurous to be virtuous. And most of this advice *is* good advice and worth attention even though it is so dull.

9:1–9 warns against the attractions of women 'Many have been misled by a woman's beauty, and by it passion is kindled like a fire.' (9:8) The passage is a reminder that these books were written by men for men. I wonder where women obtained good advice for the living of their lives? Perhaps they didn't need it.

In 11:14 the author claims that 'good things and bad, life and death, poverty and wealth, come from the Lord.' It follows that it is important to keep on good terms with God and all his advice is geared to that end.

In chapters 12 and 13 he advises people to know their own place and keep to it. 'Every creature loves its like, and every person his neighbour; all living things associate by species, and a man clings to one like himself.' (13:15–16) By this he does not mean that humans cling to other humans. The focus is narrower than that. The rich cling to the rich and the poor to the poor. The poor are warned against associating with the rich.

> 'How can the clay pot associate with the iron kettle? The pot will strike against it, and will itself be broken.' (13:2)

However sensible this advice may be, when it is carried beyond the realms of advice into the realms of divine will, it can become very dangerous and harmful indeed. There is danger in any teaching which separates one human being from another.

For those who like proverbs, mottoes and sayings, this book is a treasure trove. If this author is right in saying that 'to devise proverbs requires painful thinking' (13:26), it is perhaps better to have them provided for us.

In chapter 14 the author shows that he has no belief in any meaningful existence after death. So he advises us to live generously both towards ourselves and towards others.

163

'Do not deprive yourself of a happy day; let not your share of a desired good pass you by, Will you not leave the fruit of your labours to another, and what you acquired by toil to be divided by lot?' (14:14–15)

This could almost be a humanist writing.

The question of freedom of will is argued as fiercely in religious circles as it is outside. This author comes down firmly on the side of freedom:

'If you will, you can keep the commandments and to act faithfully is a matter of your own choice.' (15:15)

So we are responsible for our own actions and our own lives. In chapter 16 he goes on to claim that 'everyone will receive in accordance with his deeds.' (16:14) The book of Job has already demonstrated that is not true.

(Taking the book as a whole, the author is not always consistent on the question of free will – but which of us is?)

In chapter 17 he follows Genesis in claiming that man is unique in all creation, made in the image of God (what an image that gives us of God) with 'authority over the things of the earth.' (17:2) And among men 'Israel is the Lord's own portion.' (17:17) (The Lord is welcome.)

I hate that kind of teaching. Just think what we are doing with that authority. In England we have covered the equivalent of three counties with concrete and tarmac in my lifetime. World-wide we have poisoned the soil and the waterways, the sea and the air. We drive all living things back and back towards extinction, and often beyond the brink.

Perhaps it is time for the Lord to admit that it is not enough to limit human lives. (Sirach reminds us that they *are* very limited: 'a son of man is not immortal. . . all men are dust and ashes.'–17:30 & 32) He should replace us completely as he did the dinosaurs.

Or perhaps there is no Lord. In that case we shall have to get our own act together. We shall have to begin by thinking in terms of interdependence and stewardship rather than authority. We shall have to think more of our responsibility towards the world in which we live and its creatures, and less of what we can take from it. Otherwise we shall not only bring a host of creatures to extinction, we shall bring ourselves there as well.

In chapters 18ff he returns to teaching through proverbs. Occasionally there is a memorable turn of phrase such as 'a slip on the pavement is better than a slip of the tongue.' (20:18) Although I suspect that one or two people in hospital might disagree with him.

In chapter 21 he compares the behaviour of the good and the bad, the wise and the foolish, the civilised and the uncivilised man. But there isn't much reason for commentary here. We either read these chapters for what there is of worth in them, or we don't bother. If we do read them, we shall find that most of his advice is fairly mundane common sense. Occasionally he will make us sit up, and sometimes disagree.

In chapter 22 he shows that he has little time for daughters. 'The birth of a daughter is a loss.' (22:3) The only thing to do with daughters is to marry them off.

Towards the end of chapter 23 he expresses the narrow and violent attitude to wives who commit adultery that is still common in some Moslem societies. He shows no appreciation of the problems people face when marriages are not working. Nor has he room in his teaching for people to untie the knot and begin again (though we shall find him advising men to separate from evil wives).

Modern freedoms are demonstrating that many people never find happiness in marriage. And many more only find it after one or more false starts. An accepting and non-judgemental society will do its best to be flexible enough to enable people to find their own route to happiness and fulfilment with as little pain as possible.

In chapter 24 Wisdom sings her own praises.

Chapter 25 shows a fascination with numbers. It was shared by a number of Jews. 3, 4, 7 and multiples of some of these: 9, 12, 144 – all these were special numbers with special (magical) meaning and significance.

There are plenty of people today who become hooked on numbers and their magical significance in precisely the same way. For the rest of us, this is a strange and meaningless obsession.

25:16–26 suggests that the author has had some experience of the misery of an unsatisfactory marriage (which contradicts my earlier impression). It is all the fault of the 'evil wife' of course. 'From a woman sin had its beginning, and because of her we all die.' (25:24) The passage makes amusing reading (if you are a man). It leads to a recommendation to choose divorce and then in chapter 26:1–4 to a recognition of the blessings of a happy marriage. Most of the rest of the chapter continues to be about bad and good wives.

28:2 has a foretaste of some of the teaching of Jesus, 'Forgive your neighbour the wrong he has done, and then your sins will be pardoned when you pray.'

29 speaks of lending and repaying, helping the poor, and learning to 'be content with little or much'. (29:23) Since 'the essentials of life are water and bread and clothing and a house' (preferably one's own house since there is constant hassle if a house is not your own). (29:21ff)

At the end of the 20th century we have come a long way from 30:1–13 which begins 'He who loves his son will whip him often.'

There are still plenty of us who can remember frequent beatings either at home or at school or both. Sometimes such beatings were brutal and sadistic but by no means always. Although I favour a non-beating approach, beatings often had two virtues. They were immediate and they were soon over. Both those elements are important for a child.

Many of us who were beaten frequently (as I was at school) would say that we never felt damaged by it. But what kind of a father is it who cannot play or laugh with his child (13:9–10)?

13:17 claims that 'Death is better than a miserable life, and eternal rest than chronic sickness.'

Setting aside those who commit suicide, in my experience the young often fight for life long after it seems to have any value. Carers may feel that death would be a mercy, and may feel guilty for doing so, but sufferers battle on.

It is usually only later in life that death begins to be seen as a welcome friend. In old people there often comes a time when we are weary of life and ready for death as our natural end. Both my parents reached that point and I've seen it reached many, many times. Real suffering comes when people want to die and can't.

After a lifetime spent caring for the dying and the bereaved, my own conviction is that voluntary and assisted euthanasia, with proper safeguards in place, should be allowed.

Immediately after a death it is probably too early to read 30:21–23:

> 'Do not give yourself over to sorrow, and do not afflict yourself deliberately. Gladness of heart is the life of man, and the rejoicing of a man is length of days. Delight your soul and comfort your heart, and remove sorrow far from you, for sorrow has destroyed many, and there is no profit in it.'

That message is one of the most important of all for bereaved people. While we live it is essential that we give ourselves over entirely and wholeheartedly to life. That is our best tribute to those who have died. 'Gladness of heart' really is the secret of human life.

In 32:7ff he asked, 'Why is any day better than another, when all the daylight in the year is from the sun?' Why is one day holy and another not?

His answer is that God has made some days special. If we don't believe in gods we can discount that. A look at any diary will show that we are the ones who choose to make some days special. If this is the case, we are also free to ignore special days that have no relevance for us, provided that in doing so we do not give unnecessary offence.

In chapter 31ff he warns against the pursuit of wealth – the pursuit rather than wealth itself – and then goes on to encourage a modest, thoughtful, generous life of moderation bordering on the abstemious.

In 33:24–29 and 33:30–31 there are two passages about servants which are so different that they must surely have come from different sources.

In the first the servant is treated as a work animal and worse: 'Yoke and thong will bow the neck, and for a wicked servant there are racks and tortures.'

Yet in the second people are urged to treat their servants well: 'treat him as a brother.'

One of the great deficiencies of this book is that its 'wisdom' is the perceived wisdom of the time, accepted and handed on without question. Here, as in so much moral teaching, human thought is at a standstill. There is no examination of the rights and wrongs of the thought itself.

34:26 offers a caricature of true religion, a caricature frequently painted of Catholic Christianity in particular. But caricatures only work if they contain an element of truth. For that reason, this one should give religious people pause.

Chapter 36 begins with a fairly bloodthirsty prayer for blessings on Israel.

Then from verse 18 the author returns to proverbs, mostly about the value of a good wife. He has some very strange ideas about women: 'A woman will accept any man.' (v. 21) She had little choice, and in some societies that is still true. The path of progress is painfully slow.

Chapter 38 begins with a passage full of praise for physicians and pharmacists. It is tragic that the church paid so little attention to this passage and its teaching, preferring to rely on faith-healing and miracles instead, and holding back the advance of medical research and understanding.

After so much praise it looks as though another hand has added verse 15 (perhaps with his tongue in his cheek?): 'He who sins before his Maker, may he fall into the care of a physician.'

38:16–23 is about bereavement and grief. However sensible much of this passage may be, it is heartless. Grief is seen as a matter of going through the motions of outward observance 'to avoid criticism'. (38:17)

There is no genuine feeling for the bereaved, no understanding of human emotion, no sharing of the grief or empathy with the bereaved. As with most of the book, his advice is cold and calculated and lacking in real humanity.

38:24–34 expresses one of the most common misconceptions of all among academics. While he pays tribute to farmers and craftsmen of all kinds as those who 'keep stable the fabric of the world' (38:34) he still thinks of them as second class citizens. To him the top people are the scribes (academics and professional people). His attitude is expressed in unmistakeable terms: 'How can he become wise who handles the plough? The wisdom of the scribe depends on the opportunity of leisure; and he who has little business may become wise.' (38:25 and 24)

Perhaps we should ask, 'How can he become wise who has never handled the plough'? It is so often the farmer in tune with the natural world, or the craftsman handling natural objects with respect and understanding who become truly wise. They develop a depth of wisdom frequently unknown in the arid and meaningless world of philosophical debate or the business world of high finance or the juvenile university debating house that is our house of commons.

41:1–4 is a brief poem or meditation on death. It is an excellent summary and description of the way humans look at death, and it is all the better for the fact that there is no religion in it.

Chapters 41 and 42 speak of behaviour which is bad and behaviour which is good; of the anxiety a daughter brings to her father; of the nature of his god, all-knowing, all-seeing and unchanging.

Here is the god used in days gone by to try to frighten children into obedience and good behaviour: 'No thought escapes him, and no one word is hidden from him.' (42:20)

None of those closest to me used this god in my childhood but I have some memories of Sunday School teachers and preachers threatening us with his knowledge of our every move. Most children of my generation will have a few such memories. My parents' generation will have far more.

Chapter 43 is a rather pedestrian attempt to praise god the creator and then in 44:1–15 we have one of the most famous passages in the whole of the Bible. Beginning 'Let us now praise famous men' it always used to be used (perhaps it still is?) on Remembrance Sunday. It is a passage of great beauty and resonance. It introduces the author's praise for the great men of Jewish history,

Curiously, he begins with Enoch and ends in chapter 50 by singing the praises of Simon Maccabaeus the high priest, son of Onias – praised for restoring the temple, fortifying Jerusalem and providing a huge reservoir, all to enable the inhabitants of Jerusalem to withstand a siege.

The book ends in chapter 51 with the author like little Jack Homer who 'sat in a corner and said, "What a good boy am I." ' He urges others to learn from him.

There is a good deal in this book that is worth reading, but I often found that my mind strayed because so much of it is so dull. It took a real effort of concentration to pull myself back to the text, and it wasn't always worth the effort.

h

Baruch

There is nothing in Baruch to make it worth reading.

It claims to have been written in the fifth year of exile in Babylon (about 581 BCE).

Money is sent to Jerusalem and the people there are asked to pray for Nebuchadnezzar and his son Belshazzar, rulers in Babylon, 'and the Lord will give us strength and he will give light to our eyes, and we shall live under the protection of Nebuchadnezzar.' (1:12)

The troubles of the Jews are the result of their sin and disobedience. God had told them 'bend your shoulders and serve the king of Babylon' (2:21) but instead they tried to resist him.

Apparently God had told Moses that these things would happen, that the people would be taken into exile and that they would return and never be driven out again.

The whole book is the expression of the belief that as God has punished his people with exile, so he will restore his people to their own land.

The Letter of Jeremiah

This was attached to Baruch as chapter 6.

It warns the exiles not to worship idols who are not gods. Priests are accused of stripping silver and gold from the idols to spend on themselves or on prostitutes. (10–11) So the priests obviously do not believe in them as gods.

He paints a picture of gods blackened by the smoke of sacrifice, a resting place for bats, swallows and other birds, and even cats. (21–22)

> 'Like a scarecrow in a cucumber field, that guards nothing, so are
> the gods of wood, overlaid with gold and silver.' (70)

If this message is once accepted we are left only with those who believe that the gods must reveal themselves in order to be known and those who share my own belief that there are no gods at all. There is no proof either way. I cannot prove that there are no gods; believers cannot prove that there are. We must therefore agree to differ, and learn to live in harmony with one another in spite of our disagreement. That requires genuine tolerance and rules out the arrogance of evangelical zeal.

The Prayer of Azariah and the Song of the Three Young Men
(additions to Daniel inserted between 3:23 and 3:24)

In the book of Daniel; Shadrach, Meshach and Abednego were thrown into the furnace because they refused to worship Babylonian gods or the image of the emperor. The flames of the furnace never touched them.

This is supposed to be the prayer and the litany of praise they offered up to God while they were in the furnace.

Susanna
(Daniel chapter 13)

This is another of the additions made to the Old Testament book of Daniel.

It is the tale of a virtuous and beautiful woman (aren't they all?) and two lecherous old men who were judges within the Jewish community. There's nothing new in sleaze in high places.

When she refuses their advances they have her condemned to death for adultery with an invented young man.

Another young man (Daniel) claims divine inspiration, questions the judges separately and shows their testimony to be false. Susanna is vindicated and goes free. The old men are executed 'and from that day onward Daniel had a great reputation among the people.' (v. 64)

We have noticed the division amongst the Jews between the northern tribes (Israel) and Judah. It dates from the beginning.

Biblical writers frequently favour Judah and this writer is no exception. Commenting on the behaviour of the judges, Daniel says:

> 'This is how you both have been dealing with the daughters of Israel, and they were intimate with you through fear; but a daughter of Judah would not endure your wickedness.' (v. 57)

Bel and the Dragon
(Daniel chapter 14)

This is the last of the additions to the book of Daniel.

It is an unlikely and delightful demonstration of the fact that idols are not gods. It contains the famous story of Daniel in the den of lions.

But there is nothing in the story to lead to the conclusion 'Thou art great, O Lord God of Daniel.'

When the gods are shown not to be gods at all, what evidence is there that any god is left? This book offers none.

The first book of the
Maccabees

With the books of the Maccabees we return to history. This book covers a period roughly from 175–130 BCE. As history it is quite different from anything in the Old Testament. Although the fuse that lights the fires of rebellion is a religious fuse, God is no longer the central character of the story. He is pretty much sidelined. This is a story of men and battles.

Chapter one begins with the conquests of Alexander the Great and the division of his empire into four after his death. The Jews came within the bounds of the Seleucid quarter of the empire. In due course they came under the rule of Antiochus Epiphanes.

Alexander and his successors had brought Greek influence to bear on life right through the empire. Many Jews were attracted by the Greek way of life. They even 'built a gymnasium in

Jerusalem' where men performed naked. Greek influence was acceptable to many but abhorrent to some.

But Antiochus was not content with influence. He wanted an empire whose unity was cemented by uniformity of religion and custom. (1:41–42) Many went along with his wishes. Where they didn't, he used force to impose his wishes. He also took steps to demonstrate that other religions were of no account. In Jerusalem he defiled the temple by sacrificing a pig on the altar.

Many Jews suffered death rather than obey. But in Modein a priest called Mattathias rebelled and he and his five sons took to the hills. They waged guerilla warfare. Attacked on the sabbath day, many of them refused to fight and were slaughtered, a disaster which led to a change of policy.

Throughout this period there were power struggles going on all around them. These enabled the Jews to achieve a measure of independence, sometimes through military success, sometimes through diplomacy and sometimes by payment of tribute.

Such was the violence of the zeal of the guerilla fighters in the early days that ordinary people must have wondered which was worse, Seleucid or Jewish authority. Throughout the period there were Jews hostile to the Maccabean leadership.

The Maccabees proved to be remarkably able. In 165 BCE they had achieved enough success to be able to cleanse the temple and restore Jewish temple worship. At the end of chapter seven (v. 50) we are told that 'the land of Judah had rest for a few days'. It was as much as they could hope for. Although under Simon, the last survivor of the brothers, they enjoyed a rather longer period of quiet.

The book is of no interest except to Jews and historians of the period. It shows how far news of the prowess of the Spartans had spread (long after their brief period of glory), and it shows the emergence of Rome as the supreme power in the western world. It also shows the zealous determination of some Jews to remain a distinct people with a distinct religion. Without that zeal and determination there would be no separate Jewish nation today.

The Second Book of the
Maccabees

The first two chapters are a preface. The book claims to be written by Jews in Jerusalem for the Jews of the dispersion. It emphasises the importance of the Temple and its worship and it asks Jews everywhere to celebrate the new festival of the purification of the temple on the 25th day of Chislev (December). One of the reasons Christians chose this time of year to celebrate the birth of Jesus was in order to supercede other year end festivals. The same is true of Easter and of many of the lesser, largely forgotten, festivals of the Christian year. Political power over a long period ensured the success of their strategy.

The book claims to be a sort of Readers Digest condensed version of a history in five volumes written by Jason of Cyrene. After reading this book we can only be grateful that we no longer have the five volumes.

With unwitting humour the author ends chapter two 'it is foolish to lengthen the preface while cutting short the history itself.' His preface is not exactly short.

The book covers the same period as 1 Maccabees but in a very different style. It is *almost* the difference between ancient secular history and ancient religious history. The religious history, curiously enough, is not required to be factually accurate. In terms of style, 1 Maccabees is much more to modern western taste. The style of 2 Maccabees is still popular in the middle east and the Indian sub-continent. Thus 2 Maccabees is full of signs and wonders and has the Temple as its central focus of interest. Chapter 6 also mentions the Samaritan temple on Mount Gerizim. This had been important to Samaritans ever since Ezra refused to allow them to share the work and worship in Jerusalem.

Chapters 6 and 7 speak of the imposition of pagan worship and of the martyrdom of the faithful. Their sufferings are regarded as God's discipline and they put their faith in a life beyond the grave. After these two chapters the author ends quaintly, 'Let this be enough then about the eating of sacrifices and the extreme tortures.'

Chapter 8 tells of the guerrilla warfare and battles fought by Judas Maccabaeus and his brothers. Chapter 9 tells the story of the horrible disease leading to the death of Antiochus Epiphanes. Chapters 10 and 11 give us more of the battles fought by Judas aided by men from heaven 'clothed in white and brandishing weapons of gold' (11:8) and tells us about the cleansing of the temple. This is followed by a series of letters of goodwill including one from the Romans.

According to this author, in battle after battle the Jews kill thousands of their enemies without any loss on their own side. But in a battle with Gorgias 'it happened that a few of the Jews fell. (12:34)

Later, when they came to pick up the bodies they discovered that the men were wearing 'sacred tokens of the idols of Jamnia'. (12:40) So it became clear that they had died because they did not put their trust in the god of the Jews.

At the end of the chapter we are told that Judas Maccabaeus took up an offering and sent it to Jerusalem as an offering for the sins of his men. Thus he prayed and 'made atonement for the dead, that they might be delivered from sin.' (12:45)

He did this 'taking account of the resurrection for if he was not expecting that those who had fallen would rise again, it would have been superfluous and foolish to pray for the dead.' (12:43–44)

Belief in resurrection was still comparatively new amongst the Jews and remained a subject for debate. It was not a belief universally held. For those who still believe in resurrection, the question of whether there is any point in praying for the dead continues to be debated. Can their eternal destiny be altered after they have died?

For those of us who believe that death is the end, these questions are irrelevant. The book ends with more anxious times, dreams, visions, brave words and another great Jewish victory against overwhelming odds. Perhaps the best things about this book are the moments of amusement it gives to readers. The last is in 15:37–38: 'I will here end my story. If it is well told and to the point, that is what I myself desired; if it is poorly done and mediocre, that was the best I could do.' Perhaps that should be the epitaph to my own work!

1 Esdras

The book is a repetition of history contained in the Old Testament from the time of Josiah.

Chapters 3 and 4 tell the story of a challenge to the king's bodyguards to declare what is the strongest thing of all. One says 'wine' and one says 'the king' but Zerubbabel gives two answers: 'women' and 'truth'. He wins with 'truth'. The king promotes him and gives him his wish, that the exiles should not merely be allowed to return to Jerusalem, but they should be actively encouraged, supplied and supported.

Chapter five lists the returnees and tells the story of the rebuilding of the Temple and the exclusivity of the Jews who refuse the assistance of the Samaritans. In chapters 6 and 7 the temple is rebuilt and dedicated with the support of Darius the Persian emperor.

Chapters 8 and 9 describe the return of Ezra and the puritanical regime he established based on ethnic cleansing. In the name of their god, all foreign wives and their children were to be 'put away'. No thought was given to their future. I don't think I need to add my own thoughts on such behaviour.

2 Esdras

This book is particularly fascinating because at least some of it was written by a Christian. As a result, it links old and new testaments and it gives us independent evidence of the way at least some Christians saw themselves in the earliest days. The author uses a time-honoured dodge which we have already met several times. He casts some of the Old Testament books back in time, centuries before they were actually written. This enables him to 'foretell' the future right up to his own time!

He claims that Ezra's leadership was rejected by the Jews (2:33) although there is no real evidence of that either in the Old Testament or in 1 Esdras.

The first chapter is the usual kind of moan we can expect from the prophets. In spite of all that their wonderful god has done for them the Jews are 'rebellious' and full of iniquity. One day they will be replaced by 'a people that will come, who without having heard me will believe. Those to whom I have shown no signs will do what I have commanded. . . . I call to witness the gratitude of the people that is to come, whose children rejoice with gladness; though they do not see me with bodily eyes, yet with the spirit they will believe the things I have said.' (1:35–37)

It is no wonder that this was so popular with many Christians who saw themselves as the new 'people of God' of whom 2 Esdras spoke. Esdras went on to say in chapter 2 that Jerusalem would be given to this new people.

The new people of whom 2 Esdras speaks will abide by the caring standards of the Old Testament (2:20–23) and they will be rewarded with the generous mercy and grace of God and with resurrection from death.

It was never actually 'given' but two sets of new people have had Jerusalem for a time, Christians and Moslems, and now it is back with the Jews again – up to a point!

Chapter 2:23–48 is clearly the work of a Christian and reads like a Christian tract. It pretends to look forward from Ezra's time to the coming of the 'shepherd' (34), the 'Saviour' (37); and the 'Son of God' (47). Much of it is a semi-quotation from the last book in the New Testament, the book of Revelation (7:9–17) unless the reverse is the case. Both books offer a vision of a new and wonderful life after death.

Chapter 3 asks the first of a number of intriguing questions. Why were the Jews punished by being exiled to Babylon when the Babylonians were just as wicked or more wicked than the Jews?

Chapter 4:1–11a gives the angel's answer which is that it is not for us to understand 'the way of the Most High'.

That is the classic religious answer to difficult questions. Indeed we are often told that we have no business even to pose the question! 'Trust and obey. There is no other way', as the old hymn put it. Where religion is concerned, we are to suspend the use of the minds which presumably religion believes god has given us. No wonder the author says, 'It would be better for us not to be here than to come here and live in ungodliness, and to suffer and not understand why.' And he asks, 'Why have I been endowed with the power of understanding?' (4:12 and 22)

The author is given no answer to his questions. Instead the angel tells him that 'the age is swiftly hastening to its end' (4:26). Everything is mapped out by God. He has his plan and will stick to it.

In chapter five, after visions of future chaos, the author carries his earlier unanswered question one step further: 'If thou dost really hate thy people, they should be punished at thy own hands.' (5:30) And not by exile amongst the Babylonians. The answer is two fold, pretty typical, and totally unsatisfactory:

1. 'Do you love Israel more than his Maker does?' (5:33)

2. These things are beyond human understanding. (5:36–40)

If it could be shown that there was a god who was the creator of human life, and if it could be demonstrated that he was a god of love, the first answer might have some validity. But the second begs the question asked earlier: why do we have minds at all.

Nor does the writer stop asking questions. Many people have found the whole idea of a chosen people abhorrent. If there is a god who is love, how can he choose one people and not all? And when Christians open out the concept of 'the people of God to include all who respond to the message of Jesus', the question comes home with even greater force: what of all those untold millions who lived their lives without ever hearing of him? (5:41)

5:51–55: contains the curious idea that as the world grows old and tired of supporting life, its inhabitants will grow smaller. In fact, they seem to be growing much larger.

6:1–34 is an expression of the author's fascination with the end of human history on earth. 6:35 following has his outline of Genesis 1's account of creation with the addition of the two monsters Behemoth and Leviathan. It all leads us back to his original question:

If the world has indeed been created for us (i.e. not for all humans but specifically for the Chosen People), why do we not possess our world as an inheritance? Why do other 'nations, which are reputed as nothing, domineer over us?' (6:59 and 57)

At last answers are given. They are not the answers of reason but they are answers nonetheless and many Christians are content with them:

1. The Chosen People can only come to their inheritance through the narrow path of suffering.
2. Instead of focussing on the present with all its troubles, mortals should focus their minds on 'what is to come', their own death and resurrection and the end of all history. (7:16)

From 7:17 following, the author accepts the answers and the angel goes on to underline the fairness of God.

As an atheist I have found this whole section fascinating. The questions asked are the kind of questions we ask. The answers given are the kind of answers religious people still give to us – answers that I'm afraid we find totally unsatisfactory. It is also interesting to find the author acknowledging that even in his day there were those who 'declared that the Most High does not exist.'

From 7:25–44 he describes god's 'day of judgement'. His general vision is similar to many such visions. The angel speaks of God's son the Messiah. He and his followers will be revealed and those who remain shall rejoice 400 years. 'And after those years my son the Messiah shall die, and all who draw human breath.' And when the judgement comes (without compassion or patience) some will go to the pit of torment and some to the paradise of delight.

These words are addressed to Ezra. When he has heard all about the judgement he comments 'that the world to come will bring delight to few, but torments to many.' (7:47) because all of us have sinned.

God's response is to compare the few with desirable things like gold and the many with clay. 'I will rejoice over the few which shall be saved. . . and I will not grieve over the multitude of those who perish.' (7:60–61)

But notice that their punishment in the pit is not lasting as it is so often depicted. They 'are extinguished'. (7:61)

Ezra is appalled and scared. He feels it would have been better not to have been born, or not to have had a mind to be able to worry about these things. The angel comforts him and tells him not to suffer torments 'for you have a treasure of works laid up with the Most High'. (7:77)

So Ezra has *earned* heaven. There is nothing here about

needing a Saviour and nothing about the requirement of faith. We save ourselves by our own works.

In 7:78–87 he itemises what happens to 'the many' who are doomed and then from verse 88 to 99 he itemises the seven orders of the blessed. The fourth would not suit our age for people are 'gathered into their chambers. . . in profound quiet.' No musak then!

In 7:102–3 the author asks, 'What about our ungodly relatives and friends? Will we be able to intercede for them?' The answer is a firm no. 'The day of judgement is decisive.' (7:103–5)

But our author is nothing if not dogged. He deserves a good deal of respect. He points out that right through history the righteous have prayed for the unrighteous. So 'why will it not be so then as well?' (7:111) He could also have asked how heaven could be heaven if so many of our loved ones are excluded – but he didn't!

The answer he received is blunt. In this world the righteous can pray for the wicked in the hope of change. After death it is too late. And that leads our author to bewail the fact of our creation and the universal taint of Adam's sin. 'What good it is that an everlasting hope has been promised us, but we have miserably failed.' (7:120)

But the angel has no sympathy with failures. The battle between good and evil is what life is all about. The 'victorious shall receive what I have said.' But 'there shall be no grief at (the) destruction of those who fail. ' (7:129 and 131)

After all that 7:132–140 looks pretty sarcastic. I know that the Most High is now called merciful, gracious, patient, bountiful, compassionate, generous but 'if he did not pardon those who were created by his word and blot out the multitude of their sins, there would probably be left only very few of the innumerable multitude.'

It sounds as though god's creative work was and is pretty flawed and he only pardons because he doesn't fancy having the chambers of heaven almost empty. The angel claims that 'the Most High made this world for the sake of the many, but the world to come for the sake of the few.' (8:1)

Our author is not content with that. He seems to feel that life is pretty unfair 'for not of our own will did we come into the world, and against our will we depart, for we have been given only a short time to live.' (8:5) He talks of all the trouble taken in the creation of a child and asks, 'to what purpose was he made, if thou wilt suddenly and quickly destroy him who with so great labour was fashioned by thy command?' (8:14)

He prays and he doesn't hold back. He really goes for his god. 'If God is really merciful will he only accept the righteous, who have many works laid up with thee'. They 'shall receive their reward in consequence of their own deeds.' (8:33) Now, if God wants to be called merciful he will have to do better than that. He will have to 'have pity on us, who have no works of righteousness.' (8:32)

God answers, 'I will not concern myself about the fashioning of those who have sinned, or about their death, their judgement, or their destruction.' (8:38) any more than a farmer concerns himself with seed which he sows but which does not germinate. The farmer only concerns himself with seed which grows.

The author is scandalised that God should liken us 'for whose sake thou hast formed all things' (8:44) to seed. He points out that seed doesn't fail through any fault of its own. If it fails it is God's fault! Either he hasn't sent enough rain or he has sent too much! So he calls on God to 'spare the people and have mercy on thy inheritance.' (8:45)

God claims that our author cannot love 'creation more than I love it.' He goes on to praise the author's virtue and promises that he will inherit the heaven described in 8:52–54. 'Therefore do not ask any more questions about the multitude of those who are perishing. For they also received freedom, but they despised the Most High, and were contemptuous of his law, and forsook his ways.' (8:56) They have had their chance 'but they have even trampled upon God's righteous ones'. They have even 'said in their hearts that there is no God.'

Gosh! How wicked can you get? Notice that God still hasn't answered our author's questions. All that he has said is 'You're all right Jack. Forget the rest and leave them to me.' So, without being properly answered our author is put in his place. But he won't be put down. Up comes the next question:

When will these things happen?

The answer is as vague and meaningless as these answers always are – and as they must be. If we read any daily newspaper any day of any year we shall see all the signs of the end time.

Nothing he has heard has satisfied this author. He is still concerned about the sheer number of those who are doomed. But his god is no longer interested in them. He is only interested in the 'one grape out of a cluster, and the one plant out of a great forest spared with great difficulty.' (9:21)

Then the author met a grief-stricken woman whose only son has died. He tells her to grieve for the whole nation rather than just for her son.

It turns out (chapter 10) that the woman is not a woman at all but God's holy city Zion. Zion has been destroyed but the author is not to worry because he will see the new city of God.

Then in chapter 11 he has another dream, this time of a long-lasting empire (the Roman empire?) which eventually comes to an end and that will signal the end time when the Messiah 'will arise from the posterity of David (12:32) and he who is actually God's Son will be revealed.' (13:32)

The Messiah will destroy the ungodly and call to himself the lost tribes of Israel (those exiled to Assyria) who have been living in secret in another land (13:39–45) and he will also call the holy of the exiles returned from Babylon defined elsewhere as those 'who have works and have faith in the Almighty'. (13:23)

References to 'the lost tribes of Israel living in secret in another land have spawned a host of weird and wild theories such as those of the British Israelites who claim that they came to this country.

13:52 shows God underestimating the abilities of those he has made. 'No one can explore or know what is in the depths of the sea.' But 2,000 years on, we are beginning to do just that. Having reached the north and south poles and the top of Everest and having reached out to the moon, we are now beginning to explore the final unknown areas of the world, the ones under water.

Now the author is told that the world is growing old and weary so it is time for him to put his own house in order 'and henceforth you shall live with my Son and with those who are like him, until the times are ended'. (14:9) Ten and a half of the world's twelve ages are over.

God instructs the author to take five scribes to a field and he dictates 94 books, 24 for general consumption and 70 for 'the wise among your people. For in them is the spring of understanding, the fountain of wisdom, and the river of knowledge.' (14:47)

So those who only read the Old and New Testaments have got too few books and those who read the Apocrypha as well have got too many!

Some versions of 2 Esdras end at the end of chapter 14 with the author being caught up into heaven like Enoch or Elijah.

Chapters 15 and 16 read as if they come from another hand. They prophecy death and slaughter and natural disasters on a vast scale and they claim that these things will happen soon, but God's chosen will be saved:

'Behold the days of tribulation are at hand, and I will deliver you from them.' (16:74)

Now that I have been an atheist for so many years, 2 Esdras is one of the very few books of the Old Testament and Apocrypha that I would ever want to read again.

It is thoughtful in a way that hardly any of these books are. As in Job, we find a man daring to stand before 'the Most High God' and to question him. Not only that, he is a man who demands answers and who dares to go on questioning when the answers are inadequate.

Questions like his and inadequate answers like those given led me over a long period to leave all religious belief behind. I finally came to the conclusion that one of two things was true: Either God was hateful and I would hate him; or else he didn't exist. For me it was the second answer that commended itself and I have had no religious beliefs from that day to this.

The Prayer of the Manasseh

The final book of the Apocrypha which some included and some excluded is the prayer of a penitent sinner pleading for forgiveness, and giving praise to a merciful God.

It seems to me to be a natural and suitable end to part two of our study of these religious books.

Part Three

THE NEW TESTAMENT

The Gospels and the Acts of the Apostles

Introduction

The New Testament's primary purpose is to tell us about Jesus and to bring us his message. It begins with four gospels and a book of acts of the apostles. The acts will require very little of our attention but the gospels claim to be the 'good news' about Jesus.

In Christian circles it is widely believed that Mark's gospel was the first to be written and that the authors of both Matthew and Luke made use of it when they came to write their own.

It is also probable that Matthew and Luke had access to a document of the sayings of Jesus which scholars call Q (from the German word meaning a source).

These things explain the family relationship between the first three (synoptic) gospels.

John's gospel was probably written much later and independently. As a result it will receive some separate attention.

Because of the interrelationships between the gospels and the large amount of material common to more than one of them, I shall take all four together, hopping about between them in an attempt to avoid too much repetition.

But I shall use Matthew as my home base, simply because it is both the first in the New Testament and also the longest.

The Birth and Childhood of Jesus

We KNOW nothing of the birth of Jesus. We do not know where he was born. We do not know when he was born.

Most scholars seem satisfied that he was born somewhere between 6 and 4 BCE and almost certainly not on the 25th December. (BCE and CE are used nowadays instead of BC and AD.)

There are stories about the birth of Jesus at the beginning of Luke and Matthew's gospels and there is a chapter at the beginning of John which is the foundation of most serious Christian incarnation theology. In Mark there is nothing at all.

The birth stories are very readable. They have become part of the folklore with which we celebrate the passing of the old year and the beginning of the new. Many Christians treat them as myth and the rest of us set them alongside all the other fairy tales in our heritage.

As a result we are all familiar with the general outline of a baby born in a stable because there was no room in the inn; of visits from shepherds directed by angels and wise men directed by a star. Luke has plenty of other stories concerning the birth of John the Baptist, a cousin of Jesus, but none of these things with their signs and wonders need trouble us further.

The story of Herod's wrath (in Matthew 2:16–18) is also probably no more than a story with no historical basis in fact. But if it is true, one wonders at the kind of God who can cause or allow such misery. These first innocent deaths resulting from the birth of Jesus are a sign of things to come. How many thousands have suffered and died since because of the religion that bears his name?

Much is made (particularly in Matthew's gospel) of the claim that Jesus is the fulfilment of Old Testament prophecy. He is claimed to be the Jewish Messiah, a king in the line of David (which is a nonsense if Joseph was not his real father). The Jewish Messiah was a political saviour from foreign oppression. It is claimed that Jesus came to save from slavery to sin rather than as a political saviour. His kingdom is not a political kingdom. He establishes his rule in people's hearts and minds and creates a kingdom not of this world.

Apart from those who became Christians, the Jews never accepted his claim to Messiahship. For most of us all of this is a foreign language and completely incomprehensible. It was only when I ceased to be a Christian that I realised just how foreign such language has become. None of these concepts has any meaning or credence anymore.

It is also in the chapters of Luke and Matthew that we find the crude beginnings of Christian incarnation theology. Here are the claims that Jesus was not conceived in the normal way but through the Holy Spirit.

This leads to the further claim that in human terms Mary was still a virgin when Jesus was born. And that has led the Catholic church on into further realms of fantasy with its doctrines of the perpetual virginity of a woman who is supposed by the New Testament to have mothered a large family. And this is followed by the doctrine of the blessed assumption which carries Mary, unspoiled by death, direct into heaven. The best that can be said of that is that it *is* a blessed assumption.

There is plenty of evidence in the New Testament that most people regarded Joseph as the natural father of Jesus, who was the first child in a large family. His brothers are named, but with the typical attitudes of the time his sisters remain anonymous.

Over time, the doctrine of the virgin birth has been used to almost deify the mother of Jesus so that one sometimes has the impression that she is more important to Catholic Christians than any of the persons of the trinity. I remember one Irish priest actually saying that the trinity comprised the Father, the Son and the Virgin Mary!

Its original purpose was to claim that Jesus was more than just another human being. He was the fulfilment of one more (mis-understood) Old Testament prophecy which early Christians believed claimed that a virgin would conceive and have a child.

The claim that Jesus is more than just another human being reaches its fullest exposition in the gospels in chapter one of John's Gospel. John's gospel is sometimes called 'the spiritual gospel'. Certainly there is nothing crude about the theology we find here. *It is not too much to say that our whole attitude to Jesus hangs finally on our acceptance or rejection of the teachings of this chapter.*

189

This is also the gospel in which Jesus is represented as making a whole series of major claims for himself – claims which set him apart from the rest of us: the famous claims beginning 'I am the. . .' These culminate in the claim, 'I am the resurrection and I am life.'

In chapter 1:1–18 Jesus 'comes from above.' He was alive with God before John the Baptist was born ('he was before me').

These ideas are also to be found in the letters to the Philippians and the Colossians, so they were spreading throughout the Christian community. They are not solely the ideas of John, but in John they have their most complete early expression.

John links the Genesis account of creation by the Word of God with the Greek Pythagorean-Platonic philosophical concept of the logos, the Word. These Greeks saw the Word as the unifying principle behind the universe, that which sustains and holds the universe together. Having linked these two concepts, John goes on to join the two with the incarnation of Jesus.

The gospel claims that Jesus is the Word and that the Word is God. It claims that as God, Jesus was responsible for the creation of the world ('without him was not anything made that was made').

'. . .and the Word became flesh and dwelt among us.' The divine Jesus became a man. As man, Jesus has made God known to us.

It is a breathtaking proposition and has always been an inspiration to Christian philosophers and theologians but is it true? The Genesis account of creation on which part of it is based, is certainly not true. Nevertheless, the idea of some sort of creator is a hypothesis that is not necessarily destroyed by evolutionary theory.

It must also be said that the idea of a unifying principle behind the universe (some great ultimate Mind) is another hypothesis that has always commended itself to many people.

The idea that this Ultimate Mind, this Creative Principle, could become a man really is intellectually exciting in the same way as a great symphony heard for the first time is overwhelming in its power. It led Christians to develop their idea of Jesus as both Perfect God and Perfect Man. But see what follows from this:

If he is God he is beyond criticism – though a Job or an Esdras or even a Leslie might challenge that statement. If he is

190

PERFECT man he is also beyond criticism, but is he really a man? Are humans not, by their very nature, imperfect? Doesn't the idea of perfection actually take away something of the humanity of Jesus?

It certainly undermines the critical faculties of Christians. They find it extraordinarily difficult to say or to listen to anything that is in any way critical of Jesus. For many years after I left Christianity I shared that difficulty. If you believe in Jesus as God, there is no escaping that problem. But if, in spite of the overwhelming force of the intellectual and philosophical ideas of incarnation theology, you finally reject both the idea of Jesus as God, and the idea of his perfection, then you can finally examine him simply as another human being.

That will transform your approach to him.

And yet, if you are an ex-Christian, as I am, you will still have lurking hesitations and it will still bring you pain whenever you criticise the man you have worshipped. There is no easy way past this problem. My own way past may be of help to others:

We do not actually know Jesus! All we have are pictures painted by his disciples. We have no means of knowing how far those pictures are accurate. We have no means of knowing how true the gospels are. When we left my school a little record of our schooldays appeared in the school magazine. I read my paragraph eagerly, only to be disappointed at inaccuracies and things that were left out which seemed important to me. If Jesus could read the gospels how appalled would he be at the image of him found there?

When I criticise 'Jesus' in the pages ahead, as I shall do, it is important to recognise that I am not actually criticising Jesus himself. I've no idea how far he deserves my criticisms. What I am criticising is the portrait or image of Jesus handed down by his followers. As we shall see, that is an image that is thoroughly flawed. Whether as a man or as a teacher and healer, the 'Jesus' shown to us, for all his qualities which are many, leaves a great deal to be desired. I have found it difficult to write these things but I feel that they NEED to be written.

For me Jesus was just another human being, as fallible as the rest of us. It looks as though he was a man of some grace or charm and he clearly had qualities which made people want to follow him. He is not the only man to have had that kind of quality.

191

He seems to have been a quite exceptional teacher, and he believed that his teaching was 'the Truth'. We shall look at his teaching as we travel on through the gospels. As it has come down to us, much of it seems irrelevant and some of it plain wrong. How far he has a continuing value remains to be seen.

There is only one story in the gospels of his childhood. There are others which were known in the early church but the only New Testament story is in Luke 2:41–52. It describes an occasion when Jesus was about twelve, when his mother and father (note the mention of his father) went to Jerusalem. They were part of a larger group from their village and when it was time to go home, Jesus was left behind in Jerusalem.

It took his parents THREE DAYS to find him in the Temple. Like any other twelve year old boy, Jesus was surprised at their anxiety and that they were so thick that they didn't know where to look for him. A twelve year old boy? Of course he would be in the temple. Where else?

I heard recently of a little boy whose parents were sunbathing on Weymouth beach. The little boy wandered off as children do and ended up in the kiosk for lost children. Finally his frantic parents found him and he said to them, 'Where have you been?'

They were the ones who were lost, not him.

I remember a vicar's wife commenting, 'If I had been his mother I'd have given him a good hiding.' We are not allowed to these days – but I suspect that many of us have a good deal of sympathy with that vicar's wife's point of view.

John the Baptist and the Temptations of Jesus

From Jesus aged about twelve we jump to a time when he must have been about thirty.

His cousin John the Baptist came, like an Old Testament Jewish prophet, calling the people to repent of their sin and to be washed in the Jordan as a symbol of their cleansing. An ascetic whom some have linked with the Essenes (the desert community from whom the Dead Sea scrolls have come to us), his primary purpose according to the New Testament was to prepare the way for Jesus.

Yet his followers formed a sect which lasted hundreds of years. Like all the prophets, his message was primarily ethical. Stripped of its religion it can be summed up as follows:

Be generous, be honest, be peaceable, be fair, be content (with your wages), and be moral. (Luke 3:10–14)

The last of these was addressed to Herod the tetrarch and led to imprisonment and execution.

Compared with the ten commandments of the Old Testament which are largely negative, these are all positive. They mark a very real advance.

One of those who came to be baptised by John in the Jordan was Jesus. After his baptism he went away into 'the wilderness' to prepare himself for his own ministry. The story is that he was 'tempted by the devil'. Modern commentators, less graphically, see him considering his options. What sort of ministry was he to engage in?

Considering the number of miracles he is supposed to have performed, it is significant that one of the options he discarded was the option of becoming a wonder worker.

The only value these temptations could have for non-religious people is as a kind of parable. We all need to find time to take stock of our lives every so often. We need to look at our hopes and ambitions with a critical eye, and sometimes we need to change direction.

At a time of crisis in my own life, my old headmaster wrote to me encouraging me to press on with a life he depicted as a 440 yards race over hurdles. It was a good image of life, but I had to write back to him to say that my problem was that I had been running in the wrong race. I needed to start again.

Sometimes we need to take time out to look at where we are and where we are going.

j

Ministry

Luke 4:1–6:16

According to Luke's gospel, one of the first places Jesus went to when he began his ministry was his home town of Nazareth. Although he seems to have gone out of his way to irritate his hearers, his message hardly seems enough to have made the people of Nazareth want to kill him. I wonder why they were so hostile.

Had he always been too big for his boots? Had he always thought himself a cut above the rest and a bit special? To them he was simply 'Joseph's son' which is surely significant. If there were any doubts about his paternity they would have been known in Nazareth.

The same comment applies to the two (contradictory) genealogies in Matthew 1 and Luke 3. If Joseph was not the father of Jesus, neither of them has any relevance at all.

These chapters (Luke 4:1–6:16) show Jesus healing, teaching, claiming the divine authority to forgive sin, and claiming authority over sabbath tradition. People certainly seem to have been impressed by the authoritative way in which he taught.

It is difficult to know what credence to give to the stories. It looks as though he was a fairly successful faith healer (of which more later). I suspect that most of us would welcome his insistence that human need comes before rules and regulations. But there is nothing specific here that need detain us.

The Teachings of Jesus

Matthew 5–8 – *The Sermon on the Mount*

In Luke's gospel much of the same material is to be found in the 'Sermon on the Plain' – Luke 6:17–49.

Neither is an actual sermon. These are simply collections of some of the teachings of Jesus and can be treated together. They begin with the beatitudes. Matthew's version is one of the most famous passages in the New Testament.

If ever there was a case of people being seduced by language it is here. I suspect that the seduction of language has been, and still is, one of the most powerful weapons religion has in its attempt to keep its adherents and to win new ones.

I remember listening to a Hindu brahmin chanting from the Upanishads each morning. It was hypnotic. I have also heard Buddhist chants of great beauty, though they meant nothing to me. I'm told that the Quran recited in Arabic has the same kind of power, although I don't find it very impressive in English.

During the second half of the 20th century the churches worked very hard at modernising the language of their liturgies and of their Bible translations, and Catholicism switched from Latin to the vernacular.

I doubt if their modernising has attracted anyone to the churches, but it has certainly offended many who already belonged.

Seduced by the melodies of old language and comforted by teachings hidden behind incomprehensibility, people felt secure and comfortable. Now that everything is laid bare and expressed in language that often has no life or colour – no poetry or (to use a religious word) soul, both the comfort and the inspiration are gone.

The Beatitudes

The beatitudes at the beginning of Matthew's sermon on the mount read beautifully but how much do they actually mean? In Luke's version, which is more primitive and probably more accurate, the beatitudes are a series of blessings on the poor and hungry and woes to the rich. But it is all words and promises. There is no programme for change or reform. And how real are the promises? Let us look at verses 4 and 5 in Matthew chapter 5:

4 – Blessed are those who mourn, for they shall be comforted.'

When a Christian dies a funeral is arranged and usually conducted by a minister or priest who knew the person who died. Sometimes it will be a good, thoughtful funeral and there will be references to the Christian hope of heaven. For the other Christians present that will be a source of comfort.

After the funeral the Christian community will help comfort

the bereaved by surrounding them with their support and love. Those who mourn will be comforted. Sadly, even for Christians it is not always like that. And for the majority of the population in this 'mainly Christian' country (to quote the politicians), it will certainly not be like that. The funeral will often be perfunctory and conducted by a complete stranger who will take his fee and go home. If the bereaved are comforted at all, it will be by their own family and friends.

Or something worse will befall them. The cleric will regard the funeral as an evangelical opportunity, a chance to bully emotionally disturbed people into the kingdom of heaven.

Thankfully there are now alternatives. More and more people are taking matters into their own hands, creating their own ceremonies and finding their own comfort. And where people lack the confidence to do that, they are turning to organisations like the British Humanist Association whose celebrants will help them to create a funeral that is a genuinely satisfying send off, a celebration of a life rather than an offering of a hope that (being based on faith) could turn out to be nothing at all.

Yes, those Christians who mourn may be comforted, but what if their comfort is illusory? Then it will be those who have found a comfort within the framework of this life who will have found the most genuine comfort.

5:5 – 'Blessed are the meek, for they shall inherit the earth.'

Whatever Jesus may say, it is normally the rich and powerful who inherit the earth. They may pay a few of the meek to tend it, but they will lock the rest out.

Fortunately the meek have been learning to fight back through organisations like the Ramblers' Association or those like the National Trust, the Woodland Trust, the RSPB and so on which hold land all of us may enjoy, not to mention the National Parks. The meek are beginning to inherit by foregoing their meekness.

But Jesus has a point: there is a sense in which it is those who take time to appreciate the world about them who really inherit the earth – and this has nothing to do with money or power. I have tried to express this in some of my poems.

But of course, this doesn't necessarily have anything to do with meekness either. However, it could be argued that the earth's inheritors are more likely to be non-Christians in the countryside than Christians spending their spare time indoors in their churches.

On the whole the New Testament shows little interest in the natural world and there were then too few humans littering the earth for conservation or environmental issues to have surfaced – even though in parts of Greece and Italy (and even Dartmoor) the countryside was being despoiled and rendered sterile by misuse and overuse.

As the beatitudes continue they commend those who 'hunger and thirst for righteousness', the merciful, the pure in heart and the peacemakers. (vvs. 6–9)

If we ignore the promises attached to each blessing, we can agree: all such people are commendable. And it is perhaps better to suffer for 'righteousness' than to surrender our ideals and principles. But goodness, decency, high moral standards and so on are all to be chosen for their own sake. And this the New Testament consistently forgets. It always feels that rewards must be offered.

It also commonly pronounces judgement on those who do not choose what is thought to be the right path. So Luke follows his beatitudes with a series of 'woes'. (6:24–27) Neither the rewards nor the woes will cut much ice with those who have no belief in gods.

Salt and Light

And so we turn to the rest of the teaching in the 'Sermon'. In Matthew 5:13–16 Jesus urges his followers: 'Let your light so shine before men, that they may see your good works and give glory to your Father who is in heaven.'

He is right of course. 'The proof of the pudding is in the eating.' The test of moral teaching lies in the quality of those who accept it.

No one would deny that there are many fine people who are Christians. Would anyone deny that there are just as many who are not?

And what of the generality of Christians? The New Testament letters demonstrate very clearly that they were no different from any other societies of people squabbling, arguing, striving for their little bit of importance. And anybody with any experience of church communities today will have found that nothing has changed. 'Salt of the earth'? 'Light of the world'? Sadly, no.

Christianity has its share of special people, but no more than its share. They are to be found in all walks of life, of all religions and of none. Wherever people take life seriously enough to try to work out the best way to live, and the noblest ideals to strive after, there you will find the salt and the light. Religion has nothing to do with it.

Law

The rest of chapter 5 has to do with the Jewish law and the attitude of Jesus to it. The Jews believed that it came from God and was therefore binding. Jesus is anxious to demonstrate that he is an upholder of the law. No one took the law more seriously than the Pharisees, but Jesus claims to take it even more seriously than they do. We are given a number of examples:

21–26: The law said, 'You shall not kill' but Jesus goes further. He takes exception to anger and speaks of the importance of settling disputes without going to law.

Ours seems to be a society full of anger and hostility. Instead of the current sourness and hot temper, we need to learn patience and understanding; instead of hostility and suspicion, friendliness; and instead of insults and denigration, the recognition of every human being's worth.

Although he is supposed to be perfect, Jesus himself failed to match up to these standards on occasion. But they are standards anyone can aim at and life would be infinitely better for their achievement or even for the attempt.

27–32: The law said, 'You shall not commit adultery.' Jesus uses it to talk about 'lust' and divorce.

One or two Christians have taken the teaching literally with terrible personal results. Most Christians reject the letter of the teaching and they are right to do so. It is sexist. But worse than that, it shows no understanding of the nature of the marriage relationship.

The commitment of two people to one another in marriage is a unique commitment. It makes considerable demands and offers considerable rewards. There are all sorts of reasons why the commitment can prove too much for people to sustain it. 'Unchastity' is only one of them, and is probably always only a part of a greater malaise.

The ideal of marriage between two persons for life is a fine one and those who manage it, creating a relationship of real depth and strength, are to be congratulated.

Many of us, setting out with the best of intentions, do not manage it. When we fail, the last thing we need is condemnation and judgement. We are quite capable of condemning ourselves without any help from other people. The breakdown of marriage is not always traumatic, but it can be one of the most devastating experiences in life.

Those who go through it need friendship, support and help as they discover that their world has not completely come to an end. It is possible – it is ALWAYS possible to begin again whether in a new relationship or not.

Sadly, the Christian church has never been able to accept these things. It has always done a great deal to make things worse for people whose marriages have fallen apart, and to hinder the so-called 'guilty partner' in his or her attempts to start life again. The very phrase 'the guilty partner' shows how inadequate Christian thinking about marriage has been. (Officially, the Church of England has now dropped it.)

33–37: The law said, 'You shall not swear falsely.' The Quakers have suffered considerably for taking this teaching literally and for refusing to swear on the Bible in courts of law. In doing so, they and others have won for those who do not believe in the Bible, the right to affirm their human commitment to the truth regardless of religion.

5:38–48 (cf: Luke 6:27–36): According to Jesus the old Jewish law said: 'An eye for an eye, and a tooth for a tooth.' 'You shall love your neighbour, and hate your enemy.'

Frankly, that is not law. It is human nature. The teaching of Jesus asks us to conquer human nature and to instal a different set of rules. There is constant debate in Christian circles about how far we should go in following him. How realistic is he? Is there any sense in asking people to 'be perfect'?

I'm not sure that there is. I have always felt that the most we can ask of people is that they should do their best. But we do need to set our targets high. And in this sense I believe that Jesus is right.

There are times when it is not enough to let human nature be our guide. Civilisation requires the refinement of human nature in all sorts of ways, and never more than in our relationships with other people.

So I believe that we should take Jesus seriously when he says:

> 'Love your enemies, do good to those who hate you, bless those who curse you, pray for those who abuse you. To him who strikes you on the cheek, offer the other also.'

It is sometimes suggested that Jesus is exaggerating for effect; that all that he means is that it is better to endure a wrong than to go about seeking revenge. He believes that injustice should be met with generosity and kindness; hostility and enmity with love and concern.

If that is a fair extract of the substance of the teaching of Jesus, it is worth taking seriously. Mahatma Ghandi and President Mandela are perhaps the best 20th century evidence that he may well be right.

To 'love our enemies' may be unrealistic. But it is not unrealistic to try to live in such a way that we hurt nobody and seek the well-being of all those on whom our lives impinge (whether we like them or not).

Within these verses Jesus also mentions giving and lending (verse 42):

> 'Give to him who begs from you and do not refuse him who would borrow from you.'

When I was a Christian I tried to follow this teaching – to give to everyone who begged from me. The result was that every tramp told his colleagues I was a soft touch. Then, instead of giving cash, I began offering them a cup of tea. They stopped coming.

Giving to beggars and lending to borrowers can often do more harm than good. It fails to go to the root of the problem and it provides no genuine help in solving the problem. Unless we are willing to get personally involved at a deeper level, it is better to give to those who do – to those organisations committed to correcting the fault lines in our society and ensuring that no one need beg; and that people in financial trouble should be shown a permanent way out.

Show

Matthew chapter 6 makes pretty good reading. It is mostly concerned with religious matters. Jesus tells people not to parade their virtue or their generosity.

But throughout the sermon on the mount there is a constant stress on the rewards available to people who follow his teaching. As a result this has become a constant criticism of mine. Modesty, generosity, these qualities need no reward. There is no virtue in virtue which has its mind set on rewards.

Worry

Much of Matthew chapter six is about the folly of worry and about concentrating on the things that really matter in life.

'Do not lay up for yourselves treasures upon earth for where your treasure is, there will your heart be also.' (19–21)

There is a necessary and wise prudence in the handling of our affairs (which is something I have never mastered) but it is not of this that Jesus is talking. He is talking about miserliness. The novel *Silas Marner* is a perfect illustration of the teaching of Jesus here.

Silas Marner's life was dominated by the wealth he was hoarding until a baby girl (a foundling) arrived on his doorstep and transformed his life.

Jesus claims that we need to consider the question, 'What are the things that really matter? What is treasure?' When we can see things straight and true, then we can spend our energies usefully. (verses 22–24)

Verses 25–33 are extremely popular. Their general message is that we should not worry about food, drink and clothing. Instead we should seek God's kingdom and his righteousness.

Unfortunately these are precisely the things that most of us *have to worry about* whether we like it or no. Jesus lived off the generosity of his followers while his father and/or his brothers worked at the carpenter's trade to feed, clothe and house his mother and the family. His clergy do the same, safe and secure in jobs for life.

The rest of us have to find work and stay in work in order to make enough money for food, drink, clothing and housing. There is no escaping this. Curiously enough, the examples Jesus chose demonstrate very clearly just how wrong he was.

The 'birds of the air' may not sow or reap, but they have to work extremely hard building their nests and finding food for themselves and their young. Even the 'lilies of the field' have to push down roots and search for nourishment to enable them to grow and to produce flowers to attract insects to ensure reproduction.

For most of us life is hard and it is no use pretending otherwise. Where Jesus is right however, is in pointing out that anxiety and worry are of themselves quite fruitless. They achieve nothing. In fact they are worse than that: they are counter-productive. They rob us of sleep, sap our energy, and make us incapable of coping. Nothing is more debilitating.

Worry/anxiety: these are things we need to deal with promptly. We need to sit down quietly (sometimes with someone else, sometimes with expert help) and work our way through the cause of our anxiety until we find its remedy.

We also need to distinguish between necessary worries and unnecessary. Jesus was right when he said, 'Do not be anxious about tomorrow, for tomorrow will be anxious for itself. Let the day's own trouble be sufficient for the day.' (v. 34)

Over my grandfather's desk was the motto:

> 'Yesterday is dead, forget it.
> Tomorrow never comes, don't worry.
> Today is here, use it.'

If we do focus on the present, we shall almost always find that we can deal with it and often find satisfaction and fulfilment in doing so.

The Golden Rule

Matthew 7, verses 7–12 begins with one of the most famous sentences in the teaching of Jesus and ends with a version of the golden rule.

I do not believe that it is true that if you 'Ask, it will be given you; seek, and you will find; knock, and it will be opened to you.'

But it is certainly true that if you don't ask, seek, or knock, very little will be given or opened to you.

There are many versions of the golden rule beginning (to the best of my knowledge) with Confucius. There are several in the New Testament. It is one of the most popular moral teachings of all: 'Do as you would be done by.'

It's not bad as a rule of thumb but it doesn't bear too much scrutiny. Suppose other people don't want to be treated as we ourselves wish to be treated. What then?

Jesus ends the sermon on the mount with a parable which claims that his teaching makes people strong. (vvs. 24–29) If that claim is true, then his teaching is worth our study whatever our religious or non-religious beliefs may be.

Our examination of the sermon on the mount would seem to suggest that he does deserve to be regarded as one of the great teachers of the ancient world with a lot to say that is as valid today as it ever was.

But he was not infallible. He was a man with the same kind of limitations and blind spots that we all have. He was a child both of his own age and of his Jewish environment. If we remember these things we shall make the best possible use of his teaching for today. But we shall have to be selective. This is never more clear than when we consider his teaching about judgement.

Judgement

Matthew chapter 7 has a great deal in it about judgement. In point of fact there are complete contradictions in the messages about judgement.

Verses 13–23 concern the judgement of God. If anyone thinks of Jesus as 'gentle Jesus meek and mild' he should read these verses and think again. They talk of the 'many' who are heading for exclusion from the kingdom of God and for destruction.

This unpleasant and judgemental side of the teaching of Jesus is either ignored or disowned by many Christians. We shall see that it is a complete contradiction of some of his best and loveliest teaching.

But there are other Christians who love this sort of thing. They consign people like me to 'the outer darkness where men will weep and gnash their teeth' or to 'the fire' very happily.

But what is an atheist to think. On the one hand Jesus consigns him to some sort of hell and punishment. On the other hand he says (Matthew 7:1–5), 'Judge not, that you be not judged.'

There are few things that Jesus said which are more important than this, and there are few parts of his teaching more comprehensively ignored both within and outside the church.

To illustrate this sentence there is a story which almost failed to find its way into the New Testament. There are plenty of such stories which did not find their way in, and if you read them you can understand why. But this one did squeeze in. It didn't originally belong to any of the four gospels but it is usually placed at John 7:53 to 8:11. It is a little gem.

It tells the story of a woman caught in the act of adultery. The normal punishment (for a woman, not a man) was stoning to death. But she was brought to Jesus by the authorities in the hope that he would say something which would bring him into conflict with the Jewish law, and so into disrepute.

Faced with the woman he said, 'Let him who is without sin among you be the first to throw a stone at her.'

Then he looked down and doodled in the sand. One by one they all slipped quietly away, leaving him alone with the woman.

'Has no one condemned you? . . . Neither do I . . . go, and do not sin again.'

Whatever we make of the contradictions in the teaching of Jesus about judgement, this little story deserves to be imprinted on everyone's mind: we are all in glass houses and shouldn't throw stones. 'Judge not.'

Parables and other teachings
from Luke chapters 10-18 and Matthew 18:1–20:16

Whatever else is said about Jesus, he was certainly a very gifted teacher.

He impressed people by the authority with which he taught. They felt that he knew what he was talking about. He wasn't constantly referring to other authorities as if his teaching needed bolstering from others.

He was a master of the memorable phrase or sentence. Many of the things he said are in everyday usage still, even with people who have never had any close contact with his teaching: 'turn the other check'; 'a kingdom divided against itself cannot stand'; 'he who lives by the sword shall die by the sword'; 'can the blind lead the blind? Shall they not both fall into the ditch.' – and so on. Those were jotted down without even thinking about it.

But perhaps the part of teaching for which Jesus is most famous is for his parables. We came across a few of them earlier, but I ignored them because they were all parables about the kingdom of God and seemed to me to have no permanent relevance. But there are some now which do have that kind of relevance and are worth anybody's time, Christian or non-Christian.

Parables are simple, memorable stories which have the same kind of quality as poetry. By this I mean that they have several layers of meaning. Apparently simple, they have hidden depths. They have the capacity to keep bobbing up in the mind and to keep prodding us to think about moral issues. It is perhaps in his parables that we see the teaching of Jesus at its best and for many of them we need to turn to Luke's gospel.

In Luke chapter 10:25–37 one of the best of them (and one of the best known) is told in answer to the question 'Who is my neighbour?'

I say that it is one of the best known, but how well is it known nowadays? One of my brothers taught Latin. He once put this parable of the good Samaritan on the board in Latin for the last class of the day. He told his fifth formers to translate it until they recognised it. When they recognised it, they could go home early.

No one went home early.

The parable of the good Samaritan *is* worth knowing. It has all the qualities I referred to earlier.

In Luke 11:24–26 there is another tiny parable which expresses an important psychological truth. It teaches us that it is no use helping people to find freedom from their addictions unless we can find genuine alternatives to make good what they have lost. The same goes for people reaching retirement age: they need to find ways to compensate for the loss of their place in society and the activity that went with it.

There are more parables in chapter 12. In verses 13–34 Jesus illustrates the fact that 'a man's life does not consist in the abundance of his possessions.' In 12:35–48 another parable is all about privilege and responsibility: 'to whom much is given, of him will much be required.'

In Luke chapter 15 and in Matthew 18 verses 12–14 there are stories about things lost and found; and about the joy there is when something or someone valued is recovered. They all illustrate what I had to say about parables at the beginning of this chapter.

Spend time thinking about the parables of the lost sheep, the coin lost from a wedding headdress, and the lost son. They contain many lessons other than the obvious ones. I don't propose to try to spell them out. Read the stories for yourselves and draw your own conclusions. It is teaching such as this and teaching such as that found in the parable of the good Samaritan, which gives Jesus a permanent value.

Set all the supernatural stuff on one side; all the talk of heaven and hell and judgement; all the religious teaching about sin and salvation; all the tales of miracles; and there is a body of teaching of permanent value and validity. This is the pure gold of which I have spoken and it is worth sifting out.

I have skimmed over Luke 13 and 14. There is teaching in those chapters and more in chapters 16–18. Chapter 16:1–9 is often misunderstood or just not understood. Jesus commends astuteness, not dishonesty but this is not one of his wiser choices of subject. The verses which follow the story make his message clear:

'He who is faithful in a very little is faithful also in much; and he who is dishonest in a very little is dishonest also in much.'

I don't know that Jesus is *altogether* right. There must be plenty of people who are good servants of their employers and who are basically thoroughly honest, yet they have the odd pen or whatever from their place of work in their homes.

Nor is Jesus right when he says that 'no man can serve two masters for either he will hate the one and love the other, or he will be devoted to the one and despise the other.' (Luke 16:13)

He shows little understanding of a normal relationship between employer and employee. It is rare for us to be devoted to our employers but we don't normally hate them either. We are just glad to be employed and to be earning money. If Jesus had had to earn his own living he might have discovered that many of us *have* to 'serve two' or more 'masters' in order to make ends meet.

Real life is rather different from his understanding of it.

That is perhaps a good moment to turn back to Matthew's gospel. I have already referred to a few verses in chapter 18. Now I want to focus on the rest of that chapter and beyond.

Matthew 18:1–14 begins with a kind of acted parable which demonstrates Jesus' respect for children and his insistence that they be treated properly and not led astray. (See also 19:13–15) He tells his followers to be child-like – innocent and humble. It is a nice image of children, although it seems to me that if Jesus had been a parent he might have painted children in rather different colours. They don't stay innocent very long and most of them are anything but humble – cocky little beggars.

But there are qualities which children have which adults lose at their peril. Children have qualities of eagerness, openness to new knowledge and understanding, the capacity to trust, enthusiasm and zest for life. Without these things we become very dull.

Jesus also pronounces woes on those who lead children (or adults) astray. Modern hostility to paedophiles suggests that most of us share his feelings without sharing his belief in 'the eternal hell of fire', or perhaps believing that such a punishment would be appropriate.

It is no use just condemning or pronouncing woes. A paedophile is sick. What he does may be evil but the person himself is sick. The word 'evil' throws out the wrong signals. I write this just after a gifted music teacher has committed suicide following the discovery of pornographic literature in his possession. Appreciated by his colleagues for his talents and qualities, he would have been condemned by many and hounded too. He was clearly too sensitive a man to face that.

It is high time that we learned that it is more important to understand than to condemn. That may be unpopular teaching following a home secretary whose sole solution to unsocial behaviour was to lock people up for as long as possible and forget all about them. But unpopular or no, I believe it to be true.

Locking people up and scapegoating solves nothing. We need to work hard to get to the roots of social malaise and of the sicknesses inflicted by society. There is a lot of truth in the old saying 'to understand all is to forgive all', even if it is not always the whole truth.

Understanding can be the first step towards reclamation and the restoration of self-respect in people who have found that they can after all make a positive contribution to life and to the society they have damaged. It will not always be possible. But it is worth the effort of trying. What else are those parables about the lost being found all about?

In Matthew 18:15–20 we find Jesus spelling out a way in which his followers should attempt to deal with disputes. Although his advice to try to deal with things personally and carefully may be very wise, it is strange to find this 'friend of tax collectors and sinners' depicting tax collectors as beyond the pale:

> 'If he refuses to listen . . . let him be to you as a Gentile and a tax collector.' (v. 17)

Nor is there any hint of criticism of that Jewish attitude to non-Jews. This is far from the only hint in the gospels that Jesus was not as tolerant or all-embracing as he is portrayed. A number of times we find him displaying what was then a typically Jewish disdain for people of other races. Contrast this with his teaching in verses 21–35 where we find him inviting his disciples to show quite exceptional levels of forgiveness and where there is another superb parable, this one about forgiveness and punishment.

Chapter 19 of Matthew begins with another section about divorce. Jesus seems exceptionally strict and has left the whole Christian church in a hopeless muddle on this and related subjects, and its practices make not an atom of sense. Where, for instance, is the sense in a situation when, after a couple have been married in a registry office, the church says in effect: 'God does not approve of nor recognise this marriage. According to the Bible it is adultery which is why the marriage could not take place in church.'

Then in the next breath the church says, 'Please come to the church for a service of blessing and thanksgiving.' At best, that is a perfect example of the kind of confusion and muddle that exists in Christian thinking. It is an expression of the desperation of those who need to hang on to anyone who shows an interest in entering a church – even if only once.

At worst this kind of nonsense is hypocritical. It is no wonder that honest, straightforward people turn from the churches in disgust. In Luke chapter 12 Jesus condemned hypocrisy.

It is precisely because people do not wish to be hypocritical that they are turning in droves to organisations like the British Humanist Association for things like marriage or funeral ceremonies which have nothing to do with religion. It used to be the norm for people to go to church for these things even if they never set foot in a church otherwise. That is not the case any more. Honesty demands that people with no religious belief should make non-religious arrangements for themselves.

And as more and more people choose the honest path, it becomes increasingly important that the privileges of religion should be removed and that hindrances to non-religious people should also be removed. There is still far too much discrimination in favour of the Christian community and against both non-believers and also people of other religions.

People in authority constantly defer to the churches in matters of morality as if no one else thought about these things seriously. They would do well to remember that it was Jesus himself who said, 'Why do you not judge *for yourselves* what is right?' (Luke 12:57)

This is not to say that we cannot learn from the New Testament or from other religious and ethical sources. In Matthew 19:16–30 there is an important story about virtue and virtues.

As always in the New Testament virtue is placed in the context of rewards. Virtue never seems to be urged for its own sake. Here it is regarded as a matter of obeying such laws as 'you shall not kill, commit adultery . . . steal . . . bear false witness. Honour your father and mother' and 'you shall love your neighbour as yourself.'

Whilst no law can ever be regarded as absolute, these old Jewish laws are a pretty good rule of thumb start. But virtue is also seen as a matter of giving up everything to follow Jesus. Few Christians seem to take this literally – Francis of Assisi perhaps.

I am, of necessity, rushing over a lot of ground. Some of it is pretty barren and deserves such cavalier treatment. Matthew 20:1–19 does not fall into that category. It is an unpopular parable well worth study. Are our sympathies with the generous employer or with the workers who want 'justice', or both? The parable is a real challenge.

Facing both ways: Matthew chapters 9–13 and 15:1–9

In these chapters we see something more of the attractiveness of Jesus and of his message.

In 9:10–13 we see him giving his time and energy to the social outcasts of his day. In 9:14–17 it is revealed that, unlike many social and religious reformers, he was no puritan.

The compassion of Jesus (9:36) is perhaps his most attractive feature of all. In 12:1–14 there are stories which show Jesus putting people first. Their needs are of far greater importance than the requirements of ritual law or ritual purity.

And Jesus' God is a god who cares for the whole of creation – even the sparrows (10:29).

His ministry was one of care for others. He sums it up in Matthew 11:5 and the closing words of chapter 11 give as lovely an invitation as you will find anywhere:

'Come to me all who labour and are heavy laden, and I will give you rest. Take my yoke upon you, and learn from me; for I am gentle and lowly in heart, and you will find rest for your souls. For my yoke is easy, and my burden is light.' (28–30)

They are lovely words but are they true? And is the picture painted above a complete picture?

I can only speak for myself. It was not until I left the Christian religion behind that I found myself sailing in calm waters free from emotional and intellectual turmoil.

Part of that turmoil is due to the inconsistencies and contradictions of the gospel picture of Jesus. For in these very chapters that show Jesus in such an attractive light we see another side which many Christians choose to ignore.

When it comes to damning people he can be pretty vicious (10:14–15) and his God is one who 'can destroy both soul and body in hell'. (10:28 & 13:40–42)

In 11:16–24 Jesus is again in judgemental mood. He seems to have no time for any except the few who follow him and swallow his message hook, line and sinker. Is there any significance I wonder in the fact that of the twelve he chose to be his closest followers, almost all were nonentities who disappeared without trace. (10:1–4)

There are no half measures with Jesus. My old college principal's favourite saying was, 'There's much to be said on both sides.' Jesus rejects that. There is no either/or for him. There is no middle ground, no room for compromise. Everything is either good or evil. (12:30ff)

And it is quite clear that to Jesus, most of his contemporaries belonged to the category of the evil who were damned for all eternity.

What is more, Jesus almost seems to revel in the fact that his gospel is divisive. This has always been one of the most dangerous and destructive features of the Christian gospel, not only as between Christian and non-Christian but also between Christian and Christian. (See also Luke 12:51–53)

It is a divisiveness which reaches right into the heart of the family. Jesus was the eldest son in a large family. He had at least four brothers and two sisters, maybe more. (So much for the perpetual virginity of his mother.) He sets these on one side and when they come to see him he treats them with considerable rudeness. He distances himself from them. They are of less importance than his followers who are, he says, his true family. (12:46–50)

There is no reference to his father here. Had Jesus and his father quarrelled so seriously that his father did not come? Or was he just too busy earning a living for them all? Or was he dead (as Christian tradition has it)? If he was dead, then the ministry of Jesus has allowed him to duck his own responsibility to his mother and family. No wonder he expects other people to put him before their own families.

And there are plenty who have used him as an excuse to do just that. They go on to enjoy the plaudits of their fellows for the 'sacrifice' they have made for Jesus.

Again and again Jesus puts discipleship to himself before the fulfilment of family responsibility. (10:21–22 & 34–37; & 34–37; and 12:46–50) Yet he still has the temerity (15:1–9) to go on to lecture the Pharisees on honouring their parents in accordance with the old Jewish law: 'Honour your father and mother.' (15:4)

From all that has gone before it is pretty clear that he is the last person to have the right to offer that particular message. Yet of all the old commandments it is one of the most important for every age and every generation; for people of all religions and of none. We honour Parents simply because they have given us life and done their best for us afterwards.

We show our respect in the care we give to them when we no longer need their care and they begin to need ours. And this 'law' should apply in most families.

There *are* parents who are so bad that they deserve nothing from their children but they are a minority and often still receive a love and a care that they do not deserve.

To sum up: these chapters give us contradictory pictures of Jesus and we have no idea which are accurate and which are not. If we look at the *total* picture which emerges in these chapters we find that Jesus appears facing both ways, like the Roman god Janus. He appears in much the same light as the god of the Jewish Old Testament and of the Moslem Quran. He is both compassionate and cruel; merciful and judging; infinitely loving and permanently hostile.

Even in my Christian days I could never understand those who accepted this series of contradictions with relish and reverenced such a Jesus or such a god.

I could only respect Jesus by joining those 'pick and mix' Christians who claim that he was compassionate, merciful and loving and that the rest of the picture must be rejected as the work of his inferior and inadequate disciples.

Is that too easy a let out? Those who knew Jesus handed on their understanding of him and their picture of his teaching to those who followed them. Within a couple of generations, possibly less, that picture was written down and it is the picture we have in the New Testament. Whether we like it or not, *they saw Jesus in the way they depicted him.* Have we any right to paint a new portrait using only those features we like?

And if we do, how accurate is *that* portrait? Christians find it almost impossible to criticise Jesus yet the evidence of the New Testament stares them in the face. *As the early Christians understood it* there is a great deal in the teaching of Jesus that is horrible; there is behaviour that is unworthy and behaviour that is stupid; and there are matters over which time has proved Jesus wrong.

Is it not better to honestly acknowledge all that, even if it does mean that Jesus can no longer be an object of worship, and to go on to recognise that the good in the life and teaching of Jesus is too precious to be thrown away with all the rest? Like gold prospectors, it is worth all the sifting if we come up with enough gold. And there is plenty of pure gold. So let us make the most of it.

Note:
There is a good deal in Matthew chapter 13 (as elsewhere) that I have omitted. vvs. 1–23 simply state what any teacher knows from sad experience. vvs. 24–52 contain parables of the kingdom of God of no interest – except for one verse with which we can all agree:

In verse 24 Jesus claims that goodness comes from within, from the heart. The mere obeying of laws does not produce goodness and all the law-making in the world will not make us good. We shall only become good people if that is what we long to be. This is the truth behind the words of Jesus:

'Seek first God's kingdom and his righteousness. . .'

When we want virtue or goodness above all else, our hunger for it will govern all our striving and all our behaviour and we shall become what we desire to be.

The teaching of John's Gospel

John's gospel is later than all the rest and different from all the rest. It is a gospel which makes immense claims for Jesus.

I have already referred to the claim that Jesus is the 'Word', the logos, the source of all being. He claimed (8.42). 'I proceeded and came forth from God' and (8:58) 'Before Abraham was, I am.'

In the opening chapter of the gospel it is also claimed that he is the light of the world who shines through the deepest darkness. Later (8:12) he claims for himself, 'I am the light of the world.'

Other claims are that he is God ('the Word was God'); the only Son of God; and 'the Lamb of God who takes away the sin of the world.' He is said to be filled with the Holy Spirit of God and he gives that Spirit to his disciples. He is the Jewish Messiah and the Christ – the Saviour of all men.

These claims mean a great deal to Christians. But unless they

213

can be justified, they mean precisely nothing to anybody else. When Christians make these claims they might as well be speaking a foreign language for they are speaking of things which have no meaning to the rest of us.

If you do not believe in gods and if you do not believe that this world (whatever its faults) is a place of darkness and sin, then none of these claims means anything at all.

Thus, although I am giving John's gospel a chapter of its own, Christians will feel that I am giving it scant justice, especially as I shall leave its 'signs' or miracles and also the crucifixion and resurrection to be dealt with later.

We can move straight to chapter three which demonstrates the divisiveness of the Christian gospel. This is something we shall see repeatedly in John. Its message rests on the assumption that the world and its people need saving from darkness and evil and it contains what is for Christians one of the most important statements of the whole New Testament – (John 3:16):

'For God so loved the world that he gave his only Son, that whoever believes in him should not perish but have eternal life.'

Christians will be appalled but the simple fact is that if you do not start where they start; if you do not accept their premiss; this statement has no meaning at all.

John chapter 4 contains a story which Christians love. Among other things it shows that Jesus was way ahead of his time. Not only was he prepared to speak to a Samaritan (to the Jew perhaps the worst kind of foreigner) but to a Samaritan *woman*. Wow! But then in verses 22ff he spoils it all and we see the imperfections and contradictions of the man. He is a Jew of his time:

'You Samaritans worship without knowing what you worship, while we worship what we know. It is from the Jews that salvation comes.'

How arrogant and how racist. It is no wonder that Christians tend only to concentrate on verses 23 and 4 which are much more palatable.

Chapter 5 needs no comment. It portrays Jesus as the judge and life-giver and contains some teaching about life after death.

In chapter 6 he claims 'I am the bread of life' 'for this is the will of my Father, that everyone who sees the Son and believes in him should have eternal life; and I will raise him up at the last day.'

Non-believers see no evidence that Christians have a quality of life different from or better than their own. We also live on the assumption that this life is all there is for us, though we recognise that we could be wrong. So, once again, the claim of Jesus is meaningless to us, as is what follows.

For his teaching continues with reference to the central Christian rite – the communion in which Christians eat bread representing his body and drink wine representing his blood. Christians themselves are divided as to the meaning of all this though they would probably all acknowledge that it is an act of faith-union with Jesus. I shall look at it more fully elsewhere.

Early in the gospel (and again much later) we are told that none of the disciples of Jesus will be lost. Now we are told that 'many of them no longer went about with him' and we are warned that Judas Iscariot will also leave. Christians would claim that these were not true disciples and that therefore they were not lost. It is a convenient claim which covers all of us who leave Christianity behind. But it seems strange that Jesus should choose as one of the innermost twelve a man who was to prove no true disciple.

As one who used to follow Jesus (and was called 'Judas' when I stopped), I can only say that I thought of myself as a genuine disciple until I stopped believing, and I'm sure Judas did too.

However, Jesus puts us both in our place. It is those who 'continue in my word,' who 'are truly my disciples,' and they 'will know the truth, and the truth will make' them 'free'. (8:31–32)

Perhaps that is why when Pontius Pilate (who was not a disciple) asks 'What is truth?' Jesus gives no answer.

It was when I ceased to be a disciple that I felt that I was beginning to discover the truth and *that* truth has given me my freedom: freedom from intellectual and emotional anguish and freedom to come to my own conclusions about the best way to live both as an individual and as a member of society.

I do recognise the truth in what Jesus says about being a slave to sin for I have been there and I am now free from that too, but it was not Jesus who set me free. (I hasten to add that 'sin' is not a word I use any more and many of the things I was taught to regard as 'sin' or 'evil' seem to me to be nothing of the sort.)

We have already seen that John's gospel contains many claims for Jesus. It is a gospel in which he also makes great claims for himself. Some of them are very popular in Christian circles.

In John 10 he says:

> 'I am the door' [the guardian or protector] 'of the sheep. . . I came that they may have life, and have it abundantly. I am the good shepherd. The good shepherd lays down his life for his sheep. . . My sheep hear my voice and I know them and they follow me; and I give them eternal life, and they shall never perish.'

It follows from all this that the followers of Jesus are like sheep crowding together for comfort and protection, for guidance and leadership (the middle eastern shepherd led his flocks where ours drive them). And this is an image Christians love.

When will they grow up and learn to stand on their own feet making their own judgements and choices? And when will they wake up to the limitations of this self-professed shepherd? He was a shepherd who had favourites. John's gospel is the one that reveals that there was one particular follower 'whom Jesus loved' above all others.

He was a shepherd with a flock of twelve who could not even manage to keep all twelve safe. He lost Judas, and there is not much evidence that he tried all that hard to keep him.

In John 14:6 Jesus makes another claim: 'I am the way, and the truth, and the life; no one comes to the Father, but by me.' And he goes on to say (14:9): 'He who has seen me has seen the Father.'

If that claim is true it is incredibly important for all of us. But is doesn't say much for the chances of non Christians.

These claims grow more comprehensive and more extreme (14:11–13):

> 'I am in the Father and the Father in me. . . He who believes in me will also do the works that I do; and greater works than these will he do, because I go to the Father. Whatever you ask in my name, I will do it. . . Ask whatever you will, and it shall be done for you.'
> (15:7)

These things are supposed to come to pass through the Holy Spirit who is spoken of in chapter 16. I shall look at this third person of the Christian trinity later.

Christians find it wonderful to believe that God dwells in their hearts and minds and works through them. It is a belief that enriches the best of them but it makes many other Christians arrogant, narrow, dogmatic and deaf to any ideas or teaching other than their own. Because God dwells in their hearts and not in ours, they have the truth and we don't. They are always right and we are always wrong. Dialogue, conversation, debate – these things are impossible.

And there are times when Jesus appears to share their arrogance: 'I am the vine. You (Christians) are the branches.' The rest are 'thrown into the fire and burned.' (John 15:1–6)

We must assume that Jesus believed these things, and Christians certainly believe them. To those who do not believe them they can be breathtakingly arrogant so that it is no wonder that the authorities finally came to the conclusion that they must get rid of him. If people believed his claims there could be public disorder (although it is in the other gospels that this becomes clear) which led Caiaphas to say, 'It is expedient for you that one man should die for the people, and that the whole nation should not perish.' (11:50)

I find myself constantly surprised as I re-read the gospels by things I had never noticed before. It is, I think, because I have come to them with a different outlook on life and from a different point of view. The verses that follow were very precious to me in my Christian days:

'As the Father has loved me, so have I loved you; abide in my love. If you keep my commandments you will abide in my love. . . This is my commandment, that you love one another as I have loved you. . . You are my friends if you do what I command you. No longer do I call you servants. . . but I have called you friends. This I command you, to love one another.' (from John 15:9–17)

If you think of Jesus as your God, there is no greater honour imaginable than to be loved by him – no greater wonder.

But if Jesus was just a man like the rest of us then the quality of the love offered has to be called in question. It is only available to his disciples; to those who obey his commands and continue to obey them. If you cease to obey, you cease to be loved. There is no love for anyone who chooses not to be a disciple.

That seems to me to be a very limited kind of love and although he called his disciples his 'friends' they were not friends

k

on level terms. They were not friends by any definition of friendship that I would recognise. They were only friends if they obeyed him.

Ordinary human friendship and love go far beyond anything here except for one statement which I have omitted:

> 'Greater love hath no man than this, that a man lay down his life for his friends.' (John 15:13)

When we read that verse we are intended to think of Jesus. He died by crucifixion and thought of his death as a death for others. He thought of it as some kind of sacrifice by which people were to be saved from sin; as a ransom paid to release people from slavery to sin.

Whatever the limitations of the love and friendship described by Jesus, in this verse he got it right. And however misguided we may feel he was, he also deserves to be honoured for his readiness to die for others. Even if his death was lunacy it was still noble. But the nobility of it is somewhat tempered by his conviction that as the Son of God death could not hold him. He would conquer death or be raised from death.

The height of friendship lies in those who have no such conviction and still give their lives to save their friends or to save people they don't even know.

When this verse comes to my mind I find that it is not Jesus I think of but rather people like Commander Oates of the Scott expedition to the south pole who committed suicide in an attempt to give his companions a chance of survival. Or those unsung heroes of the fire service or the RNLI who risk their lives again and again for the sake of others.

Jesus turns from this to speak of the way in which he and his disciples will be persecuted (15:18–27). He speaks of love and hate, black and white.

History has shown his disciples as persecutors more than persecuted. Perhaps more than any other group of people, they have shown a capacity for hatred in their dealings both with one another and with the rest of humanity.

In spite of this, most of us neither love nor hate him or his people. We simply get on with our lives without reference to him. Those of us who know a little about him may recognise his qualities (as well as his faults) and his lasting contribution to human life. That is not hatred. Neither is it love.

But most of life and most of morality is like that – not black and white but somewhere in between.

In chapter 17 Jesus prays for his disciples.

It is worth remembering at this point all that he has said about the power of prayer and all that he has said about disciples being able to 'ask anything of the Father' and 'he will give it'. (16:23)

That is a promise which Jesus has made time and again yet when he himself makes one simple request to his Father, his Father fails miserably to grant it:

> 'Father, keep them in my name . . . that they may be one, even as we are one.' And again he prayed 'for those who believe in me' [in the future] 'that they may all be one . . . I in them and thou in me, that they may become perfectly one. . .' (17:11 & 20–21)

As we look at things like the Catholic/Protestant divide in Northern Ireland and the complete disunity of the churches – thousands of them throughout the world – it is obvious that this prayer was worthless. Jesus had said, 'there shall be one flock, one shepherd' (John 10:16) but there are masses of them and they often have very little love for one another.

So when Jesus says 'by this all men will know that you are my disciples, if you have love for one another' (13:35) it makes us wonder if he has any disciples at all. And there is nothing new in all this. When we come to look at the New Testament letters we shall find that Christians have squabbled with each other from the very beginning.

So much for the 'spiritual' gospel.

Final Teachings

The teaching ministry of Jesus goes on virtually to the end of his life. During the period of his final confrontation with the authorities – a confrontation he was convinced would end in his death – he did his best to prepare his disciples for the time when they would have to stand on their own feet.

He promised them that they would be imbued with his own spirit to strengthen them. He gave them a ritual meal by which they would feel that their communion with him continued. And he continued to teach them.

In Matthew 20:20–28 and Luke 22:24–27 Jesus laid down the principle of service. And in John 13:1–11 he washed the feet of his disciples as an acted parable expressing that principle.

In response to the ambition of some and the jealousy of others he said (Matthew 20:26–28):

'Whoever would be great among you must be your servant, and whoever would be first among you must be your slave; even as the Son of man came not to be served but to serve.'

(I have deliberately cut the quotation short and omitted 'and to give his life as a ransom for many'. Taken here it would lead to an unhelpful theological digression. I shall look at it elsewhere.)

The principle of service is reaffirmed in Matthew 23:11: 'He who is greatest among you shall be your servant.' This principle of service to others is one of the things which has made both Jesus and Christianity attractive. In India, non-Christians as well as Christians used to speak of 'the missionary spirit' as something praiseworthy. They did not mean the spirit of evangelical fervour, but the spirit of selfless service to others.

Nowhere else in the ancient world is it expressed so clearly as in the New Testament, with the possible exception of the Analects of Confucius.

In Matthew 21:18–22 there is a story of Jesus cursing a fig tree which promptly withered and died. For obvious reasons some Christians are anxious to convince both themselves and us that this did not happen. Could a countryman really not know that it was not the season for figs? Could someone perfect really be so bad-tempered?

In the Gospel the story is used by Jesus to demonstrate to his disciples the power of the prayer of faith. Should prayer be used in such trivial and destructive ways? This kind of demonstration leads naive Christians into a quagmire that we shall examine when we look at his miracles generally.

If Christians believe him they become consumed with guilt that they have so little faith that they are unable to achieve great things through prayer. And all the time spent in prayer and self-criticism is time lost in searching for real answers to human problems.

There are other Christians (perhaps the majority) who quite simply do not believe in the power of prayer – though they wouldn't say so quite as openly as that. As a result their prayers are pretty much a formality except when there is an emergency when they are a cry of desperation.

It is not the prayer of faith that 'moves mountains' but a combination of human intelligence and application.

Verses 23–27 have no importance for us and 28–30 contain a little parable illustrating the fact that

> 'It is better to do and not promise,
> than to promise and not do.'

The rest of chapter 21 and most of chapter 22 can be skipped but in 22:37–39 Jesus summarises the Jewish law. We can ignore the command to love God but what of 'You shall love your neighbour as yourself'?

'Love' is a very emotive word and there are many of us who do not have a great deal of self-love or self-respect. Neighbours of such people would not come off too well. I also remember a conversation with a seventy-year-old Christian, a man who had been a Christian all his life, who said, 'I still don't know what 'love' really is '

Although 'love your neighbours' is a pithy and effective starting point, it is clearly no more than that. In terms of everyday life it is constantly in need of interpretation and clarification

But if it persuades us to think in terms of lives of open friendliness and of a genuine concern for others that is not intrusive, then it is a pretty useful commandment. By non-intrusive I mean that service is offered on the recipient's terms and with the recipient's approval – something which the major western third-world charities have all had to learn.

Matthew 25 begins with two parables of universal worth. The scout (and guide?) motto 'Be Prepared' is illustrated by the first in verses 1–13, and the second shows that it is important to use whatever talents we have (vvs. 14 30). The rest of the chapter deals with 'the last judgement'. It might seem to be a subject an atheist would ignore or mock.

The sheep go to heaven. The goats 'into the eternal fire . . . eternal punishment'. It seems very unfair to goats that they should be identified with evil – but perhaps only 'silly sheep' could believe such things. However, within this section there is a clear and lovely picture of what is expected of a Christian. It is a picture worthy of any human being who desires to live well. Such a person will:

> '. . .give food to the hungry,
> drink to the thirsty;
> will welcome the stranger,
> clothe the naked,
> visit and care for the sick,
> and those in prison.' (Matthew 25:35–36)

Such an ideal would carry most of us beyond the limits of our present lives and yet it doesn't go far enough. Goodness requires us to go beyond the provision of care for the needy. It requires us to go to the root of the problem and to work for the eradication of all forms of deprivation.

For all the virtues of the teaching of Jesus – and we have seen that it has many virtues – it is all words and promises relating to another life that probably doesn't exist. There is no programme of reform, nothing that goes to the root of social injustice. When he summed up his own ministry he said, 'and the poor have good news preached to them.' But is it really good news if it doesn't tackle their poverty? Jesus does not go far enough.

In the passage we have just been looking at he has focussed on giving, including self-giving. In Matthew 26:6–13 and in Mark 11:41–44 there is more about giving. Both passages in their different ways offer valuable warnings about the limitations of rationalism, planned giving and stewardship.

I have just been reading an article in *Saga* magazine which speaks of the importance of planning our giving. It is important. The chances are that without planning, we shall give very little even when we think that we are generous to a fault.

But when giving becomes too rational and too organised it can become arid and suffer its own form of meanness – meanness of spirit.

Matthew 26:6–13 and John 12:1–8, remind us that there is

always room for the extravagant gesture of love.

And even though I would wish for the widow to give her mite to something more worthy, her generosity (Mark 11:41–44) should give all of us pause for thought.

Miracles

Healings

The Gospels contain a number of accounts of healings. They spend a good deal of time portraying Jesus as a healer and the gospel writers clearly regard these healings as miracles. To them, the supreme healing miracles are the occasions when they believe that Jesus raised people from death: Jairus' daughter, the son of the widow of Nain and Lazarus.

Non-believers may be quite prepared to accept that Jesus was a faith-healer but we do not believe in miracles. Although this is an area where our understanding is still very limited we believe that there is a rational and scientific explanation for every so-called 'faith' healing. If we had enough information about each of the 'miracles' of Jesus, they could be explained. Many Christian scholars are of the same opinion and their commentaries are full of provisional explanations.

A great deal of the New Testament record can be put down to credulity and exaggeration. That there was a great deal of exaggeration is already evident in the text itself. For example: it is claimed that Jesus raised Jairus' daughter from death. But Jesus himself said of her, 'the girl is not dead, but sleeping.' (9:24) Similarly with the raising of Lazarus Jesus said (John 11:4): 'This illness is not unto death.' Jesus doesn't come out of this story very well. We are told that he delayed his arrival *so that* his healing/raising might be more impressive. Let the sisters grieve if they must. But in point of fact, this story of the raising of Lazarus (written seventy years after the event) can be discounted completely along with all the miracles in John's gospel. They are highly stylised and carefully organised to provide 'signs' of the divinity of Jesus who is claimed to have authority over both sin and death.

Those who wish to treat the text as a literal account of what actually happened will find themselves with awkward questions to answer.

For example, in Matthew 8:28–34 Jesus heals two madmen (other accounts have only one). The 'demons' inhabiting the madmen say to Jesus, 'If you cast us out, send us away into the' nearby 'herd of swine.'

The story claims that Jesus did just that with the result that the pigs became so disturbed that they ran into the sea and drowned. No one, not even Jesus, spares a thought for the herdsmen who have lost their livelihood or the farmers who have lost their pigs or the pigs themselves.

I know that sensible Christians can give a sensible account of this whole affair but even their sensible account fails to deal with the questions I have raised. If these events took place (however explained), then Jesus has done more harm than good.

And it may well be that his concentration on faith healing has also done a great deal more harm than good – in two respects. Jesus seems to have believed that if people had enough faith in God they would always be able to heal the sick. He told his disciples to heal (Mark 9:17–29). A boy with epilepsy was brought to them. They tried to heal the boy and failed. To them, and to naive Christians ever since, this kind of failure is a source of bitter distress and guilt.

After Jesus had accomplished the healing the disciples asked: 'Why could we not cast it out?' (Epilepsy being thought of as a form of demon possession.)

But *failed* faith healing also brings deeper despair to those whose hopes have been raised and dashed and to their carers.

The concentration on faith healing has all that to answer for – and much more. There have been many instances over the centuries when the church has stood in the way of the advance of scientific medicine believing that faith in God was incompatible with research and the use of the human mind. The Catholic church in particular has used the forces of emotion and unreason to stand in the way of progress, and it is doing so still.

It is surely significant that the medical profession turned to Hippocrates rather than Jesus for its symbol and model. The ancient Greeks were streets ahead of Jesus in their understanding of illness and disease, however limited they may have been. It is only with the growing freedom of science from the shackles of the church that progress has raced ahead.

It has raced to the point where there are new ethical problems emerging which demand infinitely careful study, and for which there will be no easy answers. Certainly, the New Testament can provide no answers.

But the achievements of medical science have been immense and beneficial to us all. It is only by continued scientific study and the use of the best minds we have that continued progress in the world of medicine can be made.

The one contribution Jesus has made is his example of compassion for the sick and needy. The best medics share that compassion and ally it to a growing body of knowledge. But Jesus was not always so compassionate. In Matthew 15:21–28 there is a story about a Canaanite who came and asked him for help for her daughter. It is a story that bothered me when I was a Christian.

Jesus ignored her, but she pestered his disciples until at last Jesus said that his ministry was only for his own people, not for foreigners.

'It is not fair to take the children's bread and throw it to the dogs.'

Christians claim that he said that to test her. Is it fair or decent to treat a troubled woman in such a way? And I find the actual words scandalous. At that time it was a typically Jewish attitude to non-Jews. Fortunately the woman had the wit to shame Jesus into action:

'Yes, Lord, yet even the dogs eat the crumbs that fall from their masters' table.'

(Christians will be horrified by that interpretation of the Matthew story. Can they cut themselves free from their background and faith for long enough to recognise that it is a perfectly legitimate interpretation, and to one who is not a Christian, a perfectly natural interpretation?)

John's gospel shows that one of the main reasons the early Christians had for laying such emphasis on the healings of Jesus was to encourage people to believe in him. In today's world 'miracles', far from being a help to belief, are a hindrance. Indeed, they may actually be an additional reason for unbelief.

But there are healing miracles that are worth examining for reasons which have nothing to do with the subject of miracle. My favourite is described in John chapter 9. This is a wonderfully dramatic story of a man born blind who was given his sight on a sabbath day.

Whatever the truth of the healing, it is a story full of valuable lessons and insights. It demonstrates that the people who were really blind were the authorities who were so shackled by their upbringing and prejudices that they were unable to see new truth when it was staring them in the face. And it poses a question for readers of this book – a question I shall not attempt to answer:

Who shares the blindness of those authorities, the Christian or the atheist, or both? We all need always to be open to new truth and to avoid the arrogance of those who think they know it all.

The Nature Miracles

Matthew chapter 14 begins with the account of the death of John the Baptist, killed for speaking too bluntly of the immorality of Herod Antipas and his wife. (vvs. 1–12)

It continues with two miracles. Christians divide the miracles of Jesus into the healing miracles, the nature miracles and the miracles surrounding his birth and death (the incarnation and the resurrection).

We have already looked at the healings and I have suggested that there was nothing miraculous about them. It will be convenient to look at the nature miracles here and it will not take us long. Nowadays, only the most naive of fundamentalist Christians believe that they actually happened as described.

In John 2:1–11 there is a story of Jesus at a wedding in Cana in Galilee. At the wedding breakfast they were running short of wine. Jesus' mother asked him to do something about it and he worked a miracle, turning water into wine.

The story is designed by John as one of the special signs in his gospel – signs leading people to believe in Jesus. The whole thing is phoney, but if we take it at its face value Jesus doesn't come out of it very well.

First of all, he is rude to his mother – which seems a fairly regular occurrence in the gospels. On this occasion he is rude because he doesn't want her pushing him into working miracles.

But there was no need for a miracle. Cana was a small place and most of the guests would have been locals. Would none of them have had a skin or two of wine at home? It wouldn't have taken long to rustle up enough to keep everyone happy.

If we return to Matthew, in 14:13–21 we have the story of the feeding of the five thousand and in chapter 15:32–39 there is another version of the story in which Jesus only feeds four thousand people. It is significant that the other gospels only give us the version with five thousand.

Here is clear evidence of the way in which stories about Jesus grew with the telling – which is not surprising when we consider how many fishermen there were amongst the early disciples.

Most modern commentators explain these stories as a simple matter of pilgrims sharing their packed lunches. The 'miracles' never happened.

In Matthew 14:22–33 Jesus walks on the water but when Peter tries to emulate him, he goes for a swim instead. The story is so absurd as to barely need a mention except for one curious personal reason.

It helped me to escape from Christianity. I was sitting in my bed one morning reading my daily chapter of the New Testament and it happened to be this chapter. As I read about Jesus walking on the water it suddenly hit me: 'I don't believe that.'

Well of course I didn't. But what else did I NOT believe?

With new clarity and force it dawned on me that I didn't actually believe in miracles at all. And that meant that I didn't believe in the miracles of the incarnation and resurrection – the miracles surrounding the birth and death of Jesus. *But the whole Christian faith depends on those miracles.*

If they never happened then Jesus is no more than one human being among all the rest of us. I would begin to look at him in a completely different way, with new eyes.

For me it was like a conversion experience; like Paul's light on the Damascus road; like Bunyan's Pilgrim when a great weight fell from off his shoulders – especially like that.

For me, that trivial moment was a watershed and I have never looked back. I was released from years of intellectual agonising into the new simplicity and straightforwardness of a life without religion and without gods. I began to discover how lucky people were who had never had to go through the religious experience – how wonderful it was to be free. But I digress.

There is one more nature miracle to look at briefly before moving on – in Matthew 17:24–27:

Jesus pays his taxes through a miracle. How we all wish we could do the same but it isn't so easy for the rest of us. We have to earn the money to pay.

Few people will believe the story. Those who do should reflect that it doesn't actually paint Jesus in a very creditable light.

If I were a Christian I would go on at this point to write of the two great miracles, the foundation stones on which the whole of the Christian faith is built. Take them away, and the Christian faith as a separate and distinctive religion collapses. There is nothing left except some of the teaching of Jesus and his followers, and some qualities of character worth seeking.

The two great miracles are the miracles of the incarnation and the resurrection. I have said all that I have to say about the incarnation when we considered the birth stories and the theology which has grown up around them.

What little I have to say about the resurrection can wait until the end of the next chapter.

Claims, Confrontation and Death

For Christians one of the most important parts of the gospel is to be found at Matthew 16:13–17:13. It represents the moment when the closest disciples realised that Jesus claimed to be more than just a rather special teacher and healer, and more than another in the line of Jewish prophets.

Peter hit the nail on the head. Jesus claimed to be the Jewish Messiah, the Christ. But in making that claim he went far beyond anything the Jews had claimed for their Messiah. The claim to be 'Son of the living God' supported by the vision (the transfiguration) in Matthew 17, is a claim to divinity.

Here we have it in its primitive portrayal. In Paul's letters and in John's gospel we see the beginnings of the theological development of the claim which was ultimately to lead to the credal belief that Jesus is 'God of God', one of the three persons of the trinity. (It is astonishing the number of Christians who recite that week by week without ever really becoming aware that Christianity rests on the belief that Jesus is God, wholly God yet not the whole story of the godhead.)

Did Jesus actually make these claims or did his disciples go over the top? Had Jesus lost his own sense of proportion? There is evidence that he had. There is also evidence that he hadn't. According to the gospel record, the Jewish authorities certainly seem to have felt that he had developed a very inflated conception of his own significance and importance:

'You being a man, make yourself God.' 'You are mad.'

Yet there are also moments when he seems to come down to earth in a very attractive way and also to seek to bring his disciples down to earth.

In Mark 10:17–18, a little after the events described by Matthew, someone comes to Jesus and calls him 'Good Teacher'. Jesus fastens on the word 'Good' and says:

'Why do you call me good? No one is good but God alone.'

Is Jesus challenging the man to recognise his divinity? Or is he warning his disciples not to claim too much for him?

If we return to Matthew we find Jesus beginning to prepare his disciples for his death and promising them that he would rise from death. Many people see this as the teaching of the early church being put into the mouth of Jesus. It could be. Or Jesus could simply be expressing the belief he shared with the Pharisees that the dead rise to a new life with God. Or it could be a bit of both.

However important all this may be to Christians it is of no importance to those of us who think of Jesus in purely human terms.

In the story, it is Peter who makes the intuitive guess (leap of faith) that Jesus is 'the Christ'. And Jesus promptly announces that Peter will be the rock on which he will build his church. (There is a humorous play on words since petros means rock.')

Was this assertion first made by Jewish Christians to put people like Paul in their place? It has been used by the Roman Catholic Church in an incredible re-writing of history to justify the pre-eminence of the bishops of Rome and to go on to claim that the Roman priesthood is the only true Christian priesthood. The whole structure is nonsense but the claims remain – much to the distaste of all the other churches.

Peter certainly did not prove to be very rock-like and we find Jesus rebuking him in very intemperate terms almost immediately, simply because Peter shows a misplaced concern for his Master.

As the claims for Jesus grow, so the demands laid on his followers grow. The follower of Jesus is to put Jesus before life itself. So the fishermen and the tax collector were to leave their livelihoods behind and Peter and any other married men were to leave their wives behind and sacrifice everything for him. They were to live for him and if necessary to die for him.

Bertrand Russell was once asked if he was prepared to die for his beliefs. 'No,' he said. 'I may be wrong.'

There are those who, like lemmings, follow a leader through thick and thin to their deaths. There may be nobility in it. There is certainly stupidity. Jesus and his followers were certainly wrong in some of their beliefs and the evidence for that is clear even in Matthew 16.

In verses 27 and 28 Jesus refers to his second coming 'in the glory of his Father':

'For the Son of man is to come with his angels in the glory of his Father. . . Truly I say to you, there are some standing here who will not taste death before they see the Son of man coming in his kingdom.'

It didn't happen and while some Christians go on waiting others believe that it never will happen.

I have only spent time with these chapters because they are important for Christians. They have no importance for anyone else. Much the same is true of the rest of the gospel story, which means so much to Christians but has little to say to anybody else.

For we have reached the closing stages and move towards the death of Jesus. For Christians the death (and resurrection) mark the climax of the whole and give meaning to the whole of their theology.

Since I am not a Christian it will be possible to reach the end of the journey without too much further delay.

Matthew 21 begins the stories of the last days with Jesus riding into Jerusalem on a donkey and crowds proclaiming his greatness. The time for all-out confrontation with the authorities has come.

In Jerusalem he went into the Temple (John has the story placed elsewhere in the life of Jesus). In a cold fury he drove out the merchants with a whip and overturned the tables of the money changers who changed ordinary currency into temple currency.

Christians rather enjoy this explosion and call it 'righteous anger'.

It was certainly justifiable. The profiteering that went on in the temple was unbelievable.

But it was also singularly pointless. It was a protest which achieved nothing. The merchants and money-changers would all have been back in place in no time at all.

All that Jesus has shown us is that natural protest at governmental injustice and robbery is a complete waste of time and energy unless it has specific and achievable goals.

Another story of the ill temper of Jesus follows (Matthew 18:20–22). If there is any truth in the story, his bad temper was simply that. As we have seen it had no justification at all. He cursed a fig tree which had no figs. And as previously stated as a countryman he must have known that it wasn't the season for figs.

Matthew 21–23 contains a series of attacks on the priests, the scribes and pharisees of the time. Aimed at demonstrating that Jesus was wiser and cleverer than any of them, these chapters are full of venom.

In 23:1–12 he says of scribes and pharisees that 'they preach but do not practice' and so in sergeant major fashion he tells people:

'Don't do as they do.
Do as they tell you.'

He accuses them (vvs. 5 9) of seeking glory and privilege. I wonder what he would think of the bishops in the house of Lords and of the costly and colourful vestments of priests who insist on being called father by men in spite of the fact that Jesus said, 'call no man "father".'

Would he see any great difference between the churches and priesthoods of today and the temple and priests of his own day? And would today's church leaders handle him any differently or would another Caiaphas step forward to put him in his place?

In verses 13ff Jesus accused the scribes and pharisees of being 'hypocrites'. I once jokingly called an African friend of mine a hypocrite. When I picked myself up from the floor I realised that to him it was a much more serious accusation than I had realised. The central point of Jesus' condemnation was that the scribes and pharisees had 'neglected . . . justice and mercy and faith.' If he

231

was right, they deserved his condemnation – at least as far as justice and mercy are concerned. But those things are more difficult to attend to than 'faith'.

Matthew 24 is prophecy after the event, a confused and confusing mixture of passages about the fall of Jerusalem that took place in 70 CE and the second coming of Jesus that still has not taken place, and probably (I would say 'certainly') never will.

And so we come to the story of the death of Jesus told in Matthew 26:14 to 27:66. It is a dramatic story of betrayal, denial, political expediency, mob manipulation, mockery and degradation.

Through it all Jesus behaves with dignity and calm and an almost bemused numbness that finally gives way to despair.

The story begins with the last supper which is re-enacted as the central rite of Christian worship, ritualising the fellowship of the table.

It began as something very simple. It was a symbolic representation of the death of Jesus – his body and blood – which he seems to have seen as a sacrifice winning forgiveness from God for the sins of those who trust in him.

Theologians have gone beyond all reason and sense in their interpretations of the meaning of it all. In the Catholic church, for example, it is claimed that the bread and wine are actually transformed into the real body and blood of Jesus.

Jesus certainly chose an effective memorial, for the fellowship of the table has been important in every culture and every society. But is he really as great as he is painted?

He only chose twelve close disciples yet he failed to command the loyalty even of all of those. One of them betrayed him. And the one who stands out from all the rest, the one Jesus called 'the rock' lost his nerve and denied all knowledge of Jesus, while the rest ran away at the first hint of serious danger.

It is true that eleven of them returned to the Christian fold and that Peter became one of their leaders. But nothing can alter the fact that Jesus failed to hold the loyalty of Judas. At very least it calls his greatness as a leader into question.

Matthew 27:24 reports that 'a riot was beginning'. Is this the real reason that Jesus was put to death? He seems to have actively sought confrontation with the authorities. Were his teaching and actions leading to public disorder in Jerusalem? Is this why Caiaphas came to believe that it was expedient that Jesus should die, rather than that there should be wholesale slaughter and bloodshed? And is it not possible that he was right?

Here then is the sad, perhaps tragic story of a popular wandering teacher who decided to challenge the temple authorities and who perhaps began to have illusions of grandeur, but who finally and bitterly discovered how wrong he had been. Understood in this way, the final cry from the cross really was a cry of desolation – the last despairing cry of one who at last realises that he has been barking up the wrong tree:

'My God, my God, why hast thou forsaken me?'

(In fairness I should point out, as many Christians do, that these words are a quotation of the first verse of Psalm 22, a psalm that begins in despair and ends in triumph. So some Christians suggest that the last message of an exhausted and dying Jesus is rather like that of the dying Athenian who has run all the way home from Marathon after the battle: 'Oh fellow citizens, we conquer; we conquer.' For Christians it is a lovely and exciting interpretation).

The story ends with the claim that Jesus had earned the respect of a respected and wealthy man, Joseph of Arimatheia. He obtained permission to bury Jesus in his tomb.

What happened after this is anybody's guess.

The traditional Christian claim is that Jesus rose from death on the third day and that he had prophesied that he would. The gospels and the Acts of the Apostles contain a number of stories of resurrection appearances by Jesus to his disciples.

The idea of resurrection was common. It crops up throughout the gospels. People believed that any of the prophets, notably Elijah, either had or would rise from the dead. People believed that John the Baptist had risen, and now Christians claimed that Jesus had risen and backed it up with stories.

The stories contain so many ludicrous elements that they can be dismissed pretty much as the creation of emotional and superstitious people. It is perhaps significant that the earliest gospel Mark, ends with the announcement of the resurrection. No one actually sees the risen Jesus. All we have is an announcement that could easily have been misunderstood, made to three terrified women at a time when they were highly overwrought and emotionally disturbed.

All sorts of explanations of what happened have been offered. Perhaps the authorities removed the body of Jesus so that there would be no place of pilgrimage. Perhaps the Jewish explanation is right – that the disciples themselves stole the body, although I doubt if they would have had the courage. Perhaps Matthew is right when he speaks of 'a great earthquake'. In which case the body of Jesus could simply have disappeared down a fissure in the ground.

No one will ever know, nor does it matter. There are many thoughtful Christians who recognise the difficulties in the New Testament story and who quite simply do not believe in the resurrection. Those of us who are not Christian do not believe it either.

The Acts of the Apostles

Acts is full of interest to Christians because it gives a picture of the way in which Christianity spread from Jerusalem and the world of the Jews to the Gentiles or non-Jews and ultimately to Rome, the heart of the Roman Empire.

It does not have the same interest for non-Christians and can be dealt with fairly rapidly. Significantly, while Christians may read and enjoy the acts of the apostles, they rarely feel that it has anything to teach them.

The book begins with the resurrection and ascension of Jesus. I have already noted the willingness of some Christians (including some leading Christians) to dispense with the resurrection. Many who still cling to the resurrection have been willing to dispense with the ascension for a long time. There seems to have been a recognition that resurrection 'appearances' could not go on indefinitely so we have this very primitive attempt to round them off with a final appearance that clearly was final.

In place of the appearances of the risen Jesus, the disciples were to be given the spirit of Jesus to sustain them – they were to be 'baptized with the Holy Spirit'.

The Holy Spirit is the third person of the Christian Trinity and is therefore regarded as God. He has many names: the Holy Spirit, the Holy Ghost, the Spirit of God, the Spirit of Jesus, the

234

Comforter and so on. He is said to give Christians the power to bear effective witness to Jesus without fear.

Christians themselves are often very vague about the Holy Spirit. One critic of mine, a member of the clergy, wrote that I had failed to understand modern theological thinking about the Spirit. I wonder how many Christians even know what it is? She attempted no exposition! Even where Christians believe in the existence of the Spirit, they find it very difficult to speak with any precision. They speak only in the vaguest, most ethereal terms. One definition I read recently spoke of the Spirit as 'the good in everyone'.

Those who are loudest in claiming that they have received the Spirit are often a source of embarrassment to their fellow Christians. They are also often the most narrow-minded, arrogant and dogmatic of Christians. Their worship tends to be noisy, emotional, crude and tasteless.

If this is what the Holy Spirit is all about, thank goodness for atheism. I don't really believe that it is, but then, I don't really believe that the Holy Spirit is about anything tangible at all. Perhaps the old name Holy Ghost came nearer to the truth. The Hebrew word for Spirit is ruach. Its alternative meaning is 'wind'. Perhaps the Christian doctrine of the Holy Spirit is no more than that – a lot of hot air.

I've had my bit of fun, but it would be foolish to be too dismissive just because the Acts of the Apostles paints such a primitive picture of the coming of the Holy Spirit.

The words 'spirit' and 'spiritual' have a meaning for many people who would lay no claim to religion of any kind. They are words that are almost impossible to define, which is partly responsible for Christian vagueness about the Holy Spirit. But they are words that do enshrine truths about ordinary, everyday human experience.

When I was a student there were three nonconformist preachers in London who drew large crowds to hear them: William Sangster, Donald (later Lord) Soper and Leslie Weatherhead. It was said that you could tell which of them theological students went to hear because they picked up the style and gestures of their favourite.

At a much deeper level, if we are attracted by one particular teacher, hero, leader and if we stick with that person, we are

235

pretty certain to end up with at least some similar ideas and characteristics. We become imbued with that person's spirit.

When the New Testament speaks of the spirit of Jesus or the holy spirit, it seems to me that it is saying no more than that. Genuine followers of Jesus will take on board some of his ideas and their characters will develop some of his qualities. If they choose the things I have been describing as pure gold, they may well become splendid and lovely people.

In one of his letters Paul says to his readers:

'Whatever is true, whatever is honourable, whatever is just, whatever is pure, whatever is lovely, whatever is gracious, if there is any excellence, if there is anything worthy of praise, think about these things.' (Philippians 3:8)

I don't often sing Paul's praises but it seems to me that he has something very important to say there. If we focus our minds and our lives on those things which are good and true and valuable we shall become good and true and valuable people.

I suspect that that is something of the meaning the best of Christians give to being filled with the holy spirit and I can go along with that. For it has nothing to do with religion, nothing to do with the trinity, nothing to do with the supernatural. It is simply a fact of ordinary life and ordinary experience.

One of my mother's favourite sayings was 'thoughts are things'. As a child I hadn't a clue what she was talking about, but she was absolutely right. And insofar as this is what Jesus meant when he urged people to 'seek first God's kingdom and his righteousness' he was right too. Forget the god bit. If we focus our whole attention on the things that really matter in life we shall develop into decent, positive, life-affirming people.

Underneath all the religious stuff, there is something valuable here for Christian and non-Christian alike.

Apart from that, for non-Christians the most interesting part of the Acts of the Apostles is the experiment in communal living. Christians were not the first Jews to try such an experiment. The Essenes (best known as a result of the Dead Sea Scrolls) had been living in community for a long time, and their communalism was much more complete than that of the Christians. Although the Christians 'had all things in common and sold their possessions and goods' they kept possession of their homes. (Acts 2:44–46)

Their experiment was due to their expectation that Jesus was going to return very soon in power and glory. They were wrong and their experiment led pretty soon to financial hardship which had to be alleviated by collections made in the Gentile Churches.

Since then there have been all sorts of different Christian experiments in communal living, normally on a single sex basis as in monasteries and nunneries. Such experiments are not confined to Christians. They have many achievements to their name, but they also produce their own crop of problems and aberrations.

Communal living does not seem to be either superior or inferior to ordinary family life. It is simply different. If people wish to live in community, that is up to them. The non-Christian doesn't have a view either way, though he would prick the bubble of those who talk of this kind of life (which is often an escape from a tougher life outside) as a vocation.

In chapter 9 Acts gives the story of the conversion of the Jew Saul who became known as Paul. It is a classic conversion story. What many people fail to realise is that conversion can work in many ways:

Some are converted to religion; some are converted from one religion to another; and some are converted from religion to a non-religious approach to life. Most people are probably not converted at all. They simply go on with whatever approach to life their parents followed or they drift from something fairly definite to something indefinite.

In chapter 17:18 we are told that 'some of the Epicurean and Stoic philosophers met' Paul. Sadly there is no record of their conversation, if conversation it was. It would have been fascinating to read even though Paul, with the typical arrogance of his type, would have felt that he had nothing to learn from them at all.

In the course of time Christianity was to take a good deal from both groups. The Stoics were the more religious of the two and retained the respect of Christians. But Epicureans tended to be agnostic. They gathered together in groups to enjoy one another's friendship. They were gentler, more tolerant and more egalitarian than Christians – way ahead of Christians in their approach to women and children. They were non-political and had none of the evangelical zeal, the driving ambition and hunger for power of the Christians.

When Christians had achieved power, they misrepresented, maligned and persecuted the Epicureans just as they persecuted dissidents in their own ranks. As a result, it is only outside Christianity that it is possible to find a fair and balanced picture of the Epicurean life-style and teaching.

Christians may feel that I have been just as unfair towards them. But they still have the power and the privilege to enable them to get away with a very great deal. I know that I have dismissed many things that are very dear to them. I have put them down to exaggeration, emotion, superstition and so on. Is that unfair?

If ever evidence were needed for such summary dismissal it is to be found in Acts chapter 28 and the incident with the snake:

When Paul (a Roman prisoner at the time) was bitten by a snake people assumed that he was a wicked criminal and that this was the judgement of a god. But then Paul suffered no harm and people promptly changed their minds and decided that he must be a god.

With people like that, anything can be expected: virgin births, miracles, resurrections, ascension and holy ghosts.

If some of us dismiss the supernatural in Christianity no one should be surprised. When we do, we find that the Christianity that remains (in Paul's words) is about 'justice and self control'. (Acts 24, 25) Such things are of far greater value and importance than all the supernatural stuff that I have thrown away.

Section Two

From Romans to Philemon

Introduction

In one respect this second section will be much easier than the first. Whereas my examination of the gospels involved a great deal of hopping about between them, here we can proceed simply, book by book.

I was tempted to make this the first half of my book and actually prepared the first draft that way. Some of the letters are older than the gospels. Examination of them was, as we have seen, simpler. But it also seemed to me that after the gospels with their account of the ministry and death of Jesus, the rest was almost bound to be an anti-climax.

In the end I decided to follow the order of the New Testament. As a result we turn now to a group of letters attributed to Paul the Jewish pharisee whose conversion experience was recorded in the Acts of the Apostles. He became the most significant of the early Christian leaders and, more than anybody else, was the one responsible for changing Christianity from a Jewish sect to an international religion. After the letters attributed to Paul there are more letters at the end of section three of this book and then the final, fantastic apocalyptic book 'the Revelation to John'. We should be thankful that it was a revelation to him because it has always been a complete mystification to everyone else.

Christian scholars no longer believe that Paul wrote all the letters attributed to him.

They are fairly unanimous that Hebrews was not one of Paul's letters. It is so different from all the rest that I have used it to begin the last group in this study.

The rest are usually divided as follows:

Genuine letters of Paul (dating from the 50s CE): Romans, 1 & 2 Corinthians, Galatians, Ephesians, Philippians, 1 Thessalonians and Philemon.

Letters that are not by Paul: Colossians, 2 Thessalonians, 1 & 2 Timothy, Titus and Hebrews.

For my purposes it doesn't matter who wrote the letters or when or why. All that matters is that they are contained in the New Testament and are therefore foundation documents for anyone who wants to examine Christian teaching.

The set of letters from Romans to Philemon forms a convenient group and I shall look at them in the order in which they are printed.

Romans

A great deal of the letter to the Romans is taken up with theological matters which have no meaning or relevance to those who do not believe in God.

It was one of the most important books in the New Testament for the founders of the protestant wing of the Christian church. From it they derived their most fundamental doctrine, that of 'justification by faith'. This doctrine is at the root of all protestant salvation theology.

Because it is all irrelevant to non-Christians I have been very tempted to leave well alone, but the following sketch may be helpful.

Paul started from the premiss that we are all sinners from the moment of our conception. Worse than that, we are enslaved by sin and destined for death, the judgement of God and punishment.

Apart from Jesus there is no way of escape from all this. There are primitive attempts in the New Testament to show how that way of escape is offered to those who do not come into contact with the Christian gospel during the course of their lives. So it is claimed that Jesus has provided a way of escape for us all.

Through faith in him we can be released from our slavery to sin. Freed from slavery, we shall become the children of God. We shall live our lives for him and die in the knowledge that the children of God are raised from death to life in heaven where they see God face to face.

Those who believe this and who believe that they are themselves children of God, find all this very comforting. But Christian salvation theology poses all sorts of intellectual problems for thoughtful Christians. Let me mention just one: *how* does Jesus save us from slavery to sin? There have been all sorts of answers to this question, none of them wholly satisfactory to Christians, let alone to anybody else. To complicate matters further, there are many Christians today who would not accept Paul's basic premiss that children are conceived in sin.

But if you don't accept that premiss there is a fair chance that the whole structure will collapse.

Outside of Christianity these problems simply do not exist. One of the joys of ceasing to be a Christian is that so many problems that used to give me endless concern, problems for which there is no satisfactory intellectual conclusion, simply dissolve and disappear.

We are not sinners. We are human beings with all the imperfection that that implies. We do not need salvation though we shall often need help. We shall need help in growing up towards maturity. And we may need help if we go on to make a mess of our lives.

Most of that help will come from family and friends and from our own hidden resources. We shall be astonished at the depth of those hidden resources but sometimes we may also need a bit of expert help too. (It should perhaps be noted that when I became a minister we were neither trained nor equipped to provide that help.)

We shall never be anything other than imperfect human beings but if we develop ideals for our lives (including some of the ideals Christians set before themselves) we may well become better people as a result. Insofar as Christianity or Humanism or any other religion or philosophy helps us 'to be the best that we can

241

be' (to quote an old hymn), it clearly has a permanent value.

But the letter to the Romans which has been so important for Christians is one that the rest of us can skip through fairly rapidly and with only a cursory examination.

In chapter one Paul shows his low opinion of his fellows. It is God who 'gave them up to such baseness' simply because they didn't believe in him – which doesn't say very much for God either.

Chapter two is about God's judgement and can be ignored except for Paul's dictum in verse 21 that those who set themselves up as moral teachers must first live by their teaching themselves. And chapter three offers the core of Christian salvation theology (see especially verses 21 to 25). As we have seen, it is meaningless to anyone who is not a Christian.

In chapter four Paul attempts to demonstrate how it is that Christians have inherited the promises God first made to the Jews.

Most of chapters five and six continue to express Christian salvation theology. Paul has a thoroughly complex mind and his teaching is difficult for Christians to understand, and meaningless for the rest of us. But in 5:3–4 there is one statement that is worth our attention:

'Suffering produces endurance, and endurance produces character. . .'

SOME Christians say that that is why God allows or even provides suffering.

It is not always true that suffering leads to people of sterling worth. Sadly, the opposite may also be true. But we have all known sufferers whose suffering has brought out qualities of character and endurance beyond the average.

As I write I have one particular friend of mine in mind. He (and his family) had a great deal to endure over almost thirty years. Their uncomplaining courage was quite exceptional. But in John's case suffering simply brought out qualities he had always had. If I had known the other members of the family well enough, I would probably have said the same about them.

What I am getting at is this: there are undoubtedly many Christians of great quality of character and they probably believe that their faith helps them to be the people they are. But it is also true that there are many people of great quality of character who have no religious beliefs at all.

In chapter seven 14–25 Paul wrestles with the fact that we do not always seem to have control over our actions and so fail to live up to our own ideals or the ideals others have laid down for us.

There are two issues here. First of all, it seems to me that no individual has the right to lay down the law for anyone else. Society creates laws for its own protection and to keep the wheels of society running smoothly. None of these has permanent validity or authority. Every new generation has to rethink the rules laid down by its predecessors.

But the second issue concerns those crises of conscience and internal conflicts of the kind Paul addresses. They are often the result of unrealistic or false demands being made of people (often by themselves). They are also sometimes caused by external circumstances which have become more than we can control.

Paul does not really seem to understand the nature of internal conflict. Modern psychology can give us greater insight than Paul and in doing so can provide us with greater help. Once we have begun to understand ourselves we can begin to map out more clearly where we are going and resolve those internal conflicts which are tearing us apart. Paul fails to realise that human problems have human solutions. Religion often gets in the way, as do religious attitudes.

Some of those attitudes emerge very clearly in chapter eight. For Paul everything is black or white; either/or; flesh or spirit.

A full-blooded physical life can certainly follow harmful paths. No one would deny that. But what Paul fails to realise is that it is possible to combine a thoroughly physical life (in every sense of the word physical) with purity and nobility.

In point of fact, it could be argued that to be thoroughly healthy and wholesome, life must involve mind and body; what he calls spirit and flesh. The Greeks were right to emphasise the importance of a healthy mind in a healthy body. A life given over wholly to one or the other is a perversion of our natural humanity.

At the end of chapter eight (35–39) are some verses which Christians love. The language is magnificent, but it doesn't really mean very much unless it is true, and who is to say whether it is true or not?

In chapters 9 to 11 Paul claims that God is not unjust and succeeds in demonstrating just how unjust he is, and how hostile to all whom *he has 'made* for destruction.' 'Only a remnant will be saved.'

Paul goes round and round in circles and contradicts himself again and again as he revolves between thoughts of God's goodness and mercy and thoughts of his severity and judgement. If there is no God there is no problem.

At last in chapter 12 there is something for the non-Christian even if only in the most general sense.

Paul urges Christians to lead pure and wholesome lives; to respect one another's gifts and to have an honest recognition of their own gifts and limitations – this being genuine modesty and humility.

He urges Christians to use their gifts for the benefit of the community; to rise above pettiness and to show generosity of spirit. 'Repay no one evil for evil, but take thought for what is noble in the sight of all. If possible, so far as it depends upon you, live peaceably with all.' (vvs. 18–19)

In all of this Paul's standards are of the highest and worth consideration and acceptance by non-Christians. But Paul can't sustain this level. His God is a wrathful and avenging God and Paul enjoys the thought that the Christian's kindness to his enemies may actually make God punish them more ferociously.

His ideals may be such as can be worthily set before any of us to be accepted for their own sake and not because of any religious allegiance. But this is not the case with his vengeful spirit. That may be very human, but it needs to be controlled, conquered and ultimately excised.

Strangely enough, in chapter 14 Paul is much gentler, urging consideration for others and a non-judgemental approach. 'Let us then pursue what makes for peace and for mutual upbuilding.' (v. 19)

Chapters 15 and 16 can be skipped because in them Paul simply talks about his job, his future plans, and sends his greetings. But there was one matter in chapter 13 which I skipped and must now return to.

In verses 1–10 Paul urges obedience to civil authorities and to the law. He claims that government has been instituted by God and his obedience appears to be absolute and uncritical.

Few Christians and no unbelievers would accept that government is from God. Whilst good citizenship normally involves obedience to the law, the standards of government usually lag behind those of civilised opinion and the choices of government are quite often simply wrong. It is only by criticism and sometimes by civil disobedience that we can bring about change.

I can end this sketch of the letter to the Romans with the brief comment that in vvs. 8–10, when Paul sums up the law, he makes no reference to the command to love God. It is enough apparently to 'love your neighbour as yourself'.

The First Letter to the Corinthians

This is much more like an ordinary letter than Romans. But, like Romans, godless people will find little in it worth their attention. But if they do read it they will be relieved to escape the heavy theological treatise style of Romans and to move into something simpler. There is little that is noteworthy before chapter six and most of that is pretty obvious. Examples are:

- 4:2: It is required of stewards that they be found trustworthy.
- 5:8: Paul urges sincerity and truth and
- 5:11: opposes immorality and greed; idolaters, revilers, drunkards and robbers.
- 6:7: He claims that it is better to suffer wrong or to be defrauded than to go to law.

I imagine that many of us would question that. We may share Paul's low opinion of legal processes. We may also feel that trying to obtain justice is worth neither the effort nor the expense. But to abdicate completely is to hand the world over to crooks.

- 6:9: Paul loves his hate-lists. Here he lists people who 'will not inherit the kingdom of God.' Among those in his list are homosexuals.

The Bible, the 'word of God', is so hostile to homosexuals that it is difficult to understand why so many of them cling so desperately to the church. I don't think it has much to do with religion per se.

Many homosexuals have a genuine feel for language, music and ritual. They are also often very sociable people and will enjoy the sense of belonging to a community that the church can often give.

Those of us who reject the church sometimes find the need to seek out places where we can enjoy some of these things. They have no necessary connection with God or religion, but they are often to be found in the life of the churches.

6:15–16: Paul speaks of those who use prostitutes.
Prostitutes themselves are not considered.

In general, I suspect that most people would agree that prostitution, whether male or female, is something we would like to see gone. There is a great deal about prostitution that is sordid, degrading and also, simply dangerous.

But it is always a mistake to generalise and a far greater mistake to condemn. Is a woman to be condemned for taking what may be the only path open to her if she wishes to provide for herself and her family?

And which is better: that we should pay for pleasures or engage in an adulterous relationship that can hurt and damage so many people?

Much as I like the idea of the body as a temple of purity and agree with the advice to 'shun immorality', it is advice I have not always kept myself and behaviour I am often unable to condemn in others. There is an immorality which is purely selfish and which deserves condemnation. But with most of us, immorality is mixed up with all sorts of other things which may well be good and praiseworthy.

Life is rarely a matter of black and white and it can become very confused and chaotic indeed.

Certainly where two people can give one another pleasure without doing anybody else any harm there is no room for criticism, let alone condemnation. And if one of those two should happen to be a prostitute, what of it?

The climax of Paul's chapter 6 is verse 19. Here the humanist and the Christian part company very clearly.

Paul claims 'You are not your own; you were bought with a price.' The reference is to the Christian doctrine of salvation which claims that the death of Jesus on the cross is in some way the price paid to buy us from slavery to sin into the freedom of God's slavery.

Humanists have a much simpler belief. We believe that we are on our own, and that therefore we are responsible for our own lives and behaviour. It is that on-our-own-ness and sense of responsibility which is our freedom and which provides freedom's boundaries.

In chapter seven Paul turns to the subject of marriage. For him there seem to be only two reasons to marry. One is 'to promote good order'. The other is the need to exercise some sort of social control over sexual passion.

Paul's preferred option is celibacy. 'Those who marry will have worldly troubles, and I would spare you that.' (v. 28) The unmarried are free from worldly anxieties and responsibilities and can concentrate entirely on pleasing God.

You have only to look at the behaviour of many 'celibate' priests to see that just is not true. Celibacy is a denial of a major part of our humanity. I remember a lecturer at theological college saying, 'I would far rather teach contented husbands than frustrated bachelors.'

Chapter 8 is irrelevant except that Paul adopts the principle I adopted earlier: that we should try to behave in such a fashion as will cause no harm to anybody else nor lead anybody else astray.

Chapter 9 is of little interest. There is a reference in verse 5 to the brothers of Jesus. For all the semantics of Catholic theologians that makes a nonsense of their doctrine of the perpetual virginity of the mother of Jesus. It was interesting to notice in Romans 1:3 that Paul assumed a natural birth for Jesus. The idea of virgin birth comes later (in time) in the gospels.

In verses 9 & 10 Paul suggests that God has no concern for animals. One wonders what has happened to Jesus' claim that no sparrow dies outside God's care.

But in days of factory farming; vast culls of animals because of tiny risks to humans; extermination by conservationists of immigrant birds to preserve the purity of a local species; none of us can take much credit. We all tend to assume that the world is here for our benefit. We are a very long way from recognising that every creature has as much right to the world's resources as we have. Certainly there isn't a single species that causes as much harm to the world as we do.

In chapter 10 God is portrayed as a pretty horrible destroyer of all who do not please him. But verse 13 enshrines a very human truth if we take the word temptation in its other meaning of 'test'.

Paul wrote:

> 'God is faithful, and will not let you be tested beyond your strength, but with the test will also provide the way of escape, that you may be able to endure it.'

It is not always true that life will not test us beyond our strength. But it is true that there are always ways of coping with and triumphing over the tests of life if we can find them. It is also true that if we learn to tap our own human resources we shall be astonished at their depth and tensile strength.

In 10:14ff Paul goes on to speak of the sacrament of Holy Communion, the central rite of the Christian church. That rite is a kind of parable of the value all human society places on hospitality and the fellowship of the table. And so, almost by accident, Paul points us in the right direction:

In the tests or crises of life it is often in the fellowship or communion of family and friends that we find the support and strength we need – which is one of the reasons so many self-help groups have sprung up to deal with specific human crises (groups such as Alcoholics Anonymous).

In 10:24 Paul writes:

> 'Let no one seek his own good, but the good of his neighbour.'

Insofar as this is an encouragement to avoid selfishness it will have everyone's approval. But Paul goes over the top, and there are dangers associated with this teaching.

There is the danger of neglecting our own good. How many families have suffered because of the godly altruism of one of their members?

There is the danger of assuming that our own ideas of another's good are necessarily right. Many who think that they are seeking the good of their neighbours are actually doing more harm than good. Often, they end up no more than interfering busybodies.

We need to remember that we are interdependent beings and interdependent societies. The truest good for one is what is good for all. We should therefore seek the good both of ourselves and of our neighbour.

If ever we needed evidence that Christians do not really believe that the Bible is the word of God, chapter 11 provides it. Verses 2–16 is all about hair and hats and male supremacy. Fortunately Christians have followed the rest of society in discarding Paul's ideas (except where they stick to a male priesthood). But if this is not the word of God, what is? How are we to determine what is divine and what human? No two people will make the same choices.

11:17–33 demonstrates (as the letters do again and again) that for all the work of the Holy Spirit, Christians are no better than the rest of us. Perhaps the Holy Spirit is as unreal as many Christians find him.

In chapter 12 Paul speaks of our interdependence and of the importance of valuing properly each separate individual's gifts. If they used the word, humanists would say 'amen' to that for humanism is concerned to recognise each human being's worth and to value people simply because they are fellow human beings.

Parts of chapter 13 are among the best known of all Paul's writings. The Greeks had several different words to describe different kinds of love. In chapter 13 Paul uses the word 'agape' and speaks of divine love rather than human friendship or passion.

Nevertheless, for many people his words have provided a beautiful summary of what love between people can be, and people of all religions and none can use them as they would use a beautiful poem to express their ideals:

'Love is patient and kind; love is not jealous or boastful; it is not arrogant or rude. Love does not insist on its own way; it is not irritable or resentful; it does not rejoice at wrong, but rejoices in the right. Love bears all things, believes all things, hopes all things, endures all things. Love never ends.' (13:4–8a)

The chapter has a much wider reference than love alone. It speaks of human growth and development into maturity and in doing so it looks for a human completion beyond the grave.

Humanists are agnostic concerning life beyond the grave and

don't believe in holding out hopes that are uncertain. My own belief is that this life is the only one we have – it is certainly the only one we KNOW we have. If others wish to believe otherwise that is up to them. Provided they do not allow their beliefs to reduce the value and importance of the life we have, it doesn't matter.

I have always (even in my Christian days) found Paul's picture of human maturity somewhat sad. He wrote:

'When I was a child, I spoke like a child, I thought like a child, I reasoned like a child. When I became a man, I gave up childish ways.' (v. 11)

It is obviously essential that we grow up and become mature adults. But there is nothing worse than an adult who has lost the ability to see with the eyes of a child. If we have lost a child's zest for life; eagerness to learn; and capacity for wonder; we are almost dead already.

The one thing learning should teach us is that there is always more to learn. The freshness and eagerness of a child is intellectually alive, endlessly fascinated and endlessly fascinating. The only mind worth having is one that is always open to fresh insights and greater knowledge.

Chapter fourteen is about some of the excesses of religious emotional frenzy. I write this a few days after a retired Archbishop of Canterbury expressed his own anxieties about 'rave' services in the Church of England. Paul is not opposed to religious excitement as such, but he fears that much of it is no more than candy floss. He believes that if religion is to have any value at all it must be intelligible. It must make good sense and involve the use of the mind.

Within this general context Paul tells people to make love their aim. He tells public speakers to seek the 'upbuilding and encouragement and consolation' of their hearers. And he tells people (v. 15) to pray and sing with their minds.

Prayer is meaningless to me, but I wonder how many hymns and how much liturgy would remain if people really thought about the words they use.

How many could genuinely recite the Nicene Creed? Certainly many of the clergy couldn't, and even those clergy who believe the Creeds have reinterpreted them out of all recognition. What sort of a faith is it that has a meaning its formulators would barely recognise?

Paul urges Christians to be mature in their thinking (v. 20). It is amazing how many people leave their intelligence behind when it comes to their religion. I remember three highly intelligent Indian Moslems chastising me for my questioning. When I asked if they never questioned their own beliefs they replied: 'The teachings of the Prophet are not to be questioned.'

Why not?

Similarly, when the Pope speaks 'ex cathedra' he is said to be infallible. The 'infallible' statements of Popes contain some of the most complete nonsense you will find anywhere in religious teaching. But Catholics are taught to accept the authority of the church rather than to use their own intelligence.

In verses 26:31 and 33 Paul says:

'Let all things be done for edification. . . so that all may learn and be encouraged. . . for God is not a God of confusion but of peace.'

I don't normally have a lot of time for Paul but I am in complete agreement with the general thrust of this chapter. For it to have any value, any philosophy of life must make good sense and involve the use of the mind – which is what the rationalists have been telling us for centuries.

This is not to deny the value and importance of emotion But it is a reminder that emotion without reason is of no lasting value at all.

Paul ends chapter 14 on a sexist note. The Epicureans were far ahead of the early Christians They treated men, woman and children of all races and all classes with equal respect.

Chapter 15 is very important for Christians. It is perhaps the most complete exposition of the Christian doctrine of resurrection in the whole of the New Testament.

For those of us who do not believe in life after death it is quite meaningless. But it is important to notice that the whole of Christian theology and faith hangs on the resurrection. As Paul says: 'If Christ has not been raised, then our preaching is in vain and your faith is in vain.' (15:14)

There are many Christian leaders today who have no faith in any real sense in the resurrection, which perhaps helps to explain why they are so ineffectual. If you don't believe your own

251

teaching, how can you expect to convince others of its truth?

As I have already mentioned, my own departure from the Christian church came when I acknowledged to myself that I did not believe in miracles. If there are no miracles, then half the claims made for Jesus are false. There was no virgin birth, no resurrection and no ascension and there will be no Second Coming.

Christian theology goes out of the window and all that is left is a human teacher, some of whose teachings have never been surpassed.

Paul assumes that there is no point in living well if there is no resurrection (vvs. 32–34). He is quite wrong. Living well has nothing to do with belief in life after death. It has to do with our perception of the best way to live our lives.

If we believe that human beings are social animals and that life has to do with personal fulfilment, we shall soon find that contentment and satisfaction are to be found only in the pursuit of personal excellence and the well-being of our fellows.

In the concluding parts of the chapter Paul wrestles with some of the problems any teaching about life after death is likely to have to face. He is not particularly successful.

Chapter 16 has to do with finance and forthcoming announcements. His final greeting contains this generous and charitable sentence:

'If anyone has no love for the Lord, let him be accursed.'

So much for love, reconciliation and salvation.

The Second Letter to the Corinthians

This is a letter which has nothing in it for non-Christians. In chapter 6 Paul lists the credentials which should commend him to the Corinthians. Although we may admire his courage and tenacity, few of them will commend themselves as virtues. Exceptions are purity, forbearance, love and truthfulness.

Paul asks: 'What has a believer in common with an unbeliever?' (6:15)

He suggests that the answer is nothing and much of this letter would suggest that he is right. Yet both believers and unbelievers are human beings. If they actually try to work together instead of always trying to convert one another, they begin to find that they have a great deal in common, including many shared values and ideals.

Chapter 9 is one of many places in the letters where he begins the churches' long tradition of asking for money. There was probably real justification for his appeal. The communal life of the church in Jerusalem had gone badly wrong in a financial sense, leaving the Christians there in real need. Paul was also aware of course, that money talks. Money from the gentile Christians to the Jewish Christians might help the latter to give greater approval to the gentile mission of Paul and his companions.

Any human society needs money to run its affairs. But one of the scandals of the Christian church down the centuries has been the misuse of money, and the demands it has laid on society as a whole – on unbelievers and people of other faiths.

In Britain today we all subsidise the church, whether we like it or not. Church schools, church buildings, clergy homes and even clergy income all come partly from the state – which means from the mass of people who have no real religious beliefs.

If we took away that funding, how much of the church would remain?

Nor does the church use its money in accordance with its own teaching. Down the centuries it has used money for its own glorification rather than for the blessing of the poor. They have been left in their poverty and squalor.

The church has milked the poor for its grandiose schemes and cared little for the misery of needy people. It has left them to rely on God who, according to Paul, 'is able to provide you with every blessing in abundance, so that you may always have enough of everything and may provide in abundance for every good work.' (9:8)

Tell that to the starving of the world.

It is no use relying on God. We have to rely on ourselves and our common humanity. It is human concern, human compassion, human intelligence and human will that must achieve decent living conditions for all humanity. Only through these things can we bring about a society in which the world's abundance will be properly shared so that all may have enough.

In chapter 11 Paul compares himself with false teachers. Like him or loathe him, it is impossible to read verses 24 to 27 without admiring his courage, his stamina and determination. Few people could have endured so much. It is perhaps his human strength of will and valour together with his single-mindedness, far more than his complex teaching, which made him so successful.

But how successful was he? It is clear from chapter 12 that the gospel of Jesus Christ failed to make the Corinthian Christians any different from anybody else. Any examination of any Christian congregation will show that it rarely does. It is no more effective as a means of making people into better people than a thousand and one other treatments. If Christianity does not achieve its own goals, why should we believe its salvation theology?

The Letter to the Galatians

Paul begins with the central Christian message. Jesus 'gave himself for our sins to deliver us from the present evil age.' (1:3)

This message rests on a number of assumptions:

Assumption 1: That we are sinners, fundamentally and ineradicably evil.

I do not believe that. We ARE imperfect. Everybody recognises that. Part of the challenge of human life is the challenge of becoming 'the best that we can be'.

Assumption 2: That only God in and through Jesus can save us from our evil selves.

If there is no God, the assumption is meaningless.

Assumption 3: That the 'present age' is evil.

Once again, this is an assumption I do not accept. There is plenty that is wrong but there is plenty that is good and right as well. Our human task is to make 'the present age' as good as we can for as many people as possible and not to be deflected by dreams of some other perfect world beyond the grave.

It is also our task to try to leave the world in as good a condition as possible for those who will follow us in it.

Paul does not have much time for those who disagree with him, like all fanatics before or since. 'Let' them 'be accursed.' (1:8)

Since his gospel 'came through a revelation of Jesus Christ' it is indisputable. Moses' gospel came through a revelation of God. Muhammad's gospel also came through revelations. The Mormons, the Christian scientists, the Jehovah's Witnesses have all had their own revelations. They are all right without possibility of question or dispute. They are also all different!

Perhaps even revelation needs examination to discover whether there really is anything of value or not.

None of those who have received revelations would agree with that because they all have the arrogance to believe that their own teaching is wholly true and all other teaching either wholly or partly false. This kind of arrogance seems to afflict quite a wide variety of people. It led me to write a pretty awful poem some time ago:

> Beware all priests.
> They claim a special magic
> all their own
> through god's anointing oil
> and bishop's hands.
>
> Beware all prophets.
> They claim a special insight
> all their own
> through revelation, dreams,
> and god's sure call.
>
> Beware all preachers.
> They claim a special Word
> all their own:
> Upanishad, Quran, or
> Bible 'truth'
>
> Beware all politicians.
> They claim an always rightness
> all their own
> through unfair voting schemes
> and party whips.

Beware the pope.
He claims infallibility
all his own
when speaking nonsense
from his holy throne.

Beware all people
who would tell you how to live.
So often cosseted
they know far less than you –
their 'truth' disown.

Galatians is a further demonstration of the squabbling that went on in the early church – the church has not changed in this respect. The central dispute is about whether non-Jewish Christians should be made to obey Jewish law and custom.

Paul is on the side of those who say 'no' and argues his case with typically complex theological style.

The whole dispute is meaningless and irrelevant today but there are two brief moments worthy of our attention:

5:14: The whole Jewish and Christian law is summed up as: 'You shall love your neighbour as yourself.'

Is it significant that once again Paul (unlike Jesus) has dropped the law's demand that we should love God? THIS summary is no longer religious. It is solely a human law.

Insofar as it is simply urging us to treat other people with respect and consideration; to try to behave decently towards others and to strive for harmonious and friendly relationships it is surely wholly good.

It is possible to pick it to pieces (it is possible to pick any form of words to pieces) but I think most people would regard it as a worthy ideal.

In 5:22 Paul sums up the results he would expect to see from the acceptance of the Christian gospel:

'The fruit of the Spirit is love, joy, peace, patience, kindness, goodness, faithfulness, gentleness, self-control.'

Anybody with all those virtues or qualities would be a truly wonderful human being. All these things are worth striving for.

But I don't think there is any evidence that Christianity is any more likely to create people of this calibre than any other teaching. There isn't much evidence that Paul himself had all these virtues. Nevertheless, he deserves the credit for setting before us such a picture of humanity at its best. We need noble ideals as goals to set ourselves. But you don't have to be a Christian to have noble ideals.

In chapter 6 Paul shows unaccustomed kindliness and humanity. Much of it needs no comment save the stamp of any decent human being's approval:

> 6:1–2: 'If any man is overtaken in any trespass. . . restore him in
> a spirit of gentleness. Look to yourself, lest you too be tempted.
> Bear one another's burdens.'

Bearing one another's burdens is only possible to a very limited degree. We can all help one another but in the end, as Paul recognises, 'each man will have to carry his own load.' (6:5) And each woman and child too.

But when Paul says, 'Let us not grow weary in well-doing; let us do good to all' (vvs. 9–10) he always links doing good to receiving rewards. He never seems to recognise that virtue is its own reward.

We should 'do good to all' not because we believe in a god who rewards those who follow this path, still less because we believe in a god who punishes those who do not. We should 'do good to all' simply because that is the right way to live. The rest of Paul's letter is eminently skippable.

The Letter to the Ephesians

There is nothing in this letter for the non-Christian until chapter 4, and then Paul's message is similar to that in Romans 12–13.

Here he clearly has a pretty low opinion of the way most of us live our lives and he says a number of things about Jesus that are meaningless to most Christians, let alone to unbelievers.

For example: in verses 9–10 Paul speaks of the Christian claim that Jesus went to hell to preach to the souls in hell before ascending to sit at the right hand of the Father.

It was a primitive attempt to deal with a very real problem. Christians claim that God is just. They also claim that apart from Jesus and faith in him, you can't enter into the Kingdom of God either here, or hereafter.

But what of all those people who never hear the Christian gospel? The suggestion was that Jesus gave them their chance after their death.

Ephesians only begins to have any significance for non-believers when Paul begins to urge Christians to be decent people. He bids them be gentle, patient, and loving, using their gifts for the benefit of the whole (Christian) community.

He wants them to be honest and to 'speak no evil' 'but only such as is good for edifying.' (4:29)

In chapter 5 he calls them to be morally pure and to be serious minded. But he carries this to puritan extremes. He wants no levity and no drunkenness.

I must confess that I don't like drunkenness either.

His teaching about husbands and wives will not commend itself to wives – perhaps it never did: 'Wives be subject to your husbands,' etc.

In chapter 6 he shows just how limited Christianity was. It was a child of its time rather than a genuinely pioneering movement. Paul accepts the institution of slavery without criticism. He urges slaves to be obedient to their masters and masters to treat their slaves decently. In Philemon we shall see him sending a runaway slave back to his master.

Paul sees things in cosmic terms. The Christian is a soldier doing battle with the cosmic forces of evil, forces which have the rest of us firmly in their grip.

It is all very exciting and impressive but the facts of life are much more mundane. Most of us are neither great saints nor great sinners. We are not engaged in huge battles. We are simply thinking animals doing our quiet best to live our lives well and to find satisfaction and contentment in so doing.

The Letter to the Philippians

In chapter 2 Paul sets high standards for the Philippian Christians based on the example of Jesus. Verses 1–4 are worth thinking over just because of those standards. Verses 5–11 explain why Paul felt that Jesus was such an example.

It is a very attractive picture and Christians find it inspirational – but is it true? It paints a picture of a pre-existent being 'in the form of God', equal 'with God'. (Paul, the monotheistic Jew, finds it impossible to go quite the whole hog and simply say that Jesus was or is God.)

This pre-existent being 'in the form of God' left his glory behind and became a man. He suffered crucifixion and was restored to his former glory. The example he sets lies in his willingness to humble himself, to serve his fellow men, to suffer for them and to die for them.

This is the traditional Christian picture of Jesus. But is it true? If there are no gods, then obviously it is not true. If we are left with anything at all, we are left with the example of Jesus the man.

There are two signs in this letter that he may have set very high standards for his followers. If the standards Paul sets spring originally from Jesus, from his example as well as from his teaching, then they were of the highest. I have already suggested that chapter 2:1–4 is worth careful consideration. In chapter 4.8 there is as lovely an exhortation as you will find anywhere:

'Finally brethren, whatever is true, whatever is honourable, whatever is just, whatever is pure, whatever is lovely, whatever is gracious, if there is any excellence, if there is anything worthy of praise, think about these things.'

There is a great deal in this letter which is worth anybody's time and verse 8 of chapter 4 has a valuable message for all of us. If we keep our minds focussed on what is good and true and lovely there is some chance that we shall develop into good, true and lovely people.

The Letter to the Colossians

It is in this letter (1:15–20) that Paul or some unknown author makes his most explicit claim that Jesus of Nazareth is God.

When they are faced with it bluntly, many Christians find it hard to accept that this is what the church asks them to believe; that it is what they are saying every time they recite the creeds; namely that Jesus of Nazareth, their beloved healer, teacher, (saviour), was in fact the creator of the universe and is the one who keeps it all going.

It is a tremendous claim. If it were true, then Jesus would certainly deserve our worship. But is it true?

Apart from the fact that the New Testament says so, there isn't a shred of evidence for any of the superhuman claims made for Jesus. What is more, on Paul's own say so, the cosmic Christ managed only an incomplete job in his human guise so that Paul and others like him had to 'complete what is lacking'.

What sort of a god is it who needs humans in this way? At every level the claim is incredible. No wonder that (in chapter 2) Paul needs to warn the Colossians against people like me who stick to 'human tradition'. We are under the sway of 'the elemental spirits of the universe'.

But if all-loving Jesus really did create the universe, if it is true that 'in him the whole fullness of deity dwells bodily'; if 'all things were created through him and for him'; where did these 'elemental spirits' come from, and what are they doing here?

Do they pre-date creation? Are they also gods? Is the cosmic Christ not capable of dealing with them?

Paul claims that Christ HAS dealt with them. He has triumphed over them by dying on the cross and Christians are dead to them. So they are not to live as if they still belonged to the world. 'They are to set their minds on the things above, not on things that are on earth.'

This still does not answer the question, why or how there are such evil spirits if the world was created by love. All that Paul does is to raise another question. To him, all vice is of the earth – the world. But if it is Christ's world, why is it so bad? Who made

260

it like that?

To those of us who do not believe in God, none of these problems arise. One of the wonderful things about ceasing to be a Christian and ceasing to have any belief in gods at all, is that hosts of problems that troubled the mind incessantly just fall away. The mind is cleared of a mass of confusion and the whole of life becomes both clear and simple.

It is tragic that Paul and Christianity generally should feel it necessary to introduce all this theological and philosophical confusion. If we set it all on one side, we can all approve his words in chapter 3:12ff:

Here he urges people to 'put on' 'compassion, kindness, lowliness, meekness and patience' learning the arts of forbearance, forgiveness, love and thankfulness.

There is no need for a cosmic Christ or a Christian religion to inculcate these things. If they are real virtues and qualities they will commend themselves.

Sadly, Paul cannot sustain this level. He is a child of his time and not even the cosmic Christ can lift him above his age. Without the benefit of Jesus, the Epicureans left him standing, although even they failed to see the ultimate logic of their equal treatment of all kinds of people. Paul can only repeat his teaching to the Ephesians that wives should be subject to their husbands and slaves to their masters. It is very sad that he could be so limited in his vision where it really mattered.

The First Letter to the Thessalonians

1 Thessalonians is a strange mixture. There are wild flights of fancy and down to earth hopes and instructions. Almost all of the latter would fit in well with the teachings and practice of the Epicureans, which makes one wonder why the early church was so hostile to the Epicureans.

The Epicureans, like the later Quakers, were people who would harm nobody. Yet both groups suffered constant misrepresentation and serious persecution at the hands of the church.

The author of 1 Thessalonians claims that the instruction he gives comes from God. To those of us who do not believe in gods such an authority is inadmissible. On what then is our own ethic based?

On human intelligence and the human examination of 'what is right and good in conduct'. There is a reasonable consensus on general principles. But the most difficult ethical decisions have to be faced instance by instance. People face them carefully and thoughtfully and make their decisions honestly. They will sometimes never know whether they have made the 'right' decision. All that they can know is that they have done their best and that other people have no right to judge them one way or the other.

The substance of this letter begins in chapter 3:12–13 where there are two wishes or hopes: If we drop the religion, they are hopes that all of us can share:

> 'May . . . you increase and abound in love to one another and to
> all men.' And may your hearts be 'unblameable.'

Chapter 4 begins with instructions about sexual morality and marriage. Christian churches often seem to have an unhealthy obsession with sex (perhaps springing from the fact that both Jesus and Paul were bachelors. Paul had some very odd views indeed.

No one would quarrel with the call to 'abstain from immorality' or to 'take a wife in holiness and honour.' (verses 3–4)

But verse 5 equates passion and lust. It also assumes that passion cannot go with holiness and honour. What a sad point of view. The best and deepest loves are both honourable and passionate. Indeed, it is arguable that there is no such thing as love unless there is passion.

Nor do we need the warnings of verse 6 about 'God the avenger' to persuade us to do what is right and avoid what is wrong.

Verses 11 & 12 are almost pure Epicureanism: 'Aspire to live quietly, to mind your own affairs, and to work with your hands' (i.e. to earn your own living); 'so that you may command the respect of outsiders, and be dependent on nobody.'

But whatever the virtues of the advice of these verses, if we all followed it strictly, who would be responsible for government (local or national), for social order and cohesion? Quietism is very attractive, but inadequate on its own. If we ignore the flights of fancy in the rest of this chapter and move straight to chapter 5:13 onwards we shall find the part of this letter with most to say to non-religious people:

'. . . be sober . . . Be at peace among yourselves, admonish the idle, encourage the faint-hearted, help the weak, be patient with them all. See that none of you repays evil for evil, but always seek to do good to one another and to all.'

'Rejoice always': this may be asking a bit too much, yet it is certainly very much pleasanter having dealings with the cheerful and the grateful than with the self-pitying who are always moaning and groaning. So the goal is probably right even if it is sometimes beyond us.

'Hold fast what is good, abstain from every form of evil. . . Be . . . sound and blameless.'

I may have had to be selective, but the general thrust of these instructions is both positive and laudable.

The Second Letter to the Thessalonians

We can dispense with 2 Thessalonians very quickly. It has nothing to say to non-religious people at all.

It is largely about the second-coming of Jesus. There are many Christians to whom the second-coming is meaningless. To non-Christians it is a complete non-starter, a meaningless irrelevance.

I do find it curious however that a religion that teaches people not to return evil for evil should be so insistent that God WILL reward evil with evil.

The First Letter to Timothy

We can turn straight to chapter 2:8–15. Once more, women are relegated very firmly to a subordinate role.

It is curious that the Protestant churches which have always been more Bible centred than the Catholics, are the ones which have allowed women to take their place alongside men with equal standing both as lay members of the churches and also as clergy and ministers.

Once again we see the church deciding that parts of the Word are not necessarily the Word of God.

In chapter 3 the clergy are set their standards. The church would have far greater respect if they came nearer to these standards. Some do, but many do not.

It was a married clergy in New Testament times. The Catholic insistence on a celibate clergy has no Biblical authority and places impossible strains on many priests. The result is often honourable resignation but it is not always so happy.

1 Timothy is a personal letter in which Timothy is urged to live his life well; to do his job well and to encourage his fellow-Christians to aim always for the highest standards.

Although Christian theology and belief underpins the whole letter it doesn't get in the way of the main message. Without being too rigid or too precise as to details, much of it would be good advice for any member of society who wishes to lead a decent life and to make a positive contribution to society.

The Second Letter to Timothy
and the
Letters to Titus and Philemon

These can all be ignored.

No comment is called for except one concerning Philemon. Paul sends a runaway slave back to his master and this letter pleads for a decent reception for him.

There is no recognition that slavery is an evil in itself. Once again, the New Testament is of its time rather than ahead of its time.

Section Three

From Hebrews to Revelation

The Letter to the Hebrews

The letter to the Hebrews begins with the same claims made at the beginning of John's Gospel: that God created the world through Jesus and that Jesus (God's Son) 'reflects the glory of God and bears the stamp of his nature, upholding the universe by his word of power.'

It is a tremendous claim but if it is not true, it is absolutely meaningless.

The rest of the letter represents Jesus as an everlasting high priest replacing the priests of the Jewish temple. For those who have no belief in God there is no call for a priesthood, so the main thrust of this letter is completely irrelevant. But it is dangerous to say so, especially for someone who has been a Christian and is one no longer: 'for if we sin deliberately after receiving the knowledge of the truth, there . . . remains a fearful prospect of judgement, and a fury of fire . . . It is a fearful thing to fall into the hands of the living God.' (10: 26, 27 & 31)

If I believed that or any of the rest of the judgemental passages in the New Testament I would be terrified – but I don't and I'm not.

At the end of the letter the author repeats many of the

266

injunctions of Jesus. I make no apology for repeating them (somewhat selectively). In fact, there will be a number of lists in this last section of our study. As far as I am concerned they are the only parts of these books worthy of consideration. But I have been pleasantly surprised to find that there is so much that IS worthy. Here then is the list from Hebrews:

12:14:	Strive for peace with all men.
13:1–5:	See to it . . . that no one is immoral.
	Let brotherly love continue.
	Do not neglect to show hospitality to strangers.
	Remember those who are in prison. . .
	and those who are ill-treated.
	Let marriage be held in honour among all.
	Keep your life free from love of money
	and be content with what you have.
13:16:	Do not neglect to do good
	and to share what you have.
13:18:	Seek for a clear conscience
	desiring to act honourably in all things.

Christians are to be congratulated on setting high standards of personal and social behaviour, but it is perfectly obvious that you don't have to be a Christian or religious in any way to adopt such standards or such a way of life. What Christians have done is to spell it out more thoroughly and in a more concentrated way than anybody else with the possible exception of Confucius. That is perhaps their greatest contribution to thoughtful people of all kinds.

The Letter of James

The letter of James is often given short shrift by Christian scholars because there is so little religion in it. So much the better for us: it follows the down to earth set of injunctions with which Hebrews ends:

1:19:	be quick to hear, slow to speak, slow to anger.

1:21:	put away all filthiness.
1:22:	be doers and not hearers only.
1:27:	visit orphans and widows, keep unstained.
2: 1:	show no partiality.
2:13ff:	let mercy triumph over judgement clothe the needy, feed the hungry.
3: 1:	higher standards will be expected of those who presume to teach than of the taught.
3:13:	wisdom is meek and expressed in a good life and good works.
3:17:	wisdom is first pure, then peaceable, gentle, open to reason, full of mercy and good fruits, without uncertainty (?) or insincerity.
4:6 & 8:	be humble, clean and pure.
5:7–11:	be patient, don't grumble, be steadfast.
5:12:	Let your yes be yes and your no be no.

Even though some of these injunctions may be highly debatable, they do give a clear picture of the kind of standards and ideals to which Christians aspired. Once again, they have nothing to do with God or religion. Any thoughtful human being can adopt them without becoming a Christian.

The First Letter of Peter

The injunctions in 1 Peter are much more questionable than those we have considered so far in this section. There are parts of this letter that are thoroughly unacceptable to anyone who believes in living life to the full and treating people with proper respect.

1:14:	do not be conformed to the passions.
2:11:	abstain from the passions of the flesh.

This is typical of a great deal of Christian teaching. It identifies passionate behaviour with misconduct. Passion by definition is powerful but whether powerful for good or evil is another matter. Passion certainly needs to be harnessed and directed into valuable directions in much the same way as our forefathers learned to harness the power of steam. But Peter's injunction is not only wrong, it is positively dangerous. To 'abstain from the passions' is to build up such a head of steam that there is certain to be an explosion.

It is a sad and serious defect of much Christian thinking that passion and the things of the flesh or the body are seen as evil. The New Testament has none of the Greek celebration of physical beauty and achievement. It is a great loss and leads to much of the perverse and dangerous teaching on sexual matters so common in the Catholic church today. The rejection of the body and the denial of passion is sick and represents a major parting of the ways between Christians and Humanists.

Another injunction that most of us would question is Peter's charge in 2:13 to be subject to every human institution. In times of persecution there is perhaps wisdom is keeping your head down and being as obedient as possible. But it is precisely because institutions are human that we should not be automatically subject to them.

They need constant criticism, examination, reform and sometimes abolition. This is not a recipe for anarchy but we do need thinking citizens in an open society. What we do not need is a society of unthinking, obedient slaves.

A third injunction that is unacceptable hardly merits a mention. If ever we needed evidence that the Bible is a human book rather than the eternal Word of God, it is in 3:1 where wives are told to be submissive to their husbands. The author is a child of his times

though wives might approve 3:7: 'husbands be considerate. Treat wives with proper respect,'

These things apart, there is plenty in the letter that is more worthy of consideration:

1:13:	Gird up your minds, be sober
1:15:	be holy in all your conduct
1:22:	love one another earnestly from the heart.
2:1:	Put away all malice, and all guile, and insincerity, and envy and all slander.
2:12:	maintain good conduct.
2:17:	honour all men. Love the brotherhood.

For Christians the brotherhood means the Christian community, though it is surprising to find no mention of the sisterhood. But Peter demonstrates elsewhere that his approach to the sexes is far less enlightened than that of the Epicureans of his time.

'Love' is something that moves out in concentric circles. Beginning with our nearest and dearest it moves out through our friends to our social groups and ultimately to all humanity. It is obvious to anyone that we cannot love people we do not know in the same way as we love our friends. But we can develop a frame of mind that will make it natural to us to want to be welcoming and hospitable; a frame of mind that will make it natural to us to care about and to be of service to our fellows seen and unseen.

To continue Peter's list:

3:4:	be gentle, quiet
3:7:	considerate, treating others with respect.
3:8:	seek unity, sympathy, tenderness, humility.
3:11:	turn away from evil and do right,
	seek peace and pursue it.
3:15:	be gentle, reverent
3:16:	and keep your conscience clear.
3:17:	it is better to suffer for doing right
	than for doing wrong.
4:7:	Love covers a multitude of sins.
4:9:	Practice hospitality ungrudgingly
4:10:	use your gifts for one another.
5:5:	(once again): be humble, be sober.

Before we leave 1 Peter we should perhaps notice that in 2:21–24 there is a picture of Jesus, the example Christians seek to follow. I have already called in question some of the elements of that picture.

But it *is* a very lovely and moving picture of the man at the heart of the Christian religion. For Christians who can no longer accept churchianity, ritual, mystique, theology – for Christians who have lost almost everything associated with their faith but who still cling on, then this picture of Jesus may seem to be all that is left.

As we have seen throughout this study, although there is an immense amount that is unworthy of decent human beings in

Christianity; an immense amount that should be rejected out of hand; there is also a great deal that is admirable and a great deal that has never been surpassed. Both in the teaching of Jesus and in the teaching of the New Testament generally, there is a great deal that can enrich and ennoble our lives.

The Second Letter of Peter

Most of 2 Peter has to do with the end time.

At the time that atomic bombs were dropped on Japan Christians made much of the likeness of 2 Peter 3:8–10 to an atomic explosion, and as always there were those ready to tell us that the end time was very close.

There are those who concern themselves with the unknown future. But the only concern of most non-religious thinkers is the environmental concern. We are concerned about our human misuse of the planet and its resources, and anxious that we should all learn lessons from the damage and destruction for which we are already responsible. Biblical teaching about an end time is quite irrelevant. In fact, the only part of this letter which has any relevance to anything at all is the so-called ladder of virtue in 1:5–7:

LOVE

BROTHERLY AFFECTION

STEADFASTNESS

SELF-CONTROL

KNOWLEDGE

VIRTUE

The Three Letters of John and the Letter of Jude

Apart from a constant urging to keep the commandments, to do right and to love one another in deed and in truth there is nothing in these letters of any value.

There is a good deal of evidence here as elsewhere in the New

271

Testament that the churches were no better at living up to Christian teaching than they are today. I have always felt that this failure calls in question the validity of Christian teaching about the Holy Spirit.

Since my own departure from the Christian faith, this has ceased to be a problem to me for I no longer believe in the Spirit at all.

In 1 Peter I took issue with the author over his attitude to the passions. The same kind of attitude is to be found in 1 John 1:15:

'Do not love the world or the things of the world.'

This sits strangely with the claim that Jesus, acting on behalf of God (his father) created the world. If that claim is true why is the world not worthy of our love?

But we have seen that there is hardly any sign in the New Testament of appreciation of the natural world and its beauty. Nor is there any sign of environmental concern. The world is designed to be ruled by man for his own purposes. It is the scene of the cosmic battle between good and evil, and in due course it will be destroyed. What a sad and empty picture.

The Revelation to John

The Bible begins in Genesis with heaven on earth in the Garden of Eden. It ends in a magnificent finale with a new heaven and a new earth.

Much of this book is worth reading even though it may be quite incomprehensible (and who is there who would pretend to understand every detail of it?).

Beginning with a sort of OFSTED report on seven churches it continues with a series of visions and prophecies. It is a great read, but it has absolutely nothing to say to anybody who is not a Christian, and not very much to those who are. About the only passage that is well known to Christians is in chapter 7:9–17, and that particular passage gives them a good deal of inspiration. It is a vision of the new life beyond the grave. Dreams of a perfect future are as remote as tales of a perfect past. Life is about making the present as perfect as we can for those who are alive now, and establishing the best possible conditions for succeeding generations.

Those who follow the positive teachings of the New Testament, whether they are Christians or no, will make a genuine contribution towards the fulfilment of that task. In doing so they will find their own satisfaction, fulfilment and happiness. They will need no other reward.

Finale

Western Europe and much of the rest of the world owes an incalculable debt to Judaism and even more to Christianity both for good and for evil. Our Judaeo/Christian heritage is inescapable. No one in their right minds would wish to escape from a good deal of it.

For many centuries the church was almost alone in having the power and the wealth to build magnificent buildings and to commission great works of art. If 'the poor' did not 'have good news preached to them'; if they were left in their hovels and poverty to suffer disease and early death largely due to their ignorance, so much the worse for them. After all, had not Jesus himself said, 'the poor you have always with you.'

Those poor are gone and others have taken their place. Christians stand alongside everyone else in efforts to relieve and end poverty, deprivation and ignorance. And their buildings and works of art remain – in part, a magnificent heritage and in part a millstone for the shrinking band of Christians and for tax-payers who often have to pick up the tab.

If we strip Christianity of its God, its theology, its pomp and circumstance, its 'mystery' and gobbledegook, there is still a great deal left and some of it is worth both preservation and development.

Jesus and his followers have set before us in the New Testament a set of human ideals; worldly teaching as fine as anything that has come to us from the ancient world. Thanks to

274

Christianity it has the added advantage of being instantly accessible for the New Testament is still available in any library or bookshop.

We have seen, I hope, that it is worth study. Much of it is worthy of acceptance by any human being as part of his or her own ideal and standard for life. Those who filter out the pure gold for themselves will probably become better people as a result. They will certainly find means of expressing their own best ideals and values.

They will also be the first to recognise the limitations and inadequacies of New Testament teaching. This *is* ancient teaching. It is essential that we push the frontiers forwards in a world which is constantly changing and presenting us with new challenges and increasingly complex and intractable moral problems.

The New Testament is in no sense the word of God (that nonexistent figment of man's imagination). But it contains the teaching of men who were concerned to live their lives in the best possible way. As a result it will always have a value for others with the same concern. It can be a useful tool for all those who wish to become mature and decent human beings.